Margin
&
Text

Margin & Text

AMPLIFYING DIVERSE VOICES IN ARCHITECTURE

Betsy West · Kelly Carlson-Reddig · José L.S. Gámez

PA PRESS

PRINCETON ARCHITECTURAL PRESS · NEW YORK

To Dee: You are my love and my laughter. To my parents, for the deep joy of learning they instilled in me. And to our authors, who have made this project both exciting and humbling in the best way possible because they decided to share something of themselves when it would have been much easier not to.

—BW

To Tom, Nathan, and Zoe: You are my greatest of joys. To architecture: for inspiring me over the years, for being a worthy pursuit, and for becoming better by making equitable space for all.

—KC-R

To Melissa, Isa, and Moe: You've made my world immeasurably better. To Kelly and Betsy: This book would not have come together without your dedication and effort. To the authors we've worked with: Your words are inspiring. To those who read parts or all of this book, I hope you find new insights to help you shape the world around you for the better.

—JG

YAW — BENDING OUT OF THE COURSE

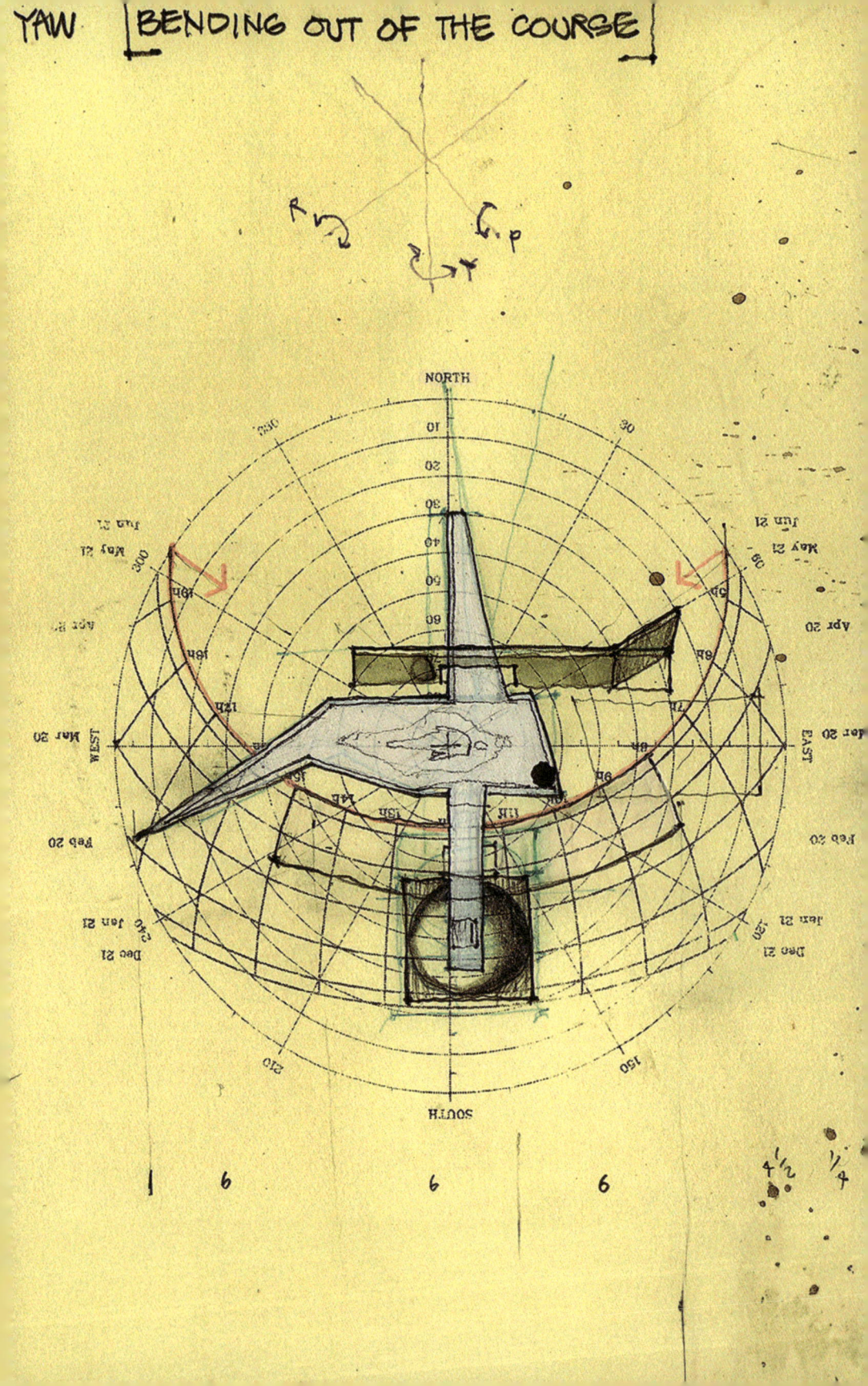

> I would like to see this thing called architecture that started out in a cocoon be blown apart to be more universal, accessible, multicultural, multicolored, multi-everything.

Gabrielle Bullock

architect

CONTENTS

- 12 **Foreword** Sekou Cooke
- 18 **Contributors**
- 20 **Introduction** Betsy West

ONE ⟶ WHOSE STORY IS IT?

- 33 **Introduction** José L.S. Gámez
- 38 **won't you celebrate resilience?** Michelle Joan Wilkinson
- 51 **Snapshot: Who's in the Room?** Manoj Kesavan
- 54 **Permanent Buildings, Fluid History: An Account of Diasporic Practice in America** *(In English with excerpts translated into Hindi)* Aneesha Dharwadker
- 77 **Benchmark: Your Thunderous Silence** Whitney M. Young Jr.
- 83 **Snapshot: Blackface Beaux Arts Ball** Melanie Reddrick
- 86 **A Case for a Black Aesthetic** Jack Travis
- 103 **Snapshot: Standing in Solidarity** Pascale Sablan
- 106 **Benchmark: Erased** Katy Gerfen
- 111 **Benchmark: Petition to the Pritzker Prize Jury Regarding Denise Scott Brown** Women in Design at the Harvard Graduate School of Design

TWO ⟶ BUILDING OTHER "AMERICAN" DREAMS

- 117 **Introduction** José L.S. Gámez
- 122 **The Trickster: Stories of Indigenous Place and Space** Chris Cornelius
- 145 **Benchmark: The Alcatraz Proclamation** Indians of All Tribes
- 148 **Snapshot: The "Exotic" Primitive Hut** Dahlia Nduom
- 152 **Frontiers of Design** *(In English and Spanish)* Ronald Rael
- 173 **Snapshot: Uncle Roy** Michelle Magalong
- 178 **Expulsion by Design** *(In English with excerpts translated into Farsi)* Ghazal Jafari
- 193 **Benchmark: #NotMyAIA** *Architect's Newspaper* editors

THREE → MILES TO GO BEFORE WE SLEEP

199	**Introduction** José L.S. Gámez
204	**Spatializing Justice at the US-Mexico Border** Teddy Cruz and Fonna Forman
219	**Benchmark: The Racist Past of Philip Johnson Comes Home to Roost** The Johnson Study Group
224	**Toward Futures That Sustain Us: The Architecture of Repair** Zena Howard and Lauren Neefe
241	**Snapshot: Derrick Bell's Interest Convergence Theory** Isabel Strauss
244	**Benchmark: Joint Statement Regarding Laws Enacted to Prevent the Inclusion of Race and Racism in School Curricula** ACSA / CELA / ACSP / IDEC
250	**A Conversation with Meejin Yoon** Meejin Yoon and Betsy West
269	**Snapshot: A Profound Act of Self-Preservation** Lesley Lokko
271	**Benchmark: Joint Statement on the Supreme Court's Decision Regarding Race-Conscious Admissions** AIA / AIAS / ACSA / NOMA
276	**Afterword** Kelly Carlson-Reddig
285	**Organizations**
291	**Glossary**
300	**Editor Biographies**

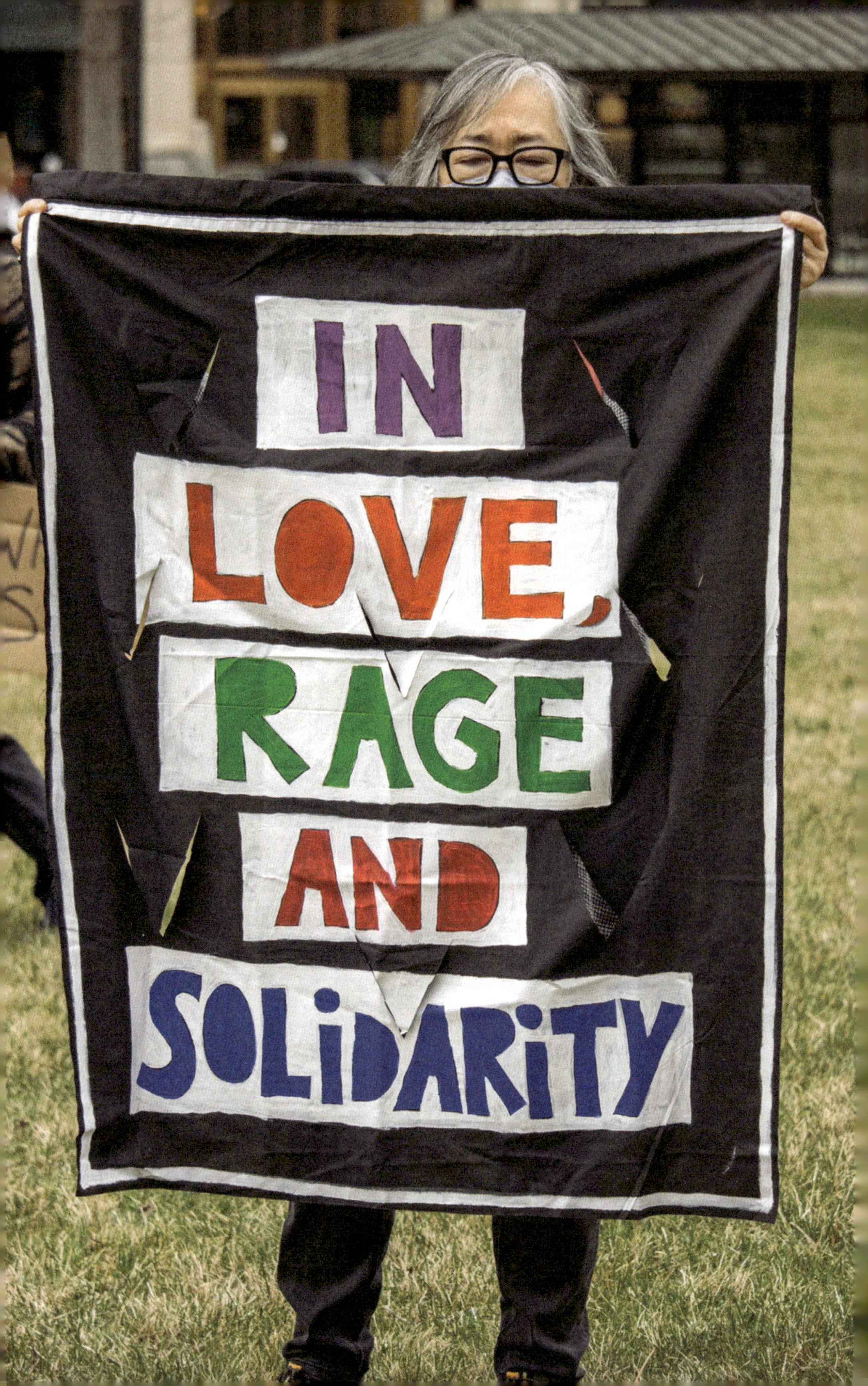
IN
LOVE,
RAGE
AND
SOLiDARiTY

"

You can't be what you can't see.

Marian Wright Edelman
activist; founder and president of the Children's Defense Fund

FOREWORD

SEKOU COOKE

Sekou Cooke is an architect, urban designer, researcher, and curator. Born in Jamaica and based in Charlotte, North Carolina, he was the director of the Master of Urban Design program at UNC Charlotte, the 2021/2022 Nasir Jones Hiphop Fellow at the Hutchins Center for African & African American Research at Harvard University, and a founding member of the Black Reconstruction Collective. Founded in 2008, sekou cooke STUDIO has completed design commissions for urban to interior-scale projects in the United States and internationally, including the Syracuse Hip-Hop Headquarters and Grids + Griots, an architectural intervention commissioned for the Chicago Architecture Biennial. Cooke's research practice centers on the emergent field of hip-hop architecture, a theoretical movement reflecting the core tenets of hip-hop culture with the power to create meaningful impact on the built environment and give voice to the marginalized and underrepresented within design practice. This work has been explored through his writings, exhibitions, lectures, and symposia, including his monograph Hip-Hop Architecture *(Bloomsbury), the traveling exhibition* Close to the Edge: The Birth of Hip-Hop Architecture, *and the 2021 exhibition* Reconstructions: Architecture and Blackness in America *at the Museum of Modern Art, New York. Cooke holds a bachelor of architecture from Cornell University and a master of architecture from Harvard University, and is licensed to practice architecture in New York and North Carolina.*

At a meeting of the Harvard Graduate School of Design Alumni Council in 2023, Dean Sarah Whiting made an incredibly profound statement in response to a question about interdisciplinarity in our fields. I feverishly wrote it down because I knew it would be the spark for this foreword and serve as a valuable introduction to the complex concepts included in this book.

"Staying in your own camp," she said, "is a way of ensuring our demise." Another way of saying this: "If we only talk to ourselves, we will reinforce our irrelevance." The note I made directly below Dean Whiting's words reads: "Disagreement is critical to progress"—a reminder to myself that only through disagreement can we identify what holds us back from the future we desire.

As Whiting continued to expand on this concept by referencing an upcoming text by Diane Davis entitled "Making Room for Conflict," I reflected on the deep entrenchment that keeps us collectively stuck in academic silos, political factions, and religious conflicts. This same entrenchment is at the heart of the debate around the inclusion of critical race theory in US schools. And it sees Israel once again in conflict with Palestine—a conflict that goes back 3,500 years, to Ishmael and Isaac.

It is the desire to interrogate our differences and break down these entrenched perspectives that motivates the editors of this book—Betsy West, Kelly Carlson-Reddig, and José L.S. Gámez—to assemble and disseminate these powerful texts. Understanding how others think and why they think what they do (what their individual perspectives are) brings us into more holistic alignment with one another and in turn helps us understand more about ourselves.

When the architecture world finally woke up (to some degree) in the summer of 2020 to acknowledge that the structural racism that permitted George Floyd to be publicly executed on camera by an officer sworn to "protect and serve" was not only an active force within US society but also the force propping up our entire industry, my own public outcry was for self-reflection. Without structural racism, this country's great works of architecture

> **Without structural racism, this country's great works of architecture would never have been built; ridding the architectural profession of its discriminatory systems would reshape it in a manner we can't begin to conceive.**

would never have been built; ridding the architectural profession of its discriminatory systems would reshape it in a manner we can't begin to conceive. Instead of feeling sorry for those affected by racism, let's reflect on our individual privileges, where they come from, and what they can teach us about ourselves and our roles in society. Instead of asking those who suffer the effects of racism on a daily basis to explain what they go through, let's acknowledge all the ways institutions and individuals (and even you) directly benefit from these same racist systems.

Since this book is an entry point into a space that may be unfamiliar and somewhat uncomfortable, let's start somewhere a bit more fundamental. Architecture, as a contemporary profession, practice, and discipline, began as an aristocratic indulgence of the white male bourgeoisie. As such, our current understanding of what architecture is (in both the academic and the para-academic arenas) has been sculpted over the last few centuries through a Western European lens. This may all sound trite or reductive, but it is demonstrably true. It is also imperative to keep repeating this fact and acknowledging its truth at the beginning of any conversation about architecture's cultural impacts. From this point—and only from this point—can we begin to build expanded narratives and imagine alternative futures.

We cannot continue to have conversations about "diversity" without an initial comprehension of what that word means (cue Mandy Patinkin as Inigo Montoya in *The Princess Bride*: "You keep using that word. I don't think it means what you think it means."). For instance, one person cannot, by definition, be diverse. There is also often a conflation of diversity in design approach with cultural, ethnic, or racial diversity. Similar terms, like "equity," "inclusion," or "social justice," are equally misinterpreted and misused. The sooner we agree upon the terms we use to communicate our most profound truths, the sooner we can begin the work of transforming architecture.

These texts present a new way forward. They present individual ideas on where diversity, equity, inclusion, and social justice exist or should exist or could exist within our profession. Each presents counterpoints and counternarratives to the dominant Western ideologies embedded within architecture. They each center what is canonically considered to be marginal, primitive, or other. As a collection, they

> **Architecture, as a contemporary profession, practice, and discipline, began as an aristocratic indulgence of the white male bourgeoisie. As such, our current understanding of what architecture is (in both the academic and the para-academic arenas) has been sculpted over the last few centuries through a Western European lens.**

describe a profession with elastic edges—able to confront difficult histories and painful pasts; able to embed itself deep within regions of conflict and disputed territories; able to redefine resiliency, monumentality, repair, and reparations; able to recognize identity as essential rather than appurtenant to architectural production and use. Bringing these transformative texts under a single heading, as West, Carlson-Reddig, and Gámez have done, re-centers their precepts as foundational to a new canon where once they were mere branches or leaves on Banister Fletcher's "Tree of Architecture." In their adoption into canon, these ideas must remain resistant to a systematic centralization. A more expansive integration of these concepts into architectural thinking is required. They must be adopted within a new multi-centric discipline instead of being co-opted by our current Eurocentric institutions.

Colonialism, a pursuit focused on acquisition and consumption, has long been invested in consuming its margins. Once margins are consumed and become part of the center, they are indiscriminately labeled, packaged, and resold for profit. This is the engine that drives gentrification: A city's industrial core loses all its manufacturing. The area becomes unsafe, undesirable, and marginal. Artists move in because they can't afford to live anywhere else. Affluent visitors and curious tourists come to see all the amazing cultural artifacts being produced. A new economy emerges. Prospecting developers attract prospecting young professionals to live in the area. The area is repackaged and rebranded as the new arts district. Property values skyrocket, and all the artists move out.

An anti-colonialist attitude would instead create a multi-centric city where each identity is celebrated and afforded room for spontaneous growth. Not commodified. Not tokenized. Not marginal.

These texts are written by individuals who identify as women architects, Black architects, Asian architects, Latinx architects, African architects, Indian architects, Native

American architects, Middle Eastern architects, and Pacific Islander architects. Each identity is laden by our society with myriad political overtones. Like me, I imagine each might enjoy a world where they are seen simply as architects—enjoying the same privileges of mediocrity as our white male counterparts. Our American way of being, however, predicates a highly present politic of being. Entering a space anywhere in the United States carrying any of these othered identities is an inherently political act, a fact that each author understands and acknowledges in their writing. To suggest that architecture could be considered in any way an apolitical pursuit, as many of our modernist and postmodernist predecessors have, goes beyond the irresponsible and borders on the criminal.

> **To suggest that architecture could be considered in any way an apolitical pursuit, as many of our modernist and postmodernist predecessors have, goes beyond the irresponsible and borders on the criminal.**

For each author there is a palpably dualistic yearning: on the one hand, to have their work and ideals be accepted as canonical and central to the architectural discipline (thus existing in the world as "architects" rather than "*architects"), and on the other, to boldly and unapologetically challenge disciplinary constraints using every political and identity-based weapon in their arsenal. Centralizing the marginal versus expanding the margins of architecture need not be mutually exclusive approaches. These texts are hopeful. About this multiplistic view of architecture's future especially, they are all hopeful.

I have been conducting a series of interviews with prominent Black architects in contemporary practice in the hopes of gaining a more holistic view of the current state of being both Black and an architect, particularly in the United States. (Given the size of the Black population within the profession, it is no surprise that some of this book's contributors are also on my list of interviewees.) Though each describes in grave detail the struggles Black architects face—the histories of monumental US structures built with slave labor, concretizing wealth built on slavery; the early legacy of exclusion within the profession; continued institutional roadblocks to successful expansion of Black practices; Eurocentric schooling; latent negative perceptions of

Blackness in popular society—they all remain hopeful. Just like our authors, they remain hopeful. All this without any clear evidence that hope is justified.

The main point of inquiry within each interview is why anyone who is either not Black and/or not an architect should care about any of the issues this tiny group faces. Who cares if some obscure profession has diversity challenges? "If I'll never hire an architect, why would it matter to me whether an architect is Black, white, or other?" The answer is simple: architects and urban designers make decisions every day that impact the lives of millions. Everyone's surroundings are affected by design decisions. And having an entire realm of our daily lives controlled exclusively by those trained in a white colonial tradition is detrimental to all involved.

The texts in this publication, and their collective juxtaposition, stand directly in opposition to this reality. Restructuring the core of how architecture operates as a practice, a profession, and a discipline by neutralizing the idea of marginalization itself, as these texts hopefully suggest, removes any need to qualify architecture as anything but built reflections of cultural identities. Then we can all be architects.

CONTRIBUTORS

BETSY WEST

KELLY CARLSON-REDDIG

JOSÉ L.S. GÁMEZ

SEKOU COOKE

MICHELLE JOAN WILKINSON

MANOJ KESAVAN

ANEESHA DHARWADKER

WHITNEY M. YOUNG JR.

MELANIE REDDRICK

JACK TRAVIS

PASCALE SABLAN

CHRIS CORNELIUS

DHALIA NDOUM

RONALD RAEL

MICHELLE MAGALONG

GHAZAL JAFARI

TEDDY CRUZ & FONNA FORMAN

ZENA HOWARD

LAUREN NEEFE

ISABEL STRAUSS

MEEJIN YOON

LESLEY LOKKO

THE SUPREME COURT JUSTICES

INTRODUCTION

BETSY WEST

> "Who decides what is margin and what is text? Who decides where the borders of the homeland run? Absences and silences are potent.... In every country there are gaping holes. People fall through them and disappear. Yet on every side there are also doors to a wider place."
>
> —Janette Turner Hospital, "Litany for the Homeland," in *North of Nowhere, South of Loss*, 2003

To practice architecture in any of its myriad guises is to design a piece of the world—our own piece or, most often, somebody else's piece. We enjoy what we do and believe it might even be important. We like to think of our endeavors as operating somewhere on the spectrum between benign and beneficent. It's particularly painful, then, to admit that we have crafted a profession that throughout its history has been, almost by definition, overwhelmingly white and overwhelmingly male. And it still is.

We can say this is "disturbing" or "regrettable" or "reprehensible," but the most damning thing we can say is, "it still is." To believe that we got here and have stayed here by mistake is to practice a sustained and determined act of willful ignorance. And to assert that we have no responsibility in the matter is an untenable position. Therefore, in these pages we have attempted to reveal what we can and make a space for others to speak. It is their ideas and voices we celebrate and honor, and it is they who have taught us a great deal along the way.

So how did we get here, to this book, with these people and their lived experiences? It did not start in the world of architecture.

On November 8, 2016, Donald Trump was elected president of the United States. Inspired by racism, sexism, and xenophobia, he made these toxic ideologies de rigueur.

Then, on May 25, 2020, George Floyd was murdered like so many Black and Brown men and women and boys before him. But this time we all watched it happen. This time it happened in our living rooms, and we watched him die a brutal, senseless, cruel, heartbreaking death over and over and over. Cities across the country lit candles, laid wreaths, went into mourning, and went up in flames.

> **It's particularly painful, then, to admit that we have crafted a profession that throughout its history has been, almost by definition, overwhelmingly white and overwhelmingly male. And it still is.**

George Floyd memorial outside Cup Foods in Minneapolis, where he was killed

Riots in Minneapolis following the death of George Floyd, 2020

And finally, on January 6, 2021—as if we needed the point to be driven home—armed rioters stormed the Capitol, threatening to prevent the transfer of power, hang the vice president, and kill the speaker of the house. Almost without exception the insurrectionists were white, and the police and military—despite being beaten, choked, tear-gassed, and overrun for hours—did not open fire on them.

The whole world watched these events and their aftermath. Collectively it was one of those moments when things fall apart—especially for white folks. Things like our extremely comfortable worldview, which turned out to also be extremely fragile; the belief that those in our justice system would not and could not turn into extrajudicial killers; the chimera that we were well-informed, enlightened, and empathetic; and the security of our carefully constructed and well-worn identities as upstanding citizens in a functioning democracy.

Now here we are, architects practicing in a #Black LivesMatter, #StopAsianHate, #MeToo, #FreePalestine, #FuckPutin world. Here we are, emerging from a pandemic that laid bare deep economic and social disparities in access and infrastructure that very literally determined

BETSY WEST

top: Insurrection at the US Capitol, January 6, 2021
bottom: Overcrowded US Border Patrol station

24 INTRODUCTION

> **We're waking up to the erasure of both individuals and whole groups of people who have made extensive and critical contributions to the profession. We're waking up to those who have been and continue to be locked out of architecture entirely.**

who lived and who died. Here we are, the symbolic architecture of the People's House scarred, our democracy tested, attacked, and perhaps mortally wounded. And here we are, mostly white people in our mostly white profession of architecture in the middle of this milieu, confronted by our past half measures of understanding and action, living in an unsettled and unsettling present and trying to figure it out so we can do better, be better.

To greater and lesser degrees, architects who are in the majority are waking up to the deliberate divide in the culture of architecture that is, as in all of society, both structural and strategic. We're waking up to the long history of vitriol aimed at people and ideas outside the Eurocentric US culture of architecture. We're waking up to the erasure of both individuals and whole groups of people who have made extensive and critical contributions to the profession. We're waking up to those who have been and continue to be locked out of architecture entirely.

In response to our decidedly non-diverse history, there has emerged an insistence among majority architects that difference doesn't matter—that we don't see people in terms of skin color, ethnicity, nationality, socioeconomics, politics, gender identification, etc. This is a contemporary response to historical wrongs, and while it may be well-intentioned, we are becoming ever more aware that difference actually does matter. To believe otherwise is in fact part of the problem, not the solution, because those in the minority in every culture—including the culture of architecture—are eyes wide open when it comes to difference. Experience confirms with absolute clarity that difference matters. A lot.

There exists a split decision among minority professionals as to whether it's more desirable and more effective to be identified as Black architects, Latinx architects, female architects, queer architects, etc., or simply as architects. What is clear, however, is that to deny difference is to deny architecture's great potential for diverse meaning, substance, and vitality. The built version of humanity

BETSY WEST   **25**

to which we aspire can only grow out of a rich accumulation of different lived experiences, different histories, different values, and different translations of the world. Absences in that tapestry are, indeed, potent. Gaping holes do indeed exist.

The nouns "diversity" and "inclusion" are used so often that they roll off the tongue almost as one—diversityinclusion. The power, though, is in the verbs "include" and "diversify." We don't yet have all the right words or know all the right actions to engage one another with the respect, humility, and humanity we desire and deserve. For good reason, trust is limited and hurt and anger abound, and we all have to recognize our roles in that. But for the first time in generations there seems to be a genuine desire to move the needle toward the moral thing, the effective thing, the joyful thing, the just thing.

So where do we start? The past, the present, the future? Does it even matter? Doing even a very little something that we're not quite sure of is better than doing a whole lot of nothing. History is long, and it will take time to come to a deep and panoramic understanding of our past, not to mention a fulsome understanding of our present and a collective, overarching vision for an equitable future—a future where everyone has a seat at a table that is truly round and a voice that is listened to and respected.

But working together for equity and justice in the immediate present is doable even without that. As the blackspace.com manifesto suggests, we can "move at the speed of trust" and do the work now, as our views of the past, our negotiations of the present, and our hopes for the future unfold. Amid burning buildings, protests in cities large and small, police brutality, hate crimes, mass shootings, the devastation of COVID-19, and the deadly rhetoric of weaponized politics, we must recognize architecture's agency to stabilize and uplift or exclude and oppress. It's just that simple, and just that complex.

As Sekou Cooke noted in the foreword, we engage collectively in this endeavor with hope. Hope that we can open the doors wide, hope that together we can speak and work

> **Amid burning buildings, protests in cities large and small, police brutality, hate crimes, mass shootings, the devastation of COVID-19, and the deadly rhetoric of weaponized politics, we must recognize architecture's agency to stabilize and uplift or exclude and oppress.**

for the benefit of others—for disenfranchised communities who have little reason to believe that beautiful, healthful architecture has anything to do with them; for past, present, and future students who are surprised when we bring BIPOC lecturers and critics to our universities when that should simply be the norm; for minority faculty and practitioners who are forging a path, sometimes precarious and oftentimes in relative isolation; for our present and future clients; and for every member of our professional community, including not only architects and educators but all those who collaborate and participate in every stage of the design and building process. In all these settings it is, indeed, critical for everyone to see as many people as possible who "look like them."

Hence this publication, *Margin and Text*. Our contributors are a rich amalgam of Black, white, Indigenous, Latinx, Asian, African, Middle Eastern, Indian, and Pacific Islander. Each is a unique manifestation of their lived experience. They are different genders and generations, they come from different cultures and traditions, they have different points of view about architecture, and together they give us an unfamiliar but exciting picture of what architecture in the United States could be. They have all endured the weight, the stress, the frustration, and the pain of being in the minority. But they are all speaking to both the difficult and the celebratory, often one and the same, with honesty, courage, and vulnerability.

The book is comprised of nine primary texts, supported and surrounded by photos, quotes, statistics, benchmarks, and snapshots. The benchmarks record events—some historical, some current—that have had or are having, for better or worse, an impact on society and on architecture. The snapshots are personal stories that elicit a range of emotions, from "yes, that's happened to me, too," to "oh my god," to stunned silence. The photos that are not directly associated with the essays don't depict architecture per se, but illustrate the context in which architecture exists at this specific moment in time. Not since the 1960s, with its messy, ugly, revolutionary cultural upheaval, has there been the level of awareness and activism, protest and conversation, that is taking place in the United States right now. In the 1960s, big and lasting gains were made across society in terms of Black rights, women's rights, gay rights, and beyond. The photos we've included may indeed be capturing another once-in-a-generation troubling of the waters that could further advance issues of diversity, not just for architects, but for all.

We invite you to explore the book in all its variety of material. We invite you to start at the beginning and read straight through, or dip your toe in here and there as mood or curiosity leads you. Most of all, we invite you to write in the margins. Literally. Writing in the margins as we read is a learned behavior. That's where we raise questions. That's where we record definitions. That's where we add emphasis and mark things that pique our interest and spark our imagination. That's where we make connections between ideas.

The margins illuminate the text.

Existing on the margins—not in a book, but out in the world—is also a learned behavior: Avoid the police. Keep your hands where they can be seen. Don't expect too much. Keep your head down. Work harder than anybody else. Be quiet. Know your place. Behave.

In that world, nothing is illuminated.

So which is it to be? In this moment, on the radically shifting threshold of an unknown future, are we on the verge of something of import? Real import versus hypothetical import? Real progress versus the desire to progress?

Some of the answers may lie in the questions. Who decides what is margin and what is text? Who decides where the borders of the homeland run? And who opens the doors to a wider place?

Collectively we all do.

> **We invite you to explore the book in all its variety of material. We invite you to start at the beginning and read straight through, or dip your toe in here and there as mood or curiosity leads you. Most of all, we invite you to write in the margins.**

IN THIS HOUSE, WE BELIEVE:
BLACK LIVES MATTER
WOMEN'S RIGHTS ARE HUMAN RIGHTS
NO HUMAN IS ILLEGAL
SCIENCE IS REAL
LOVE IS LOVE
KINDNESS IS EVERYTHING
©KRISTIN JOINER
CAFEPRESS.COM/THEWAWHSHOP

→ ONE

WHOSE STORY IS IT?

Essays by

Michelle Joan Wilkinson

Manoj Kesavan

Aneesha Dharwadker

Whitney M. Young Jr.

Melanie Reddrick

Jack Travis

Pascale Sablan

Katy Gerfen

Women in Design at the Harvard Graduate School of Design

> **The challenge is always to talk about these things without causing disabling despair.**
>
> Jack Travis
> architect and educator

INTRODUCTION
José L.S. Gámez

Chapter 1 of this volume addresses pervasive discriminatory forces that shape architectural education and practice, the social systems that shape the built environment, and the narratives that are embedded within them all.

The structural systems that tend to stifle architecture's diversity are not new, as the benchmark pieces included in this chapter attest. Whitney M. Young Jr.'s 1968 keynote speech to the American Institute of Architects and the 2013 Pritzker Prize jury petition supporting Denise Scott Brown point to seminal moments when key organizations in the architectural establishment were called out for discrimination or inaction and, when confronted, failed to act. We see the continued impacts of institutional failures in the firsthand experiences of Manoj Kesavan, Melanie Reddrick, and Pascale Sablan, recorded in their snapshots. Their stories expose the everyday nature of microaggression, and the regular failure to adequately and equitably represent communities of color. They remind us to remain skeptical of larger mainstream narratives that suppress diversity as they shape the social and physical environments that we inhabit.

Michelle Joan Wilkinson, Aneesha Dharwadker, and Jack Travis add depth to these discussions by exploring ways that designers may engage practices rooted in a cultural voice as a way to critically reconstruct history and create new narratives. Their reflections challenge architects to ask a new set of questions. Whom should we design for? How do we express our culture through design? Where should we implement our work? And are buildings an appropriate vehicle for confronting questions tied to heritage, representation, and race today? In their attempts to provide answers, Wilkinson, Dharwadker, and Travis point to persistent forces of marginalization, each with an eye toward undermining those very same forces. As a curator at the National Museum of African American History and Culture, Wilkinson, in a discussion about resilience and weathering—both of

Black bodies and buildings—reminds us that architecture itself can serve to represent and express histories that have been suppressed or untold, and extend that expression into the present and the future. But in so doing, the body of architecture may itself become a site of violence, subject to attacks that mirror the plight of those whose history it seeks to protect. For Travis, the question of representation gives rise to a desire for a culturally rooted set of principles that could form a Black aesthetic. He challenges architects and designers to find patterns and parallels specific to the profession but already present and recognizable in Black fashion, music, art, and spirituality that might inspire qualities for racial identification in architectural works. Dharwadker's discussion of growing up in the American South sets the stage for reflection on the influence of ethnicity in her architectural education and practice. She discusses the potential for a robust diasporic practice imbued with care and concern for the ordinary, the everyday, and the overlooked.

Practices such as these engage a form of storytelling that helps reestablish heritage while simultaneously creating identities in the present.

> **Architecture itself can serve to represent and express histories that have been suppressed or untold, and extend that expression into the present and the future. But in so doing, the body of architecture may itself become a site of violence, subject to attacks that mirror the plight of those whose history it seeks to protect.**

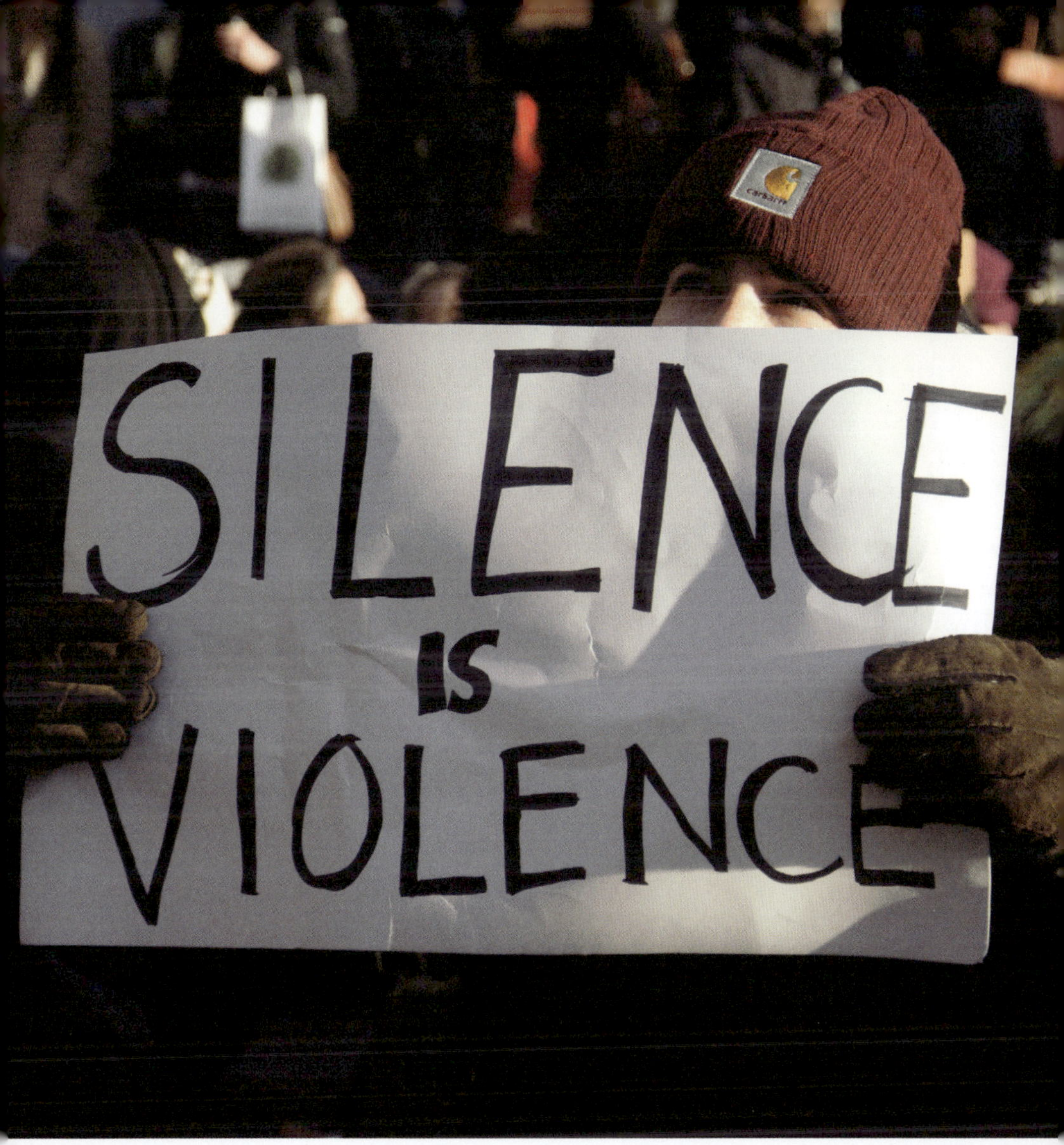
SILENCE
IS
VIOLENCE

Resilience

Resilience refers to the ability of something to recover from impact or harm; for instance, inanimate materials must be strong, tough, and/or flexible to withstand a potentially destructive force without damage. When applied to human beings, the concept is less straightforwardly positive. While it may seem like a compliment to describe a person or community as resilient, it also implies an unfair and unrealistic expectation that they should be able to recover readily from psychosocial stresses associated with bias, microaggressions, discrimination, overt racism, and violence.

> **Stop commending people for being resilient and instead redesign the systems that make people suffer.**
>
> Tweet by Bilal
> @theveryblackproject

WON'T YOU CELEBRATE RESILIENCE?

Michelle Joan Wilkinson

Michelle Joan Wilkinson, PhD, is a curator of architecture and design at the Smithsonian's National Museum of African American History and Culture (NMAAHC). In 2018, Wilkinson organized NMAAHC's three-day symposium "Shifting the Landscape: Black Architects and Planners, 1968 to Now." Prior to her role at NMAAHC, Wilkinson was director of collections and exhibitions at the Reginald F. Lewis Museum of Maryland African American History & Culture. She has also worked at the National Gallery of Art, the Smithsonian American Art Museum, and the Studio Museum in Harlem. As a fellow of the Center for Curatorial Leadership in 2012, Wilkinson completed a residency at the Design Museum in London. Her research project V Is for Veranda, about architectural heritage in the Anglophone Caribbean, has been presented to international audiences in Suriname, England, India, and the United States. Wilkinson's most recent work, the Rendering Visible project, focuses on the Black architectural imagination and issues of representation in architectural renderings. She is also a co-curator of Making Home, *the seventh installment in the Smithsonian Design Triennial, at the Cooper Hewitt, Smithsonian Design Museum. Wilkinson holds a bachelor's degree from Bryn Mawr College and a PhD from Emory University. In 2019–20 she was a Loeb Fellow at the Harvard Graduate School of Design.*

"African American history and culture has taught me that Black people are very resilient. But at some point it's like, let's stop being resilient. I want to be able to say, 'And then they fought, and then the battle was won, and people could stop being resilient and just move on into victory.'"

—Interviewee, content development for the National Museum of African American History and Culture, 2015

The word "resilient," part of the English language since the 1600s, is invoked in myriad fields, from engineering to material science to business to the military. Then beginning in the late twentieth century, concepts of resilience were applied to individuals, especially children.[1] Today, phrases like "emotional resilience" and "climate resilience" indicate the widespread application of the term to people, places, and ideas. Within architecture and design, resilience figures prominently as a goal in shaping the natural and built environment. "Understanding Resilience," a resource tool from the American Institute of Architects, describes resilience as "the ability of a system and its component parts to anticipate, absorb, accommodate, or recover from the effects of a hazardous event in a timely and efficient manner, including through ensuring the preservation, restoration, or improvement of its essential basic structures and functions."[2] This definition encompasses what happens before, during, and after the hazardous or traumatic event. It suggests that we must anticipate (imagine) the trauma, absorb the damage that is inflicted, and recover whole. It presumes that the object or individual impacted is equipped with the assets needed to preserve itself. Across all these fields, resilience broadly conveys an ability to recover (seemingly well) from physical or mental adversity.

NARRATING RESILIENCE

I am a curator of architecture and design at the National Museum of African American History and Culture (NMAAHC), where resilience is a potent framework for the museum's storytelling. As such, I have started interrogating how resilience lives at the intersections of race and architecture and how it operates when pulled apart from that intersection.

---

1. For a close look at how the word has evolved over time, see Alastair McAslan's report "The Concept of Resilience: Understanding Its Origins, Meaning and Utility," published online by the Torrens Resilience Institute (Adelaide, Australia 2010): https://www.flinders.edu.au/content/dam/documents/research/torrens-resilience-institute/understanding-community-resilience.pdf.

2. IPCC glossary of terms, in "Managing the Risks of Extreme Events and Disasters to Advance Climate Change Adaptation," in *A Special Report of Working Groups I and II of the Intergovernmental Panel on Climate Change (IPCC)*, ed. C. B. Field, V. Barros, T. F. Stocker, D. Qin, D. J. Dokken, K. L. Ebi, M. D. Mastrandrea, K. J. Mach, G.-K. Plattner, S. K. Allen, M. Tignor, and P. M. Midgley (Cambridge, UK, and New York: Cambridge University Press, 2012), 555–64. The AIA borrows this definition of resilience from the IPCC: https://archive.ipcc.ch/pdf/special-reports/srex/SREX-Annex_Glossary.pdf.

From the earliest years in NMAAHC's development, the word "resilience" appeared throughout promotional materials for the yet-to-be-built museum.[3] Resilience was used to explain many conceptual elements of the building, including the exterior form, referred to as the corona (crown) by the designers on the architectural team of Freelon Adjaye Bond/SmithGroup: "As the outer layer of the building, the corona draws on imagery from both African and American History, reaching toward the sky in an expression of faith, hope and resiliency."[4] This reference to resiliency refers to the upward and outward angles of the three bronze-colored tiers of the building envelope, which echo the angle of the capstone atop the nearby Washington Monument. This crown-like silhouette draws on Yoruba sculptural shapes and intends to convey triumph and jubilation—as if one's arms were raised up to express a much-anticipated, long-awaited achievement.

> **As the outer layer of the building, the corona draws on imagery from both African and American History, reaching toward the sky in an expression of faith, hope and resiliency.**

Even before its opening, the museum positioned resilience as an ingrained American value that underpinned success and national identity, like American exceptionalism, the American dream, and other stories of national progress and pride. The intention was to introduce resilience as a shared value, but also to teach visitors how resilience became a defining element of the African American experience. This interpretation of resilience informed the museum's curatorial work as well. Curatorial staff referenced resilience in speeches and presentations, and it is a major thread in the museum's permanent exhibition titled *Making a Way Out of No Way*. Describing the exhibition, our website notes that "by embracing the belief that change is always possible, even in the bleakest of circumstances, African Americans have exemplified a resilient spirit that is also fundamentally American."[5]

There was bipartisan support for the creation of the museum and staunch advocates who worked over many decades to bring it into existence. But from the beginning there was also hostility—people who opposed both the content and the location. There were threats against the museum itself, as well as threats against its employees.

---

3. Congress passed the legislation creating the NMAAHC in 2003. After more than a decade of fundraising, site selection, design, construction, hiring, and planning, the museum opened to the public in 2016.

4. NMAAHC design and construction media fact sheet, released September 1, 2016, https://www.si.edu/newsdesk/factsheets/design-and-construction.

5. See https://nmaahc.si.edu/explore/exhibitions/making-way-out-no-way.

Exterior of the NMAAHC with corona profile

MICHELLE JOAN WILKINSON

Interior of the NMAAHC: "We are determined…to work and fight until justice runs down like water and righteousness like a mighty stream." Martin Luther King Jr., 1955 / "I cherish my own freedom dearly, but I care even more for your freedom." Nelson Mandela, 1991

42   WON'T YOU CELEBRATE RESILIENCE?

> **Imagine, then, how dangerous an undertaking it was to build a museum of African American history and culture on the National Mall.**

As symbols of Black life, Black achievement, and Black potential, African American structures and communities have long been targets for terror. Churches, homes, and other places of "Black aliveness"—to invoke Kevin Quashie's term—have been sites for attack and spaces of resilience.[6] The same holds true for museums. Imagine, then, how dangerous an undertaking it was to build a museum of African American history and culture on the National Mall. At a National Conference on Cultural Property Protection held prior to the museum's opening, deputy director Kinshasha Holman Conwill and others discussed the building's design and the security challenges particular to the project. As it turns out, the museum's rich conceptual underpinnings, iconic silhouette, and beautiful, porous skin were marginal to more crucial deliberations about ensuring physical survival. The building incorporates various defensive elements, for instance, architectural features intended to slow or mitigate structural threats that go beyond the usual considerations of fires and flooding. Ruppert Landscape, the company that installed the landscaping, noted that "there was a need for high security. Granite-clad concrete security walls and bollards were installed early on in the project. Crews built [three-foot] ramps to move materials over the barriers—all of which were constructed and deconstructed daily."[7]

Centuries of attacks on spaces of Black life have taught us to imagine the trauma of an attack before it happens and equip ourselves with the attributes necessary to recover. Still, it is sobering to consider that a museum that champions the resilience of African Americans would, itself, need to take special precautions to ensure its ability to withstand physical attack, not only from natural disasters, but also from destructive human forces seeking to eliminate its very existence.

One of the museum's themes that traverses all three history galleries—from the days of slavery to segregation to today—is called "Living with Terror." Illustrating this continued truth, a noose was found inside the museum in 2017, a year after the opening. Writing about the incident in the *New York Times*, founding director Lonnie Bunch III called it "a cowardly act of leaving a symbol of hate in the midst of a

---

6. Kevin Everod Quashie, *Black Aliveness, or a Poetics of Being*, Black Outdoors: Innovations in the Poetics of Study (Durham, NC: Duke University Press, 2021).

7. "Project Profile: The National Museum of African American History and Culture," Ruppert Landscape blog, December 11, 2017, https://www.ruppertlandscape.com/project-profile-national-museum-african-american-history-culture/.

View of the NMAAHC showing protective design features woven into the landscape

tribute to our survival." Bunch opined, "If you want to know how African Americans continue to persevere and fight for a better America in the face of this type of hatred, you need only visit the museum, where the noose has been removed but the rest of the remarkable story of our commitment to overcome remains."[8] Given this kind of history, a history that is repeated time and time again, I understand why we praise resilience. What other option exists in the face of the inescapable terror of capture, confinement, enslavement, and degradation? The terror of rape, beating, lynching, and murder? The daily ongoing terror of walking while Black, sleeping while Black, driving while Black, praying while Black?

WEATHERING AND RESILIENCE

The ability to persevere is a distinguishing feature of resilience, and indeed the ability to adapt and adjust is often lauded. But how has the continuous need for resilience impacted African Americans and African American communities over time—psychologically, physically, and socially? The resilience required to survive and thrive in the face of racism is connected to negative health outcomes, from

[8]. Lonnie G. Bunch III, "A Noose at the Smithsonian Brings History Back to Life," *New York Times*, June 23, 2017, https://www.nytimes.com/2017/06/23/opinion/noose-smithsonian-african-american-museum.html.

premature aging and heart disease to diabetes, cancer, and stroke.[9] Researcher Arline Geronimus describes the corrosive effects of racism on Black public health as "weathering."[10] Unlike the gradual weathering that affects all buildings[11]—the result of a material's exposure to its environment—this type of weathering is more in line with what scholar Christina Sharpe has called "weather that produces a pervasive climate of anti-blackness."[12] The atmospheric conditions that are weathering Black people are the same conditions instilling their resilience.

Because resilience speaks to the ability to absorb and surmount even the most oppressive circumstances, the word unsettles me. It triggers a cascade of ideas and images of what Black people and Black communities have had to endure, from casual indignities to legalized terror. Lucille Clifton's poem "won't you celebrate with me" (1993) is both mantra and lament on the ways she is made to be resilient in the face of daily attempts at her eradication:

> won't you celebrate with me
> what i have shaped into
> a kind of life? i had no model.
> born in babylon
> both nonwhite and woman
> what did i see to be except myself?
> i made it up
> here on this bridge between
> starshine and clay,
> my one hand holding tight
> my other hand; come celebrate
> with me that everyday
> something has tried to kill me
> and has failed.[13]

Clifton ensured her self-preservation. But is sidestepping eradication enough? Is not dying enough?

I am not the only Black woman recoiling at the notion of a precarious resilience. Tracie L. Washington of the Louisiana Justice Institute brought this point to the fore in her comments at a 2015 summit on the tenth anniversary of Hurricane Katrina. The summit focused on strategies for a "Resilient New Orleans," which was also the title of an accompanying document. Regarding the expectation

9. Carol E. DeSantis et al., "Cancer Statistics for African Americans, 2019," *CA: A Cancer Journal for Clinicians* 69, no. 3 (May 2019): 211–33, available at https://doi.org/10.3322/caac.21555.

10. Arline T. Geronimus, *Weathering: The Extraordinary Stress of Ordinary Life in an Unjust Society* (New York: Little, Brown Spark, 2023).

11. See Mohsen Mostafavi and David Leatherbarrow, On *Weathering: The Life of Buildings in Time* (Cambridge, MA: MIT Press, 1993); Dario Camuffo, "Weathering of Building Materials," *Air Pollution Reviews* 5 (2016): 19–64.

12. Christina Sharpe, "The Weather," *New Inquiry*, January 19, 2017, https://thenewinquiry.com/the-weather/.

13. Lucille Clifton, "won't you celebrate with me," in *The Book of Light* (Port Townsend, WA: Copper Canyon Press, 1993), 25.

to always be resilient, Washington explained: "I'm not gonna live being forced to be resilient. I don't want to hear that word again. I'm sick and tired of people saying 'y'all are so resilient'; 'resilient' means you can do something to me. No. I'm not resilient. I have a right not to be resilient."[14] Washington's words were met with applause and cheers. Later, in an interview with commentator Melissa Harris-Perry, Washington added: "We weren't born to be resilient. We're conditioned to be resilient, and I won't accept that…. We should condition the government to ensure our environment…is healthy enough so that I can make a good living; I can send my child to a good school; I can have great health care."[15] She addressed the root issues and reframed accountability and action from the individual to the collective: make our society equitable, ensure our environment is healthy, hold elected officials accountable, and stop expecting me to bounce back from persistent trauma. Stop expecting me to recover from the next terrible thing before I even know what's coming.

Somewhere between Clifton's poem and Washington's pronouncements is the act of deflecting intentional harm—a precautionary practice that is familiar to Black women, Black people. Take a look at Elizabeth Catlett's sculpture of a Black woman, *Rejecting Injustice* (2003). Her hand is held up in a defensive gesture, projecting both strength and the need for protection.

THE PRECARITY OF RESILIENCE: THE ONUS IS ON US

Design can offer protection, preservation, and potentially the ability to recover well. But we can no longer talk about communities being resilient in the same ways we talk about structures designed to be resilient. In architecture, "resilient design" generally means infrastructure intended to prevent or mitigate damage. Protections are incorporated into the building's structure and systems so that if it sustains trauma, the damage, if any, is not beyond repair. When used to describe Black people, though, resilience presumes a proven capacity to survive regardless of the extremity of the damage, and irrespective of the completeness of the

14. See also Maria Kaika, "'Don't call me resilient again!': The New Urban Agenda as Immunology… or…What Happens When Communities Refuse to Be Vaccinated with 'Smart Cities' and Indicators," *Environment and Urbanization* 29, no. 1 (2017): 89–102, available at https://doi.org/10.1177/0956247816684763.

15. Melissa Harris-Perry, "Unequal Recovery for Those in New Orleans," MSNBC, August 29, 2015, https://www.msnbc.com/melissa-harris-perry/watch/unequal-recovery-for-those-in-new-orleans-515724355991.

left: Elizabeth Catlett, *Rejecting Injustice*, 2003. Bronze, 73 × 11 × 42 in.
right: Kennedy Yanko, sculpture inspired by Lucille Clifton's poem "won't you celebrate with me"

rebound. Though resilience is frequently used and affirmed in architecture and design discussions, when speaking across buildings, environments, and communities, we must reexamine what we mean and, most importantly, who we imagine when we use the word. For Black people, Black communities, Black cities—too often, the onus is on us. It's on us to recover well, shepherd the recovery of a community, and bankroll the recovery of a city, a state. The onus is on us to withstand traumatic events but to appear as though nothing remarkable has happened.

Calls for resilience presuppose our ability to recover like machines rather than the human beings and human settlements that we are. In chronicling what happens to "human bodies as they attempt to withstand and overcome the challenges" of systemic oppression, including racism and classism,[16] Geronimus's weathering framework provides

16. Sharpe, "The Weather," https://thenewinquiry.com/the-weather/.

MICHELLE JOAN WILKINSON

an important counterpoint to the celebration of resilience. For groups suffering inequities, resilience is necessary, but should not go unquestioned. An unquestioned insistence on resilience maintains our investment in the existing state of affairs—a status quo allowing continued harm. At the NMAAHC we examine how resilience is forged and understand that it is a by-product of "making a way out of no way." But "making a way out of no way" is not simply an uplifting aphorism; it speaks to the immense emotional, psychological, physical, and spiritual labor required to persist, to continue existing, in spite of conditions designed to hasten your demise.

> **Expectations of resilience correspond directly to race and place—to zip codes with buildings and populations and futures that are vulnerable to weathering if not outright attack.**

In sum, making the connection between resilience and the design of conditions that require resilience is paramount. We can recognize that resilience is not only a point of pride but also a potential burden, an unwanted responsibility foisted on some but not others. Expectations of resilience correspond directly to race and place—to zip codes with buildings and populations and futures that are vulnerable to weathering if not outright attack. Reconceptualizing resilience through this lens challenges our thinking and prompts a line of questioning that goes beyond architectural discourse to architectural duty.

- How might architects protect the health of communities weathering racism?
- How will designers ensure the safety of those living with terror?
- How can architecture provide for the welfare of those who refuse resilience?

If architectural licensure requires continuing education about the public's welfare—that is, our projected ability to fare well in our natural and built environments—then architecture as a field must be willing to rethink resilience from the perspective of those who don't want to be celebrated for it and repair the harmful conditions that make resilience a prerequisite for Black life.

__Representation__

Representation refers to the action of speaking or acting on behalf of an individual or group, such as the way an elected politician works on behalf of their voting constituency. Equal representation suggests that all people deserve this right, and further, that proportional representation by individuals who share characteristics of identity (race, gender, ethnicity, etc.) would create fairer representation and advocacy for all people, especially those historically underrepresented. In an equitable and inclusive society, institutions and centers of power would reflect the diversity of those whom they serve. To speak of historically underrepresented groups points to the fact that the perspectives, experiences, and needs of large groups have gone unheard by those in power. The disadvantage of underrepresentation compounds over time through the concretizing of systems and structures that disempower and disable.

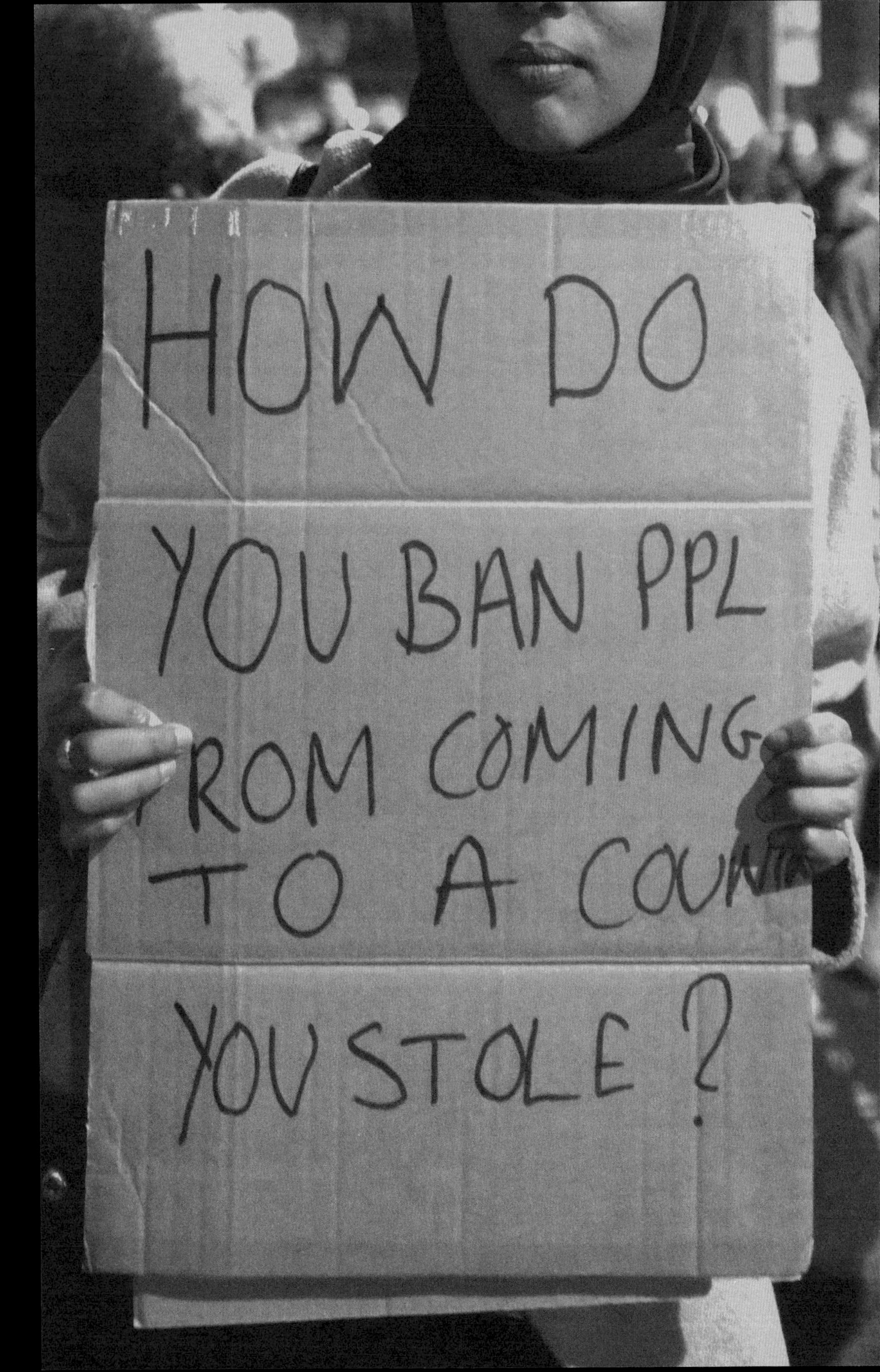
HOW DO
YOU BAN PPL
ROM COMING
TO A COUN
YOU STOLE ?

[SNAPSHOT]

WHO'S IN THE ROOM?

Manoj Kesavan

Twelve to fifteen years ago, following the runaway success of the High Line in New York, every city seemed to be trying to create their own version. Charlotte's response was a Rail Trail that would run along a new light-rail line, and I was on the advisory panel overseeing the project and offering guidance in design and planning. The goal was to connect downtown with the South End—an area then mostly full of warehouses, strip clubs, some funky eateries, and music venues. It also had some of the very little affordable housing close to the center of the city, including Brookhill Village—a mostly Black, low-income neighborhood. The design team held several community meetings in the area, asking the attendees what kinds of things they wanted to see along the Rail Trail. Guess what rose to the top? Not more affordable housing but beer gardens and dog parks.

Fast forward to now: most of what used to be in South End a little over a decade ago is gone, replaced by high-end apartment complexes, eateries, and businesses. And there are close to twenty breweries—most of them dog friendly. This "beer and dogs" phenomenon is a reminder of how the preferences of a small, mostly white, young, upwardly mobile demographic—with the luxury of expendable time to attend these meetings and the confidence to walk into these spaces and make their voices heard—get prioritized over the more pressing needs of everyone else. It's a reminder that there are unseen and unheard communities who are rarely in the room at even the most well-intentioned community meetings and listening sessions where their future may well be decided.

opposite: Protester responding to Trump's blanket ban on people entering the United States from several Middle Eastern and Muslim-majority African countries

> **To be a trailblazer is not an act of courage, but an act of survival and resistance.**
>
> Michelle Magalong
> urban planner and educator

Marginalization

To be marginalized is to be ignored or treated as insignificant, unimportant, or powerless. People who are marginalized are usually not part of the dominant culture; this often includes women, racial and ethnic minorities, people with disabilities, LGBTQ+ individuals, people living in poverty, and so on. Marginalized individuals and groups are actively and often systemically restricted by unfair social, cultural, political, economic, and structural barriers that make it difficult for them to advance.

PERMANENT BUILDINGS, FLUID HISTORY: AN ACCOUNT OF DIASPORIC PRACTICE IN AMERICA

Aneesha Dharwadker

Aneesha Dharwadker is an assistant professor at the University of Illinois Urbana-Champaign, with joint appointments in the School of Architecture and the Department of Landscape Architecture. Her teaching and scholarship examine globalization, design, colonialism, and contemporary social issues in relation to the built environment, including public health and literacy. Recent publications include "Dystopia's Ghost" (Places Journal, 2022), "A Reading List for the End of Architecture" (Dialectic VII, 2019), and "The Imagination Station" (Telesis vol. 5: Adaptive Practice, 2023). In 2022, she received the New Faculty Teaching Award from the Association of Collegiate Schools of Architecture. Dharwadker is a licensed architect in Illinois. She is the founder of Chicago Design Office, where she executes both speculative and constructed works at a range of scales. She holds a master in design studies in the history and philosophy of design from the Harvard University Graduate School of Design, and a bachelor of architecture from Cornell University.

> **I could reinforce the pernicious stereotype of the humble, acquiescent minority, and be complicit in the centuries-long silencing of subaltern voices, or take the risk of being loud, and appear petty and defensive about things that no one else cared about anyway.**

Growing up in a small university town in the American South, I learned too quickly about the chasm between what my ethnicity meant to me and what it meant to others. There was the—let's be real, totally bogus—confusion about which "kind" of Indian I was ("dot" or "feather"?), which evolved by the mid-1990s into persistent questions about whether Apu from *The Simpsons* was my uncle. What to me was a rich, multidimensional cultural experience, growing up as a first-generation American with deep ties to India, was to others a farce, an excuse for humiliation disguised as curiosity. I cherished and dreaded school, never knowing which America—the triumph or the crucible—I would experience on a given day. But writing, art, and music were an inexhaustible escape: explorations of color, texture, structure, and composition eventually led me to architecture, a field of study but also a state of mind where everything could potentially coalesce.

And yet, at eighteen, immersed in contemporary architectural discourse in a competitive undergraduate program, I discovered the next incarnation of the same othering impulse—more sinister somehow when couched in a venerable institution. I expected a culturally expansive approach to the world history of architecture, but India, which has a nearly five-thousand-year-old urban history and gave civilization the written zero, yoga, chess, and the Taj Mahal, was casually omitted from the syllabus. I ran into what became a lingering paradox in my time as an architectural student: I could reinforce the pernicious stereotype of the humble, acquiescent minority, and be complicit in the centuries-long silencing of subaltern voices, or take the risk of being loud, and appear petty and defensive about things that no one else cared about anyway. The message appeared to be that Brown people did not make buildings, typologies, or urban schemes that were relevant to our modernist education, and furthermore, educators trained in categorically European traditions couldn't be expected to learn this ostensibly separate history in order to teach it to us. In a course built entirely on the memorization of dates

"ठोस इमारतें, तरल इतिहास: अमरीका में प्रवासी साधना का एक विवरण" (तीन अंश)
अनीशा धारवाड़कर

फिर भी, अठ्ठारह वर्ष की उम्र में, जब मैं अपने प्रतिस्पर्धी विश्वविद्यालय में समकालीन वास्तुविज्ञान के प्रवचन में तल्लीन थी, मुझे उसी अन्य-करण या "अदरिंग" के आवेश का अगला अवतार मिला – जो, किसी कारण से, और भी भयावह था, क्योंकि वह एक सम्मानित संस्था में स्थापित था। मेरी अपेक्षा यह थी कि वहाँ वास्तुविज्ञान का विश्व-इतिहास एक प्रशस्त सांस्कृतिक दृष्टिकोण से पढ़ाया जाएगा। परंतु उस पाठ्यक्रम से भारत को अकस्मात हटा दिया गया था – वही भारत जिसका नागरीय इतिहास लगभग पाँच हज़ार वर्ष लम्बा है और जिसने विश्व-सभ्यता को शून्य का लिखित चिन्ह, योग, शतरञ्ज, और ताज महल दिए हैं। इसलिये वास्तुविज्ञान की पढ़ाई के दौरान मैंने लगातार एक अंतर्विरोध का अनुभव किया: मैं या तो एक विनम्र, सहनशील, अल्पसंख्यक वर्ग की छात्रा बनकर उस "स्टीरियोटाइप" को और मज़बूत कर सकती थी, जो सदियों से आधीन आवाज़ों को चुप रखने में सह-अपराधी हो; या फिर मैं जोखिम उठाकर, क्षुद्र तथा "डिफ़ेन्सिव" बनकर, ऐसे मुद्दों पर आवाज़ उठा सकती थी जिनके बारे में लोग वैसे भी परवाह नहीं करते। मेरी शिक्षा का संदेश यह था कि भूरी-त्वचा के लोग उन इमारतों, वर्गीकरण के भेदों, और नागरीय योजनाओं को नहीं गढ़ते जो हमारी आधुनिकतावादी शिक्षा के लिए अनिवार्य हैं। इसके अतिरिक्त, यह भी स्पष्ट था कि जिन अध्यापकों की अपनी शिक्षा केवल निश्चित यूरोपीय परंपराओं के अनुसार हुई थी, उनसे यह आशा करना संभव नहीं था कि वे एक अलग इतिहास को ख़ुद सीखेंगे और हमें भी पढ़ाएँगे । एक ऐसी कक्षा में, जिसका पूरा पाठ्यक्रम तिथियों व कालक्रमों को रटने पर निर्भर था, मैंने वास्तुविज्ञान के इतिहास की एक अपनी, निजी परिभाषा को रचना शुरू किया – ऐसी परिभाषा जो कालबद्ध स्वरूपों, व्यवस्थाओं, और सम्बन्धों पर आधारित थी, जो रैखिक कालक्रम से श्रेष्ठ थी और उस पूर्वग्रह से ऊँची थी जो, कहने को, अतीत के "निष्पक्ष" प्रलेखन में दिखाई देता है। मुझे लगा कि इतिहास को कालक्रम से अलग करना और इतिहास-लेखन का गहरा विश्लेषण करना, जिससे यह स्पष्ट हो कि वस्तुनिष्ठता तथा निष्पक्षता के पर्दे के पीछे क्या होता है, एक मूलभूत और क्रांतिकारी प्रस्थान था। साम्राज्यवाद के सिद्धांतों और उपनिवेशवाद की साधनाओं का निष्ठ और सख़्त प्रलेखन करते समय, एडवर्ड सईद ने जिन ज्ञान-मीमांसाओं का विश्लेषण मानवशास्त्र के विषयों के लिए किया था, उन्हीं का वातावरण वास्तुविज्ञान में भी था – मार्मिक, सर्व-व्यापक, और बिल्कुल अदृश्य।

उसके बाद, ग्रैजुएट स्कूल के अंतर्गत, एक ऐसी जगह जो निष्ठित रूप में प्रगतिशील प्रतीत होती थी, मुझे फिर से अनपेक्षित वास्तुविज्ञान-इतिहास

> **Some essential questions, ones I am still asking, began to form: Where do you think Europe came from? Modernity at that scale required massive amounts of capital—where do you think that came from? And, for god's sake, what do you think happened to all that cotton?**

and chronologies, I started cobbling together my own definition of architectural history—one based on patterns, systems, and connections across time, one that transcended linear narration and the bias built into "objective" documentation of the past. To separate history from chronology, and to critique historiography—to really unpack what was going on behind that curtain of objectivity—felt like a radical departure. Imperialism (the philosophy) and colonialism (the practice) were, as Edward Said had documented so rigorously for the humanities, the epistemological atmosphere for architecture as well: vital, ubiquitous, and invisible.

Later, in graduate school, I (again unexpectedly) uncovered a deeply conservative approach to architectural history in a place that appeared sincerely progressive. During office hours with a respected faculty member, I learned that being a self-professed "Europeanist" did not require any knowledge of, or burden to be educated about, colonialism, either in general or in relation to architectural and urban history. I was intellectually and emotionally ill-equipped at the time to respond with anything other than silence, but some essential questions, ones I am still asking, began to form: Where do you think Europe came from? Modernity at that scale required massive amounts of capital—where do you think that came from? And, for god's sake, what do you think happened to all that cotton? The economic dimension of colonialism, which materially transformed the colonial metropoles into superpowers that dominated, among so many other things, architectural theory, was constantly overlooked. This position reinforced the deeply problematic perception that architecture is willed into existence through sheer tenacity, and that "context" is only local. Colonialism was the original globalization of capital, and the architectures that flowed from it were one lasting expression of the violence in its hinterlands.

It became increasingly clear that few were asking these kinds of questions, because who they were—their life experiences, educational trajectories, and spatial imaginations—would be fundamentally at odds with the terrifying

सम्बन्धी एक गहरा रूढ़िवादी दृष्टिकोण मिला। एक माननीय प्राध्यापक से उनके दफ़्तर में बात करते समय मुझे पता चला कि आत्म-वर्णित "यूरोपीयवादी" होने पर उपनिवेश-अवस्था के बारे में न तो किसी ज्ञान की आवश्यकता है, और न ही उसके बारे में शिक्षित होने का बोझ, चाहे उपनिवेशवाद सामान्य रूप में समझा जाए या वास्तुविज्ञान तथा नागरीय इतिहास के सम्बंध में। उस समय, बौद्धिक और भावनात्मक स्तर पर, मुझमें मौन रहने के सिवा किसी और प्रतिक्रिया की शक्ति नहीं थी, परंतु कुछ आवश्यक प्रश्न, जिन्हें मैं अभी तक दोहरा रही हूँ, मेरे मन में उभरने लगे। आपकी समझ में यूरोप कहाँ से पैदा हुआ? उस पैमाने पर आधुनिकता के लिए विराट पूँजी की ज़रूरत होती है – आपकी समझ में उतनी पूँजी कहाँ से आयी? और, भगवान के लिए, आप की समझ में उतनी सारी रुई का क्या हुआ? उपनिवेशित अवस्था के आर्थिक आयाम की हमेशा उपेक्षा की जाती रही थी, जबकि इस आयाम ने साम्राज्यवादी महानगरों को महाशक्तियों में बदल दिया और, कई और वस्तुओं के साथ-साथ, वास्तुशास्त्र के सिद्धांतों पर भी अपना क़ब्ज़ा बनाए रखा। इस नज़रिए ने उस गहरी समस्यात्मक धारणा को बल दिया जिसके अनुसार वास्तुविज्ञान केवल निरी दृढ़ता से उत्पन्न किया जाता है, और उसका सन्दर्भ केवल "लोकल" या स्थानीय होता है। उपनिवेशवाद पूँजी के विश्वव्यापीकरण का पहला और मूल रूप था, और उससे जो वास्तुकलाएँ विभिन्न रूपों में प्रवाहित हुईं, वे आंतरिक इलाक़ों में हुई हिंसा की स्थायी अभिव्यक्तियाँ थीं।

*

मेरी कुण्ठा और बढ़ी क्योंकि मैं जानती थी कि अन्य विषयों तथा सर्जनात्मक साधनाओं ने कुछ दशक पहले इन समस्याओं से जूझना शुरू कर दिया था, जब १९८० के कुछ बाद अंग्रेज़ी भाषा के संस्थानों में उत्तर-औपनिवेशिक सिद्धांत उभरे। इस विश्लेषण के साधन आसानी से उपलब्ध थे अगर हम जानते कि उन्हें कहाँ ढूँढा जाए, परंतु वास्तुविज्ञान को अपने अनुशासनात्मक स्तर पर अपने साहित्य और विचारधारा को अस्थिर करने में अत्यधिक मुश्किल हो रही थी। वास्तव में, जब तक कोविड-१९ की महामारी तथा अमरीका में जॉर्ज फ़्लॉयड की हत्या का संकटकाल नहीं आया, और जब तक उनसे फलित सामाजिक अपेक्षाओं का पुनर्मूल्यांकन नहीं हुआ, तब तक वास्तुविज्ञान के प्रवचन – व्यक्तिगत लेखक और साधनाकार के पैमाने के ठीक पार – इस सारे झंझट में अपना स्थान खोजने की प्रक्रिया शुरू न कर पाये। नयी व्याख्यान-शृंखलाओं के स्पष्ट विषय; डिज़ाइन-अध्यापकों की नियुक्ति में नयी प्रधानताएँ; कम्पनियों की वेबसाइटों पर नस्लवाद-विरोधी नए बयान; नयी सामान्य स्वीकृतियाँ, कि पूंजीवादी निर्माण-क्रिया के लगातार शोर ने समाज और पर्यावरण को बहुत हानि पहुँचाई है। "डी-कलोनियल" तथा "सेटलर-कलोनियल" जैसे शब्द अकादमिक विशेषताओं की परिधि से चलकर ठीक हमारी साझा शब्दावली और सामूहिक जन-प्रवचन में उतर आए ("सोशल

> **The tools were readily available if one knew where to look, but architecture was having enormous trouble unsettling its own literature and ideas at a disciplinary level. It was not really until the crises of the COVID-19 pandemic and George Floyd's death, and the recalibration of social expectations that resulted from both, that architectural discourse, beyond the scale of the individual writer or practitioner, began to grapple with its place in this mess.**

answers. To address these questions honestly would require upturning every basic fact about architecture, history, and modern life. Or, perhaps more precisely, it would require completely recontextualizing the processes and outcomes of European urbanism after 1492, with many new layers and voices added to the core narratives of design history and theory classes. From my vantage point, the fixation on the European nation-state as a bounded entity from which we derived the primary historical data, philosophies, and outcomes of architecture and urbanism (despite the massive global footprint, monetary drain, and enduring social impact of colonial empires) was unalterable. The discipline appeared to have fallen for the self-exonerating narrative that any activities in the colonial hinterland had little impact on the architectural development of the metropole. But in the bluntest way, Liverpool and Manchester prove otherwise, as cities built of cotton mills in a country that couldn't grow an ounce of the fiber.

Compounding my frustration was knowing that other disciplines and creative practices had begun grappling with these issues decades before, when postcolonial theory emerged in English-language institutions in the 1980s. The tools were readily available if one knew where to look, but architecture was having enormous trouble unsettling its own literature and ideas at a disciplinary level. It was not really until the crises of the COVID-19 pandemic and George Floyd's death, and the recalibration of social expectations that resulted from both, that architectural discourse, beyond the scale of the individual writer or practitioner, began to grapple with its place in this mess. We began to see new, unequivocal lecture series themes; new priorities in faculty hires; new anti-racism statements on firm websites; general acknowledgments that the steady thrum of capitalist building has caused great social and environmental harm. Terms like "decolonial" and "settler colonial" entered our shared vocabulary, moving from the periphery

मीडिया" के आवश्यक वाहन द्वारा)। यह उभरता आंदोलन मान्यता-प्रदायक और अतिदेय है, परंतु नाटकीय प्रदर्शन में घट जाने का जोखिम भी रखता है – सक्रियता का एक और ढंग जो विभिन्नता को तभी तक स्वीकार करता है जब तक सत्ता की संरचना को वह वास्तव में हिलाने न लगे। अमरीका में डिज़ाइन की शिक्षा-पद्धतियों को बदलने के लिए आवाज़ों की जिस "सुनामी" की ज़रूरत है उसका अभी तक भूम-बिछल नहीं हुआ है; जब होगा, तब वह वास्तुशास्त्र की ज्ञान-मीमांसा में एक ऐसी समता लाएगा जो वास्तुविज्ञान-विद्यालयों के पाठ्यक्रम से लेकर पेशेवर साधनाओं तक फैलेगी, और उसके बाद – बिलकुल सकारात्मक अर्थ में – लौट जाने की कोई सम्भावना नहीं रहेगी। वह डिज़ाइन के कार्य-क्षेत्र से एक ऐसा मानवीय दृष्टिकोण माँगेगी जिसे हम अभी पहचान भी नहीं सकते, पर जो पीड़ाजनक इतिहास और संदिग्ध इतिहास-लेखन में शिक्षा देने, शिक्षा लेने, और वास्तुनिर्माण करने के तरीक़ों को शुद्धि से बदल देगा।

*

विदेश-प्रवासियों की साधना लोगों और योजनाओं को नए दृष्टिकोण से देखने का तर्क कर सकती है और परिपालन भी। इससे संचार और सहानुभूति – जिनका "सॉफ़्ट-स्किल्ज़" के नाम पर अधिकतर उपहास किया जाता है – दोनों ही "डिज़ाइनर" के कार्य-भंडार में मूलभूत साधन और साधना के केन्द्र बन सकते हैं। वास्तुविज्ञान के इतिहास का कथानक, जो बहुत संकीर्ण तथा पीड़ाजनक है, अठ्ठारवीं शताब्दी के यूरोपीय "एन्लायटन्मेंट" की विचारधारा के अधीन था। वे डिज़ाइनर, जिनका वंशगत इतिहास उपनिवेशित स्थानों से जुड़ा है, अपने निजी अनुभवों को शास्त्रीय सिद्धांतों में बदल सकते हैं, और डिज़ाइन के इतिहास को लिखने, उसे पढ़ाने, तथा उसे समझने की पूरी प्रक्रिया का विस्तार कर सकते हैं। प्रवासियों की साधनाएँ ऐसे बृहत् और सूक्ष्म नवप्रवर्तनों का केंद्र बन सकती हैं जो मिलकर अपने स्थान और कथानक से उपनिवेशवादी और पूँजीवादी "इन्फ़्रास्ट्रक्चर" और ज्ञान-मीमांसाओं के विरुद्ध प्रतिकार करें। वास्तुशास्त्र को अंदरूनी आंदोलनकर्ताओं की ज़रूरत है, जो उतना ही विनाश और विध्वंस करें जितना कि सृजन और उत्पादन। इससे हो सकता है कि प्रवासी साधनाएँ कुछ कम उत्खनन, कम निर्माण, और कम हस्तक्षेप की माँग करें – कम संग्राम भी करें, उन पार्थिव तत्वों से जिन्हें हमने विद्रोही तत्व बना दिया है।

अनुवाद: विनय धारवाड़कर और अपर्णा धारवाड़कर (विस्कॉन्सिन विश्वविद्यालय, मैडिसन) तथा ब्रजेश समर्थ (एमरी विश्वविद्यालय, एटलैंटा)
टाइपसेटिंग तथा डिजिटल-संपादन: ब्रजेश समर्थ; ज़ारा चौधरी (विस्कॉन्सिन विश्वविद्यालय)

of academic specializations into collective public discourse (with social media as a critical vehicle).

This evolving movement is deeply validating and long overdue, but also at risk of being reduced to a superficial performance—another form of activism that accepts diversity until it actually destabilizes our power structures. The tsunami of voices required to change the course of design in the United States has yet to make landfall, but when it does, it will bring an epistemological equity that will stretch from architecture school curricula to professional practice, from which there will be, in the most positive sense, no turning back. It will demand a humanist approach to design at a scale we don't yet recognize—one that can distill a painful history and a dubious historiography into new ways of teaching, learning, and producing architecture.

WHAT MIGHT CONSTITUTE A DIASPORIC PRACTICE?

The United States has always been about land: how to acquire it, cultivate it, and build on it in order to extract profit from it. Behind the philosophies, debates, and radical manifestos that helped establish this nation and change the course of others is this inescapable material fact. The approach was never about stewardship, of course, but about exploitation, and we are now deeply aware of the climate ramifications of this behavior. The fraud at the center of the colonial enterprise was that human rights violations were an acceptable outcome of, and in turn a vehicle for, control over land. The Dutch, Portuguese, French, and British empires outsourced these abuses to their respective hinterlands by plundering natural resources (spices, minerals, fibers) from climate zones different from their own, committing genocide of Indigenous populations, and systematizing indentured servitude and slavery at a transcontinental scale. After the Treaty of Paris, the political relationship between Britain and the

> **The fact of British decolonization in the United States did not expunge the colonial mindset; rather, it created a new paradigm where colonialism, slavery, and capitalism all overlapped spatially, under a vast project of land management, to produce the global-scale economic shifts whose results we still live within today.**

ANEESHA DHARWADKER

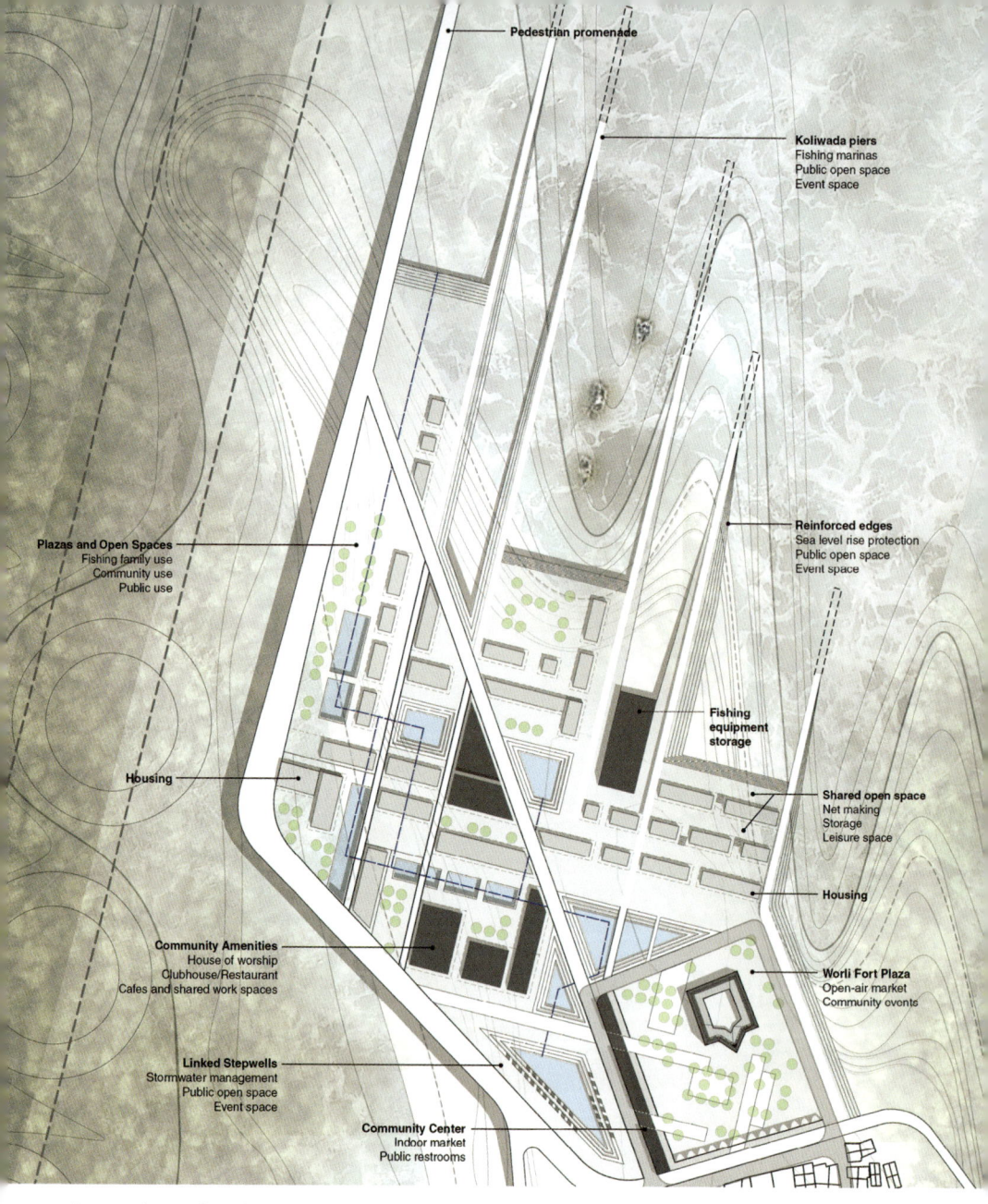

above and opposite: Chicago Design Office and Hinterlands Urbanism and Landscape, "Mangrove Metropolis," 2018, a speculative proposal for mangrove restoration for the Worli Koliwada fishing community in Mumbai. The proposal includes a catalog for site-specific ecology, culture, and commerce, addressing the seasonality and time-based fluctuations of the site conditions.

PERMANENT BUILDINGS, FLUID HISTORY

Other Mangrove Species

Mammals
- Indian Jackal — *Canis aureus indicus*
- Indian Grey Mongoose — *Herpestes edwardsii*
- Indian Wild Boar — *Susserofa cristatus*

Insects
- Small Salmon Arab — *Colotis amata*
- Teak Defoliator Moth — *Hyblaea puera*
- Carpenter Bee — *Xylocpa spp.*

Reptiles
- Little File Snake — *Acrochordus granulatus*
- Common Garden Lizard — *Calotes versicolor*
- Dog-Faced Water Snake — *Cerberus rynchops*
- Indian Rat Snake — *Ptyas mucosus*
- Common Monitor Lizard — *Varanus bengalensis*

Marine Life
- Striped Barnacle — *Balanus sp.*
- Blue-spotted Mudskipper — *Boleophthalmus boddarti*
- Ring-Legged Fiddler Crab — *Gelasimus annulipes*
- Telescope Snail — *Telescopium telescopium*
- Olive Ridley Turtle — *Lepidochelys olivacea*
- Mantis Shrimp — *Oratosquilla sp.*

Birds

Resident Birds (Year-round presence)
- Grey Heron — *Ardea cinerea*
- White-Throated Kingfisher — *Halcyon smyrnensis*
- Mangrove Kingfisher — *Halcyon senegaloides*
- Brahminy Kite — *Haliastur indus*
- Black-Winged Stilt — *Himantopus himantopus*
- Little Cormorant — *Microcarbo niger*
- White-Eared Bulbul — *Pycnonotus leucotis*
- Black-Headed Ibis — *Threskiornis melanocephalus*
- Lesser Whistling Duck — *Dendrocygna javanica*

Migratory Birds
- Common Sandpiper — *Actitis hypoleucos* — Winter migration from Europe & Asia
- Black-Headed Gull — *Larus ridibundus* — Winter migration from Central Asia
- Lesser Flamingo — *Phoeniconaias minor* — Winter migration from Gujarat

Commercial Species

Fish
- Bombay Duck — *Harpadon nehereus*
- Barramundi — *Lates calcarifer*
- Flathead Grey Mullett — *Mugil cephalus*
- Silver Pomfret — *Pampus argentus*
- Cobia — *Rachycentron canadum*
- Indian Mackerel/ Bangdu — *Rastrelliger kanagurta*
- Kingfish / Seer Fish — *Scomberomorus guttatus*

Benthic Macroinvertebrates
- Indian White Prawn — *Fenneropenaeus indicus*
- Asian Hard Clam — *Meretrix meretrix*
- Short-neck Clam — *Paphia malabarica*
- Carpet Clam — *Paphia textile*
- Tiger Prawn — *Penaeus monodon*
- Kulate — *Perna viridis*
- Blue Swimmer Crab — *Portunus pelagicus*
- Giant Mud Crab — *Scylla serrata*
- Blood Cockle — *Tegillarca granosa*
- Squid — *Uroteuthis duvaceli*

Red lines indicates when to refrain from fishing and eating certain species in order to avoid overexploiting depleting fish and macro invertebrate stocks. Doing so helps pregnant and juvenile fish or macro invertebrates survive.

Months: January, February, March, April, May, June, July, August, September, October, November, December

Monsoon Season

Holi — March 20-21, 2019
Eid — August 10-11, 2019
Diwali — October 27, 2019

Mangrove Vegetation

Mangrove Associates
- Common Night Glory — *Rivea hypocrateriformis*

Shrubs
- Toothbrush Tree — *Salvadora persica* — April - January Bloom Time
- Sea Purslane — *Sesuvium portulacastrum* — April - January Bloom Time
- Sea Holly — *Acanthus ilicifolius* — April - January Bloom Time

Trees
- River Mangrove — *Aegiceras corniculatum* — April - September Bloom Time
- Grey Mangrove — *Avicennia marina* — May - July Bloom Time
- White Burma Mangrove — *Bruguiera cylindrica* — May - July Bloom Time
- Broad-Leaf Orange Mangrove — *Bruguiera gymnorrhiza* — January - December Bloom Time
- Milk Mangrove — *Excoecaria agallocha* — January - December Bloom Time
- Tall-Stilt Mangrove — *Rhizophora apiculata* — May - September Bloom Time
- Red Mangrove — *Rhizophora mucronata* — July - October Bloom Time
- Sonneratia Mangrove — *Sonneratia apetala* — March - July Bloom Time

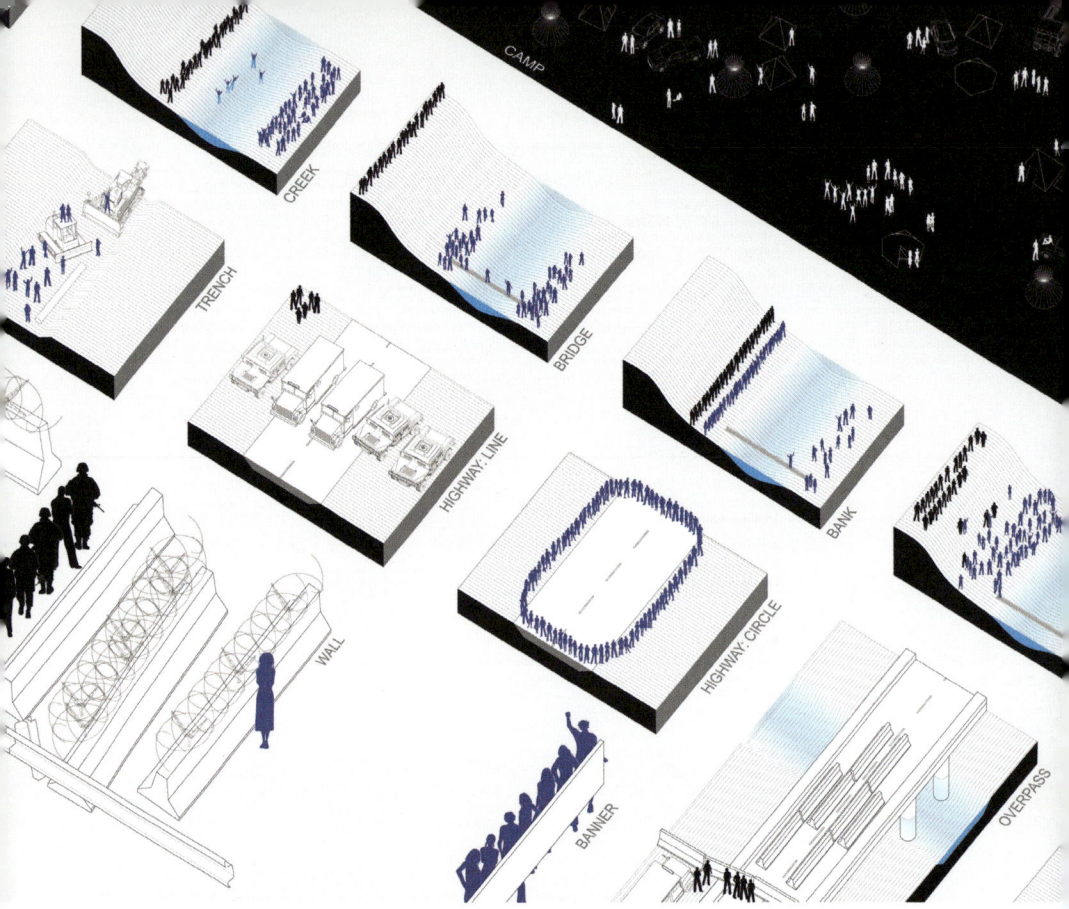

above: Chicago Design Office, "Native Citizenship," 2018, drawing included in *Form N-XOO: New Forms for Citizenship*, the online gallery of the US pavilion at the International Architecture Exhibition in Venice. This image documents forms and spaces of protest at Standing Rock Reservation in North Dakota in 2016, revealing how subversive forms of citizenship unfolded in Indigenous territory.
opposite: Chicago Design Office, "The Imagination Station," 2022, design workshops with Chicago's North Lawndale community; Chicago Design Office and Hinterlands Urbanism and Landscape, First Followers Learning Lab, 2018–20, a community reentry center in Champaign, Illinois. This project was carried out in collaboration with the nonprofit First Followers and engaged previously incarcerated young men in the processes of design and construction.

colonies transformed rapidly into an economic partnership, establishing cash flow for the new nation and bringing an avalanche of raw cotton to the kingdom's shores. The fact of British decolonization in the United States did not expunge the colonial mindset; rather, it created a new paradigm where colonialism, slavery, and capitalism all overlapped spatially, under a vast project of land management, to produce the global-scale economic shifts whose results we still live within today. Simon Lewis and Mark Maslin cite 1610 CE— early in the expansion of colonial enterprises but well into

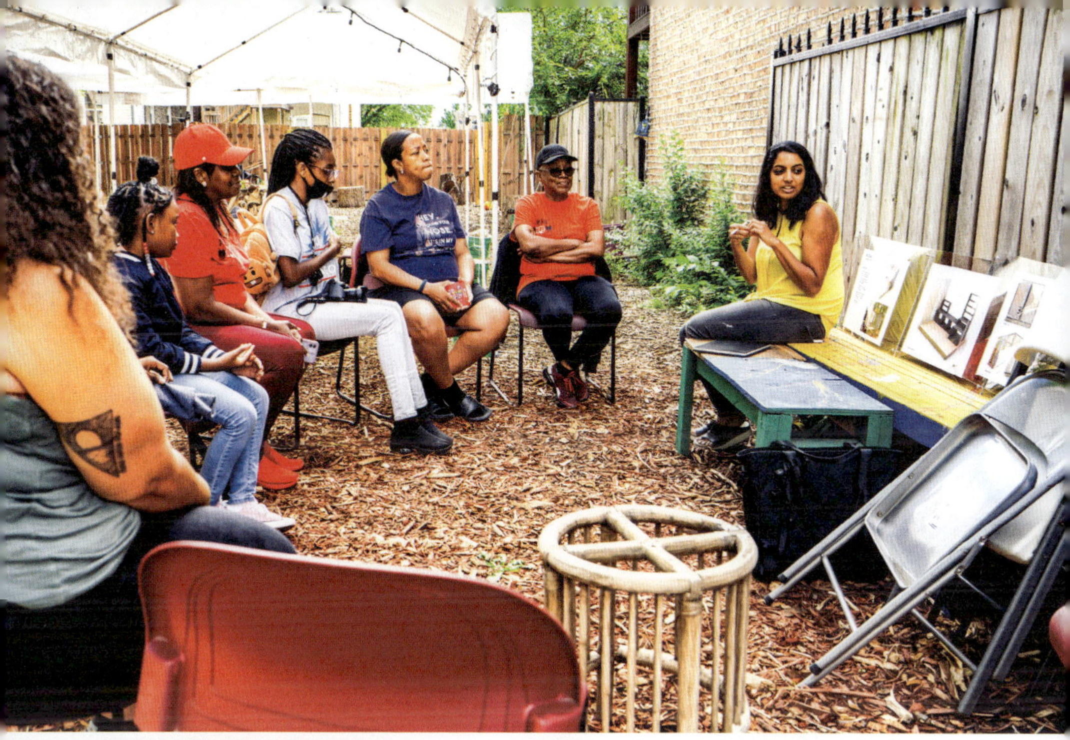

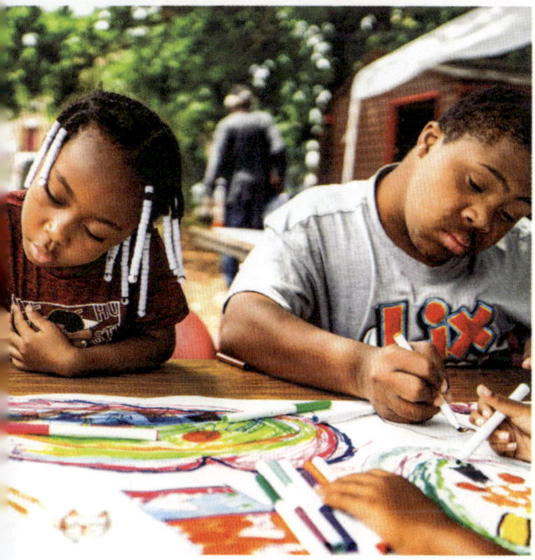

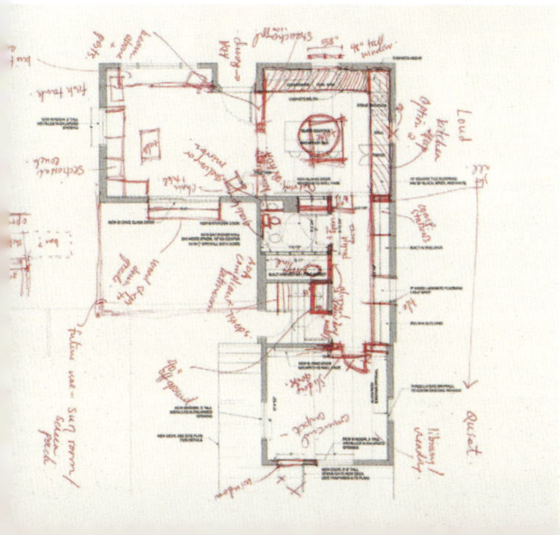

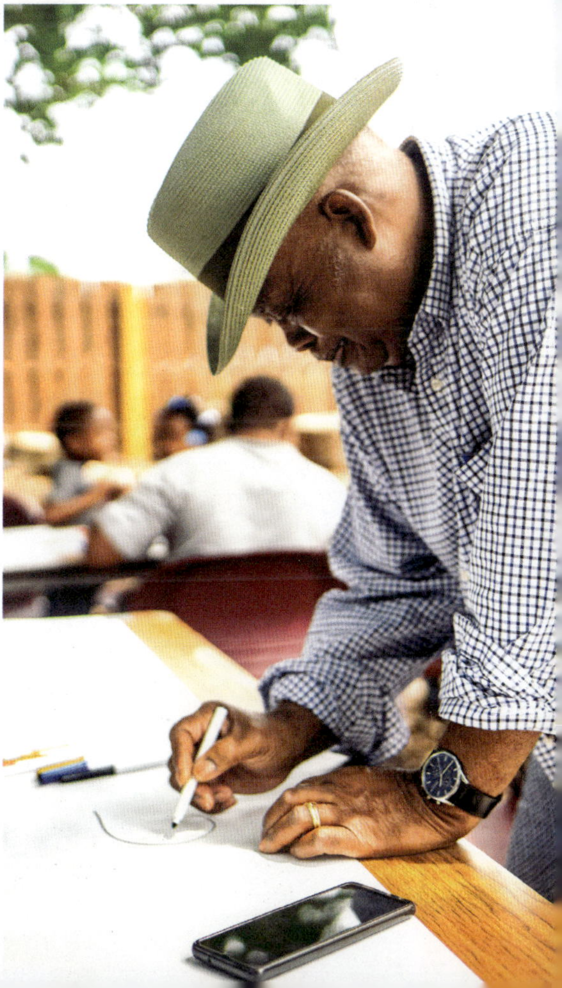

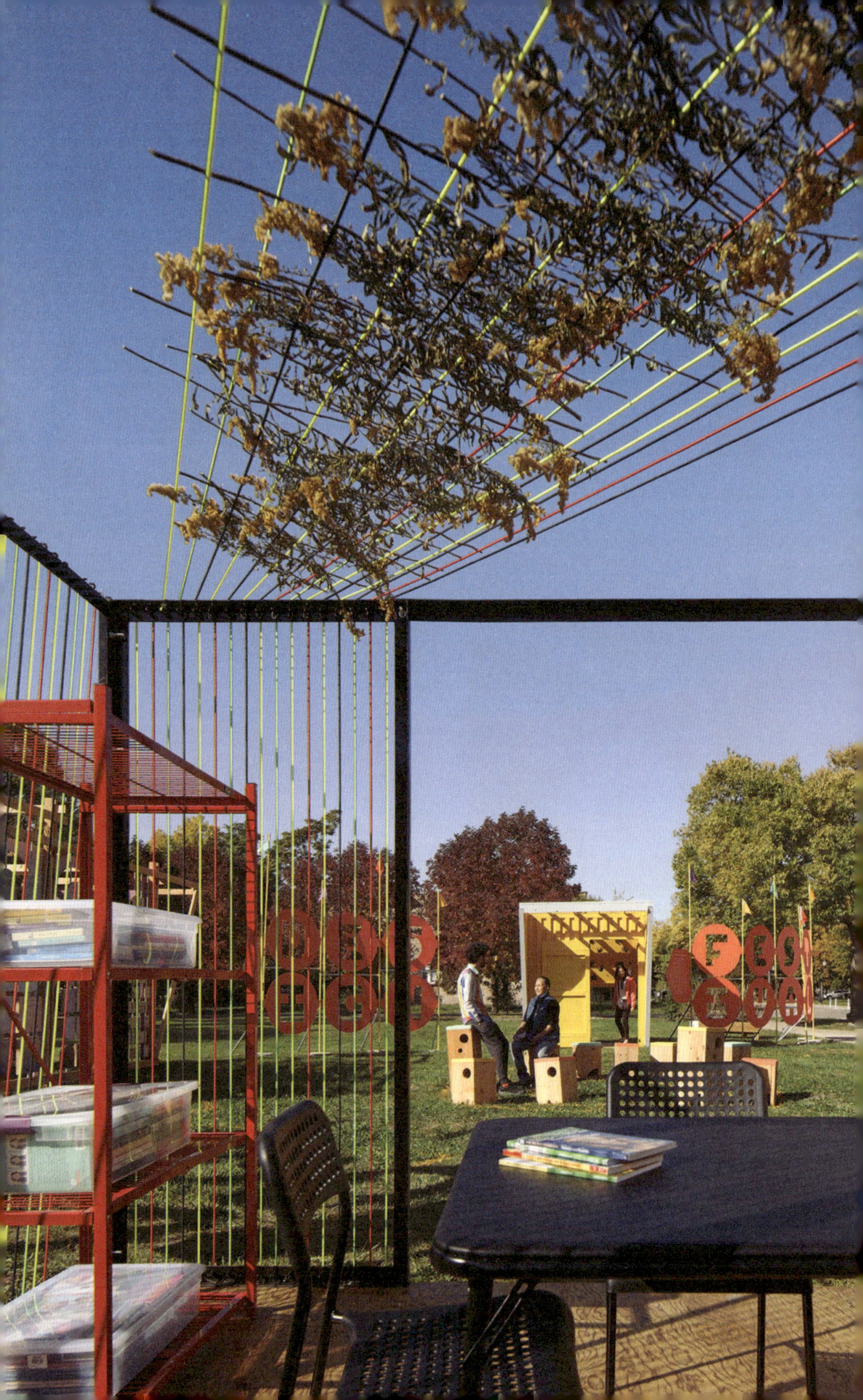

above and opposite: Chicago Design Office, "The Imagination Station," 2022, a flexible literacy pavilion for children and adults in North Lawndale, Chicago

ANEESHA DHARWADKER

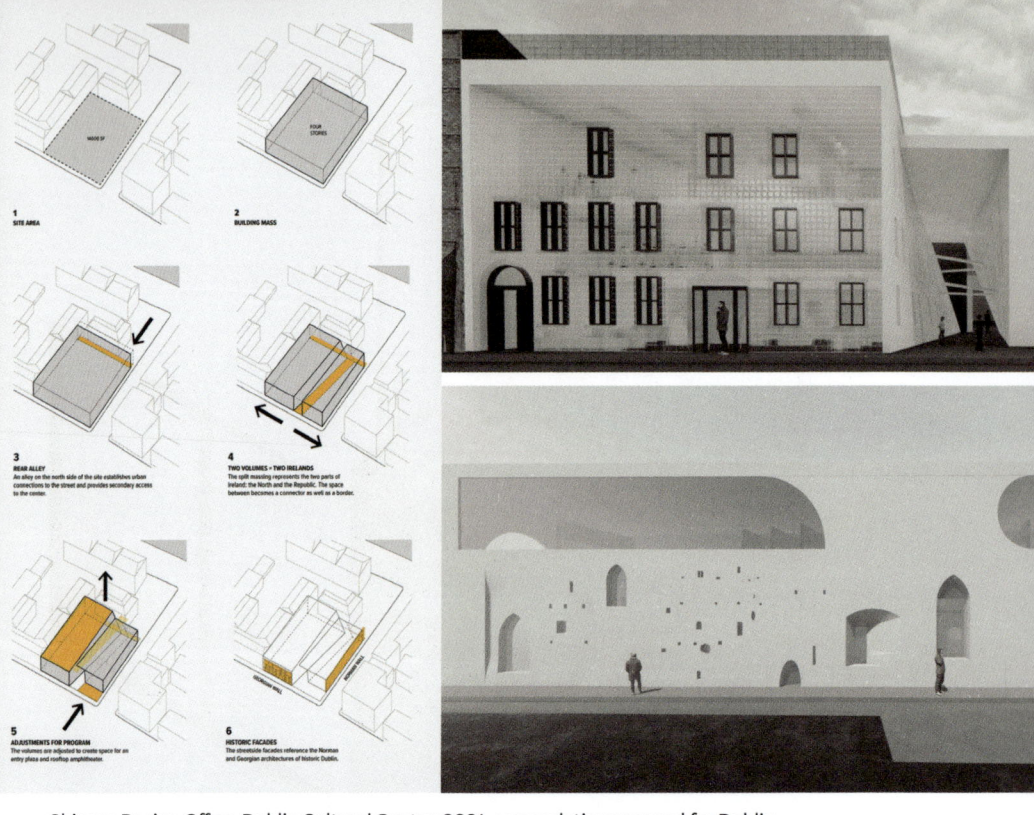

Chicago Design Office, Dublin Cultural Center, 2021, a speculative proposal for Dublin. Ireland has long been considered the original testing ground for British colonialism, and now—a thousand years later—is still divided along a partition line between the North and the Republic. This proposal is divided into two volumes with a porous hall between, reflecting the ongoing relationship between the two parts of the island. Contemporary interpretations of historic facades are projected onto the exterior, addressing the inextricability of colonial history from the present built environment.

the Columbian exchange, which, after 1492, generated an unprecedented movement of people, goods, technologies, diseases, flora, and fauna across the globe—as the year marking the identifiable start of the Anthropocene. This is the date at which geologists can point to material changes in the soil composition of North America as a result of new human activity.[1] Land has both abetted and registered colonialism, a critical component of producing this new epoch. Even today, after so many acts of decolonization and civil rights movements across the globe, our experience of the built environment is one of negotiating property boundaries that are imperialist in spirit. We are dictated by where we can and cannot go, and architectural practice, with rare exceptions, only reinforces those hard edges.

[1]. Simon L. Lewis and Mark Maslin, *The Human Planet: How We Created the Anthropocene* (New Haven, CT: Yale University Press, 2018).

68 PERMANENT BUILDINGS, FLUID HISTORY

Being a member of a postcolonial diaspora in the United States is thus fraught with complexities and contradictions. It is a constant balancing act of knowing this history, being powerless to do anything about it, and trying to survive day to day within current economic pressures. Practicing architecture—in its own way, an act of colonization over earth, water, and natural ecosystems—further complicates the situation. I care about architecture because I care about the aesthetics, usability, and environmental performance of the buildings we inhabit, and I believe all three can be carried out far more thoughtfully. Put another way, there is enormous room in architectural practice to make transformative gestures, large and small, that change both the process and the product of architecture in ways that might begin to address the damage wrought by colonial activities and mentalities. Within the existing structures of the private market, this might come in the form of an unwavering commitment to material sustainability and a reduction of construction waste at every stage of building.

The work of my practice, Chicago Design Office, oscillates (sometimes hourly) between the radical and the mundane. Certain projects address fundamental, decolonizing questions about practice, like who we should be designing with and for, where we should be implementing work in the world, and if buildings are even the answer to the questions we are asking. My past experiences of social and disciplinary parochialism undergird my approach to this work; they are a motivation and a reminder that we all exist in a deeply flawed system, and that any progress, however incremental, is imperative. One recent example is "The Imagination Station," a deconstructible reading pavilion for a children's organization based in North Lawndale, a predominantly Black neighborhood on Chicago's West Side. The grant-based funding mechanism allowed small organizations that might not otherwise have the resources to pay for design work to experience the benefits of it—an incremental effort to repair both the environment and social interactions within it. The design process involved community meetings, workshops, list making, and informal exchanges with the eventual users, resulting in a multidirectional conversation informing the ninety-six-square-foot design.

Other projects are constrained by external factors like building codes and driven by the conventions of architectural

MASS Design Group, hanging stelae at the National Memorial for Peace and Justice, Montgomery, Alabama, 2018

project management (construction detailing, cost estimating, RFIs, field notes). Rethinking those entrenched systems, too, is a stubborn disciplinary challenge, as it can be hard to identify where empathy and anti-colonial reasoning can be folded into the most technical aspects of building production. The permanence of buildings as an outcome is at odds with potential design approaches, like resisting construction efficiency or reducing rentable square footage in order to create unexpected spaces of public-ness and community. But that very well may be the fulcrum of change: where the integrity of a building's internal logic can be sacrificed for the people it is supposed to serve as well as the people it isn't.

A diasporic practice can argue for and implement new approaches to projects and people, centering communication and compassion (derided so often as "soft" skills) as essential tools in the designer's repertoire. The narrative of architecture history is painfully narrow and dominated by Enlightenment-based thought, but designers with ancestral history in colonized spaces can channel the personal into the disciplinary, expanding how design history is written, taught, and understood. Diasporic practices can be sites for both sweeping and minute innovations that together make spaces and stories that retaliate against colonialist-capitalist infrastructure and epistemologies. Architecture as a discipline also needs agitators from within, un-doing and un-making as much as creating and producing. Diasporic practices might end up arguing for less excavation, less building, and less intervention. Less battling against the earthly elements we've turned mutinous.

Certain practices and projects are taking on this enormous responsibility in powerful ways: studio:indigenous, helmed by Chris Cornelius, designs for Indigenous clients with Indigenous typologies and construction techniques in mind, reconsidering building, drawing, mapping, and design narratives all at once. Marshall Brown Projects focuses on collage as an architectural generator and as a critique of miscegenation laws in the United States. Reddymade, founded by Suchi Reddy, centers empathy and its neurological benefits in its design processes. The Settler Colonial City Project, launched by Ana María León and Andrew Herscher, overlays colonial history in the United States onto the everyday spaces of our cities, with a focus on Chicago. At a larger scale, MASS Design Group's justice-based approach to public works, their structure as a nonprofit across two continents, and their attention to the material processes and impacts of construction offer a roadmap for expanding postcolonial issues into institutional missions. The National Memorial for Peace and Justice in Montgomery, Alabama, in its unsparing abstraction and modulation of cross section, acknowledges the grotesque reality of the history of lynching while offering moments for visitors and family members to reflect and heal. These approaches indicate what diasporic difference might look and feel like, where ingrained ways of knowing are challenged through design interventions and reconfigurations. Diasporic practices are uniquely positioned to take on the spatial and the epistemological at once, with finesse.

Diversity is a strange beast in this discipline. So much is gained from having people with different upbringings in conversations about architecture because it allows us to recognize how careless and destructive many modern design decisions have been (in particular with regard to housing design and planning). We can't fix problems that we can't identify, and we need all those perspectives to articulate what those problems are in the first place. But when it comes to the application and construction of design, we risk suffocating a diversity of ideas with the requirements for licensing, permitting, and code compliance. This is not to say that life safety issues aren't paramount, but the way architectural knowledge is approached in these technical arenas leaves little room for subversion. Diasporic practice, as a paradigm, could offer a way forward in this regard, especially if it can center questions of audience and process as well as materials and construction techniques in relation to climate impact.

In short: In a world where all buildings can be legally sorted into five categories, what is Construction Type VI?

> This is the myth [of a zero sum game]—that "If you gain, I lose."…It is as if I don't want you to come to my dinner table because I think that you will just come and eat up all of the food, without recognizing that you are bringing all kinds of cakes and pies and roasts and fruits and salads with you. It comes from two deeply held beliefs, that you have nothing of value to offer and that I have everything that I need at my table. Neither of those beliefs is ever true. Each of us has something to teach, and each of us has something to learn.

Camara Phyllis Jones
physician and anti-racism activist
"Seeing the Water: Seven Values Targets for Anti-Racism Action," 2020

> **The communication is probably more candid, though more painful than ever before, and this is progress.**

Whitney M. Young Jr.
American civil rights leader
Keynote address to the American Institute of
Architects National Convention, 1968

Racism and **Anti-racism**

Racism is the conscious or unconscious belief that different races possess distinct characteristics, abilities, or qualities that make them innately inferior or superior. These beliefs can manifest outwardly as overt harassment, humiliation, violence, neglect, oppression, inequitable opportunities, or unfavorable outcomes. Racism is often associated with a dominant white culture, but prejudice and discrimination based on race and ethnicity exist across all cultures. Racism can be fueled by action or inaction. Doing nothing or not speaking up when something unjust is happening is, in effect, racist.

Anti-racism is the practice of acknowledging one's own prejudices, taking steps to identify and describe existing racism, and actively working to dismantle racist systems. The goal of anti-racism is to proactively change systems, institutions, laws, policies, behaviors, and beliefs that perpetuate racist ideas and actions.

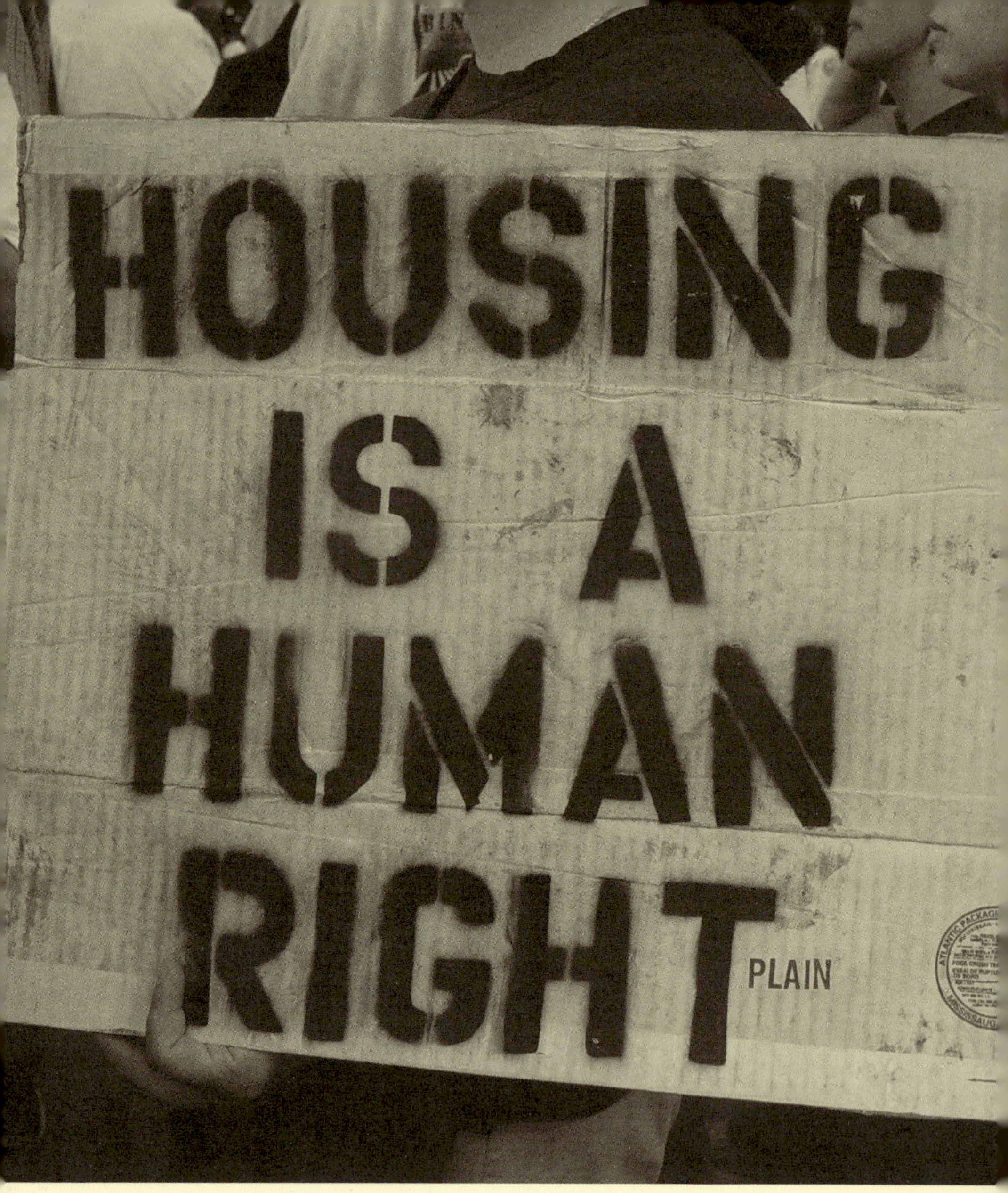
HOUSING
IS A
HUMAN
RIGHT
PLAIN

[BENCHMARK]

YOUR THUNDEROUS SILENCE

Whitney M. Young Jr.

In 1968, Whitney M. Young Jr., executive director of the National Urban League, delivered a speech at the American Institute of Architects National Convention calling for more diversity in the profession and challenging architects to act on critical social issues facing urban communities. It is excerpted below.[1] *In 1972 the AIA created the Whitney M. Young Jr. Award, which is given annually to an architect or architectural organization that actively embodies social responsibility.*

It would be the most naive escapist who today would be unaware that the winds of change, as far as human aspirations are concerned, are fast reaching tornado proportions. Throughout our world society, and particularly in our own country, the disinherited, the disfranchised, the poor, the Black are saying in no unmistakable terms that they intend to be in or nobody will be comfortably in…

The disinherited in our society today, unlike the past, are fully aware of the gap between their standard of living and the large majority of Americans. No longer are they the sharecroppers on farms and in rural areas where they have not the benefit of newspapers and radio. Today, for the most part, the poor live within a stone's throw of the affluent. They witness on their television sets and read in their newspapers and see personally how the other half, or the other eighty percent, live. The poor no longer assume that their status is God-made. They no longer believe that they are

---

[1]. The full text is available at https://content.aia.org/sites/default/files/2018-04/WhitneyYoungJr_1968AIAContention_FulLSpeech.pdf.

congenitally and innately inferior because of their color or because of a condition of birth. The poor are fully aware today that their conditions are man-made and not God-decreed or constitutionally derived....

We are a racist nation, and no way in the world could it be otherwise given the history of our country. Being a racist doesn't mean one wants to go out and join a lynch mob or send somebody off to Africa or engage in crude, vulgar expressions of prejudice. Racism is a basic assumption of superiority on the part of one group over another....

You are not a profession that has distinguished itself by your social and civic contributions to the cause of civil rights, and I am sure this has not come to you as any shock. You are most distinguished by your thunderous silence and your complete irrelevance...

But I have read about architects who had courage, who had a social sensitivity, and I can't help but wonder about an architect that builds some of the public housing that I see in the cities of this country. How he could even compromise his own profession and his own sense of values to have built thirty-five- or forty-story buildings, these vertical slums, and not even put a restroom in the basement and leave enough recreational space for about ten kids when there must be five thousand in the building. That architects as a profession wouldn't as a group stand up and say something about this is disturbing to me.

You are employers, you are key people in the planning of our cities today. You share the responsibility for the mess we are in terms of the white noose around the central city. It didn't just happen. We didn't just suddenly get this situation. It was carefully planned... It took a great deal of skill and creativity and imagination to build the kind of situation we have, and it is going to take skill and imagination and creativity to change it.

When you go to a city—Champagne-Urbana—the University of Illinois is about the only major institution, and within two or three blocks are some of the worst slums I have seen in the country. It is amazing how within a stone's throw of the School of Architecture you have absolutely complete indifference—unless you have a federal grant for research, and even then it's to study the problem...

As a profession, you ought to be taking stands on these kinds of things. If you don't as architects stand up and endorse model cities and appropriations, if you don't speak out for rent supplements or the housing bill calling for a million homes, if you don't speak out for some kind of scholarship program that will enable you to consciously and deliberately seek to bring in minority people who have been discriminated against in many cases, either kept out because of your indifference or couldn't make it—it takes seven to ten years to become an architect—then you will have done a disservice to the memory of John Kennedy, Martin Luther King, Bob Kennedy, and most of all, to yourselves....

So, what's at stake then is your country, your profession, and you as a decent civilized human being. Anatole France once said, "I prefer the error of enthusiasm to the indifference of wisdom." **For a society that has permitted itself the luxury of an excess of callousness and indifference, we can now afford to permit ourselves the luxury of an excess of caring and of concern.**

"All Negroes didn't riot in Watts. All Negroes didn't riot in Newark. One out of three in Newark were whites, and one out of five in Watts, and that's why there was more violence in Newark. White people are more experienced."
   —Whitney M. Young Jr., Address at the American Institute of Architects National Convention, 1968

Protester in Minneapolis following the death of George Floyd

Microaggression

Microaggressions are intended or unintended verbal, nonverbal, and environmental slights or insults—often subtle or indirect—that communicate negative, dismissive, or exclusionary messages. These can include backhanded compliments; tone of voice, words, or gestures that convey annoyance or impatience with another's point of view; making assumptions based on stereotypes; interrupting or talking over someone during meetings or discussions; or facial expressions and body language that convey disrespect or condescension, such as crossing arms or avoiding eye contact.

Le Corbusier and Josephine Baker at a celebration aboard the SS *Lutetia*, returning to Europe from Latin America, circa 1929. The person in blackface is not identified.

[SNAPSHOT]

BLACKFACE BEAUX ARTS BALL

Melanie Reddrick

It's 2001, and I'm walking down the hall toward the studio when I see a poster advertising the Beaux Arts Ball. I look closer, and I realize it includes a photograph of Le Corbusier and friends at a dinner party. And…someone in the photo is wearing blackface makeup. I wasn't really surprised to see Le Corbusier in that group. I was, however, floored by the fact that our (their) student architecture organization used that photo to advertise our (their) Beaux Arts Ball.

There seemed to be an epidemic of racist incidents at the university that year. That same semester, several white fraternity members posted photos of their blackface parties on social media channels. Their target: one of the Black fraternities. And a biracial student running for president of the Student Council was attacked and beaten on the way back to her residence hall. She reported from her hospital bed that the attackers used racial slurs and referenced her presidential run as the reason for the assault.

The State Bureau of Investigation got involved, and finally so did I.

I was one of only two Black graduate students in architecture at the time, and we (along with another minority graduate student) started a NOMAS chapter, bringing minority speakers to campus and creating a support system for one another, grads and undergrads alike. The organization was open to all, which was initially viewed with suspicion by some. A group of fellow students even reported to the school's administration that one of our flyers was "obscene."

Nevertheless, we doubled down and decided to start a series of juried art shows around themes of diversity and inclusion. The first year it was titled *Outsider/Insider*. One of the works in the show was a sculpture I created in collaboration with a fellow (white) graduate student. The show was a great success. The following year, the theme was *Homeland*, and the show featured another excellent collection of work.

So, despite the malice and hurt and anger that was so pervasive at that time, in the end we fought back the way architects do—with creativity and hard work.

> It is often said that culture is the sum total of the stories we tell ourselves, about ourselves. Whilst it is true, what is missing in the statement is any acknowledgement of who the 'we' in question is. In architecture particularly, the dominant voice has historically been a singular, exclusive voice, whose reach and power ignore huge swathes of humanity—financially, creatively, conceptually—as though we have been listening and speaking in one tongue only. The 'story' of architecture is therefore incomplete. Not wrong, but incomplete.

Lesley Lokko

architect and educator

Code Switching

Code switching refers to the actions of a member of a stigmatized group or minority culture to change their behavior—speech, appearance, dress, expression—in ways that conform to the dominant culture in order to optimize the comfort of others and gain social acceptance, fair treatment, and better employment opportunities. Code switching can have significant implications for personal well-being and even physical survival.

A CASE FOR A BLACK AESTHETIC

Jack Travis

Jack Travis established his namesake design studio in 1985. Since then he has been involved in more than one hundred projects of varying scope and size with clients that include Spike Lee, Wesley Snipes, and Giorgio Armani. He acted as "cultural design consultant" on two of the largest projects in Harlem: Kalahari Condominiums with Frederic Schwartz Architects (2004–09) and the Harlem Hospital New Patient Pavilion with HOK Architects (2006–11). Travis investigates Black history and includes forms, motifs, materials, and colors that reflect this heritage in his work. He has appeared in all of the prominent design publications as well as in the New York Times, New York Newsday, *and the* Daily News, *and on shows including the BBC television program* Building Sites. *Travis has taught at Parsons School of Design, Pratt Institute, the Fashion Institute of Technology, and the School of Visual Arts in New York. He founded AC/DC Studio (Afri-Culture/Design-Culture) in 1994, which seeks to collect, document, and disseminate information on Black culture as it relates to environmental design. He is associated with mentorship programs including Walks of Life and Learning Through Art & Architecture. In 1991, Travis edited* African American Architects in Current Practice *(Princeton Architectural Press), the first publication to profile the work of Black architects in the United States. Travis is a Fellow in the AIA, and a 2006 inductee in the Council of Elders of the National Organization of Minority Architects. He was awarded the AIA Fellows Mentor of the Year in 2015.*

Architecture in the United States is perhaps the most segregated of all the professions in the Western hemisphere. Through my fifty-year career in practice and academia, I have become acutely aware of a pervasive and profound lack of the following:

- a Black cultural expression in form-making strategies for the built environment disciplines;
- a significant and visible cadre of professional role models for women and minorities in these disciplines;
- an awareness among children of color that these disciplines and related fields can provide viable career opportunities; and
- an atmosphere, in the studio or the profession more broadly, where people with widely differing perspectives are allowed to speak to a diverse audience, especially people of color in their own communities.

These absences are stark when compared to Blackness in other creative arenas. For instance, though we might have individual interpretations depending on our own backgrounds, generally we can conceive of "Black music" art forms, or at least Black identity in musical genres. Most of us have some idea that gives that phrase meaning. Jazz, for instance, is considered by many experts as having an identity associated with Black culture. Bebop, R&B, soul, hip-hop, and rap are others. Likewise, one can easily think of Black dance, literature, poetry, or fashion. But is there a comparable notion or awareness of a Black culture in the environmental design disciplines?

During the 2009 National Organization of Minority Architects conference in St. Louis, a Black real estate entrepreneur named Mike Jones was one of the keynote speakers. He reflected:

> As I thought about tonight, and the honor and responsibility associated with being your keynote speaker, I struggled with the need to be relevant because of the profound regard I have for your profession. In doing my research, I was blown away by the myriad of types of architecture. They spoke to every human era, and every place on the planet, with a notable exception. There was nothing on Africa. And in the modern canon or citations on America, we were conspicuous by our absence.

Frederic Schwartz Architects and Jack Travis, Kalahari Condominiums, Harlem. The brick facade of this mixed-use 248-unit complex incorporates references to scarification as well as traditional African patterning and symbolism.

His statements echoed those of Whitney M. Young Jr. some forty years prior, as the first Black keynote speaker to address the American Institute of Architects at its 1968 national convention:

> You are not a profession that has distinguished itself by your social and civic contributions to the cause of civil rights....[Instead] you are most distinguished by your thunderous silence and your complete irrelevance.[1]

[1] Whitney M. Young Jr. keynote speech, American Institute of Architects national convention, Portland, Oregon, 1968, available at https://content.aia.org/sites/default/files/2018-04/WhitneyYoungJr_1968AIAContention_FulLSpeech.pdf.

88 A CASE FOR A BLACK AESTHETIC

Clearly the environmental design disciplines, especially architecture, have failed the Black designer and, ultimately, society in this regard. The field of architecture remains a bastion of white supremacy, and it is difficult indeed to identify, define, or clearly understand a Black design aesthetic.

TEN PRINCIPLES OF A BLACK AESTHETIC IN DESIGN

> **I propose a collection of principles not as a dogmatic set of fixed criteria but as a work in progress, presented for discussion, debate, and inquiry. It informs a hypothesis: that a Black aesthetic in architecture in the United States does exist, but under so many layers of denial and resistance that it remains hidden in plain view.**

Through decades of practice, teaching, and writing, I have consistently pursued issues of Black culture, representation, and resources. My goal is to make a broad case for a Black aesthetic in the environmental design disciplines—architecture, landscape architecture, urban planning, urban design, and interior design—and to employ that aesthetic to reinforce social connectivity in urban Black communities. I propose a collection of principles not as a dogmatic set of fixed criteria but as a work in progress, presented for discussion, debate, and inquiry. It informs a hypothesis: that a Black aesthetic in architecture in the United States does exist, but under so many layers of denial and resistance that it remains hidden in plain view. The goal of these principles is to bring this aesthetic into the light of day, where it can be understood and further developed.

The first four design principles refer to basic infrastructure of resources and services so often missing in Black communities. Because a lack of resources is a condition common to almost every person on the planet who identifies as African, a truly Black architecture requires the following practicalities.

1. **Economy:** a positive response to financial limitations
2. **Simplicity:** use of local materials and labor to avoid transportation costs; straightforward solutions that can be replicated

JACK TRAVIS

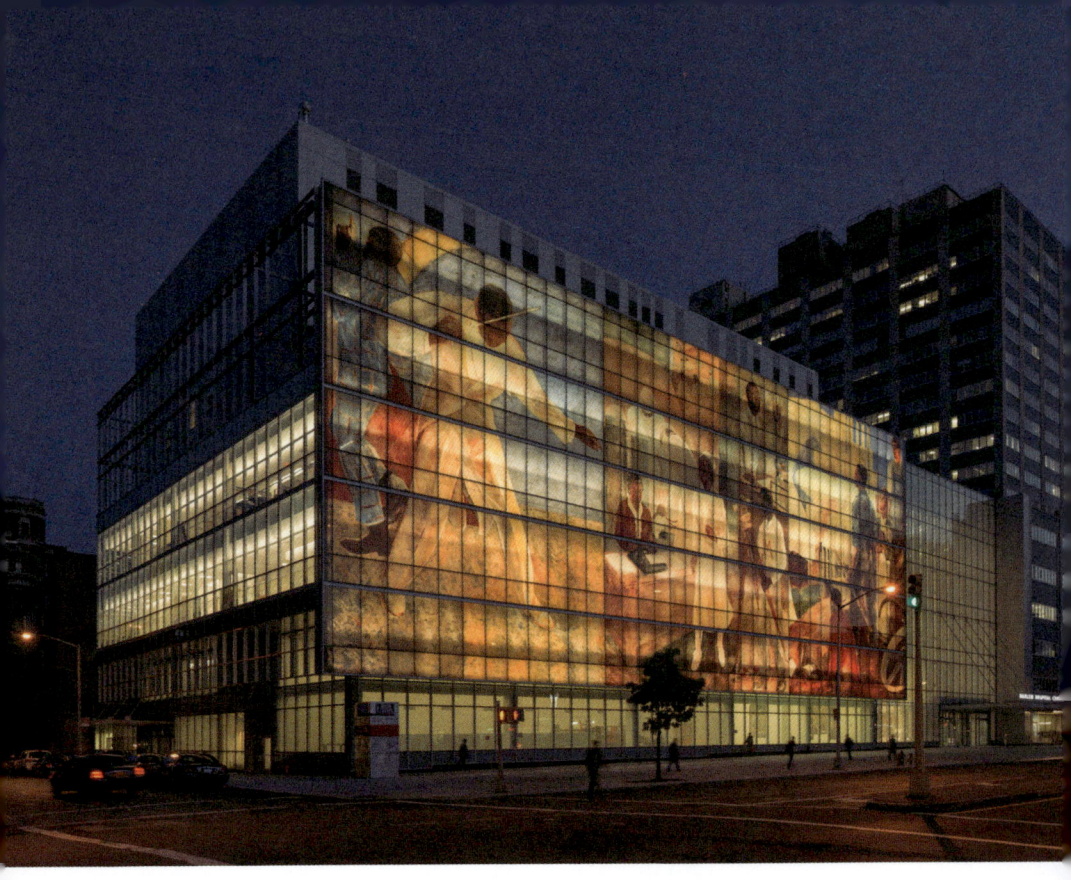

HOK Architects and Jack Travis, Harlem Hospital Center Modernization. This iconic hospital, a long-standing fixture of Harlem, incorporates a community atrium and gallery containing murals by several Black artists commissioned in the late 1930s as part of Works Progress Administration programs. The sixty-five-foot-high curtain wall facade, digitally "painted" with ceramic ink, spans an entire city block, replicating three colorful panels from a WPA mural uncovered and restored during the hospital's modernization. Depicting scenes from the African diaspora, it is a visual manifestation of the building's prominent place and historical importance in the community.

3. **Ease of Construction:** a direct approach to materiality and detailing, including prefabrication and modularity, to make the most efficient use of resources
4. **Ease of Maintenance:** durable, easily cleaned materials intended for long-term use; maintenance that does not require specialist expertise

The next three design principles address the celebration of Black culture within architecture as distinct from other cultures, particularly Eurocentric ones.

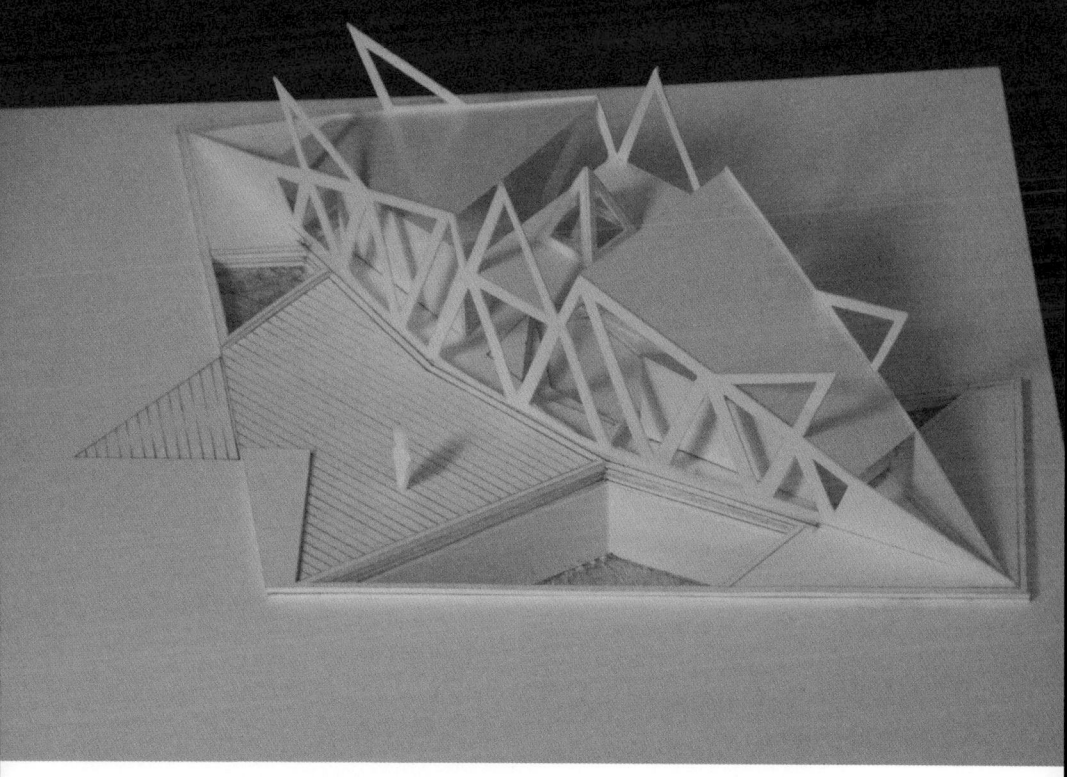

This is part of a series of studies by Jack Travis for several Black artists' houses: James Baldwin, Samuel Jackson, Amaza Lee Meredith, and Nina Simone. This residence, designed for the writer and civil rights activist James Baldwin, explores identity, structure, and site. Integrated into the earth, it creates a visual synergy between inside and outside but also cultivates a sense of privacy and solace for a man very much in the public eye. The enclosed spaces are connected by cultural memory and meaning.

5. Spirituality: a deep understanding and reverence for an "other" place, beyond where and what we know
6. Heritage: knowledge of and connection to past cultural practices—albeit severed and often diminished—necessary to go forward
7. Duality: the condition of being Black in which we seek to express both an African and an American identity

The next three principles relate to important space/form relationships that are also environmental, green, and sustainable.

Jack Travis's design for Saunders House expresses duality at its core. The Saunderses are Black, but also have French, Native American, and European heritage. Their house weaves these different sensibilities together via an existing Eurocentric house, a new addition, and a passageway that connects the two on multiple levels as the occupants move back and forth between moments in their lives when they have to be more American than African, and other moments when they can be more African than American.

8. Earth Centered / Earth Nurturing: a relationship to the land that is environmentally sustainable and healthy for both people and the planet

9. Strong Indoor-Outdoor Relationship: blurred boundaries between inside and outside; biophilic conditions

10. Color, Pattern, and Texture: the use of bold motifs to create a vivid and varied expression of beauty

FURTHER MUSINGS ON A BLACK AESTHETIC IN DESIGN

The ten principles above provide foundational strategies for relevant and meaningful environmental design solutions that are indicative of the Black and African experiences and characteristic of our collective nature, whether on the continent in sub-Saharan countries or in the Black diaspora worldwide.

> **The next ten [musings] are intended to address how Black designers can help non-designers see themselves in their environment and recognize that architecture can be meant for them.... They celebrate Black culture through decidedly non-European/American aesthetics.**

The next ten "principles" are in a formative stage, requiring more research, so for now I will call them musings. They are intended to address how Black designers can help non-designers see themselves in their environment and recognize that architecture can be meant for them, even in the current moment when there is virtually no architecture that adequately addresses their needs or expresses who they are.

The first five musings invoke a Black aesthetic through a deep connection to past cultural landscapes. They celebrate Black culture through decidedly non-European/American aesthetics.

> **11. Sustainable by Circumstance:** a worldwide lack of resources that compels us to "make do," using and reusing what we have in order to sustain ourselves
> **12. Dynamic Use of the Wedge, Diamond, and Triangle:** a preference for the three-point structure as opposed to the four-point structure, and the angular line over the orthogonal
> **13. Asymmetry/Symmetry:** use of balanced versus axial relationships with less structured imagery and proportion
> **14. Heightened Sensual Interpretations:** taking joy in visual extravagance, excess, and indulgence
> **15. Belief in and Understanding of an "Imperfect Perfect":** a formal/informal dynamic; seamless integration of the conceptual and the literal

The final five musings draw on cultural practices that have enabled Black people to express moments of glory, celebration, and triumph in artistic media and daily living. In them, we find ways to exult in a particular moment (time or space) specifically because we know it exists in the midst of so much anguish. How we might embody these in architecture is an open question.

> **16. Syncopation and Scat:** a disturbance or interruption of the regular flow of rhythm; the placement of rhythmic accents where they wouldn't be anticipated,

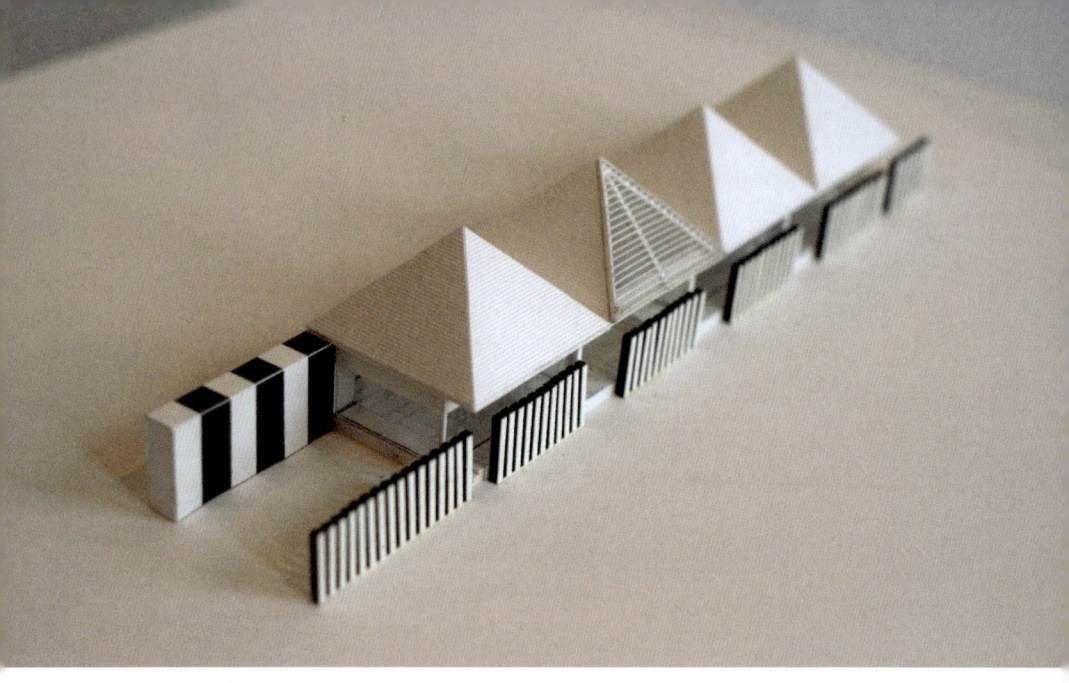

Jack Travis's study for a house for Nina Simone consists of four beach huts in a row. The black and white refer both to her struggle with racism and to the stripes of a zebra (an African reference), which, like a human fingerprint, are unique to each animal. The pavilions face south to catch the sun all day. One is an open-air courtyard where Simone could be outside unobserved. It also separates her bedroom suite from the public part of the house.

sometimes in the form of a backbeat, as used in virtually all contemporary popular music

17. Sampling and Borrowing: unapologetic use and reuse of content owned by others, as in music, to enhance a new contemporary sensual experience

18. Inclusivity by Nature: generosity in word and deed; shared care for the community

19. Call and Response: a succession of two distinct phrases where the second phrase is a direct response to the first, as often experienced in music, sermons, or speeches

20. Soon Come and "CP" Time: fashionably late; anticipation and celebration of when someone will be with you again

Marcus Garvey, an eminent Black activist and "Back to Africa" advocate from the turn of the twentieth century, cautioned, "If the Negro is not careful he will drink in all the poison of modern civilization and die from the effects of it."[2] With similar sentiment a century later, the aforementioned Mike

2. "Philosophy and Opinions of Marcus Garvey," ed. Amy Jacques-Garvey, https://guides.hostos.cuny.edu/lac118/5-1.

94 A CASE FOR A BLACK AESTHETIC

Jack Travis's design for the personal space for a young African American child (his daughter) is intended as private space, sanctuary, and refuge. Spaces for rest, study, play, and storage are all incorporated into a small, flexible, multifunctional area expressive of the child's cultural identity and lifestyle.

Jones said: "If you really want recognition and success, you must free yourself from the tyranny of dead ideas. You must fight for public policy that speaks to and supports what is best about cities. You must produce a vision and an approach that exemplifies that policy in such a unique and compelling way that no barrier can stand against it." Almost a hundred years apart, Garvey and Jones articulated prescient warnings that continue to demand both resistance and action in the pursuit of a Black aesthetic.

> **To truly establish a foundation in the hearts and minds of design professionals and students alike, a non-monolithic aesthetic vision must emerge that captures and propels the Black experience in unapologetic terms.**

Resistance: Black designers must resist elitist ideals, architectural code switching, and the sociopolitical practices that have historically marginalized us. We understand the limits of design and have lived through conditions of scarcity, but we also recognize the nascent possibilities for social and aesthetic transformation in the design fields.

Action: Black designers must proactively pursue an architecture of our own, one in which culture and ethnicity are significant spatial, formal, and environmental factors—bedrocks of design. Technique and process alone will not set the work apart or express the nature of who we are, who we remain, and the plight of our journey through time. It will matter greatly how we "image" this work, how we create a vision from our African-ness, our Blackness (with a capital B), how we create an architecture that is truly from us, for us, and by us. Black artists of all kinds—musicians, painters, poets, dancers—have been able to bring that understanding into their work. Black designers must as well.

And representation matters, from academia to the profession. Design education must instill cultural awareness and understanding of the profound impact that projects can have in their communities. Black architects, interior designers, landscape architects, urban designers, urban planners, and educators must be people who believe that architecture can reach out into community, be collaborative, be theoretical and literal, be conceptual and decorative. Black designers must push for greater cultural dialogue in place making, or the future of even our most vibrant communities will be at risk.

To truly establish a foundation in the hearts and minds of design professionals and students alike, a non-monolithic aesthetic vision must emerge that captures and propels the Black experience in unapologetic terms. This is, in part, the inspiration for the principles and musings articulated above. They have afforded my own work the heightened possibility for cultural dialogue in place making, and their continued goal is a broader and more inclusive environmental design palette. This is a tall order indeed, but we must not waver in our resolve to expand the relevance of our work by expanding our visions.

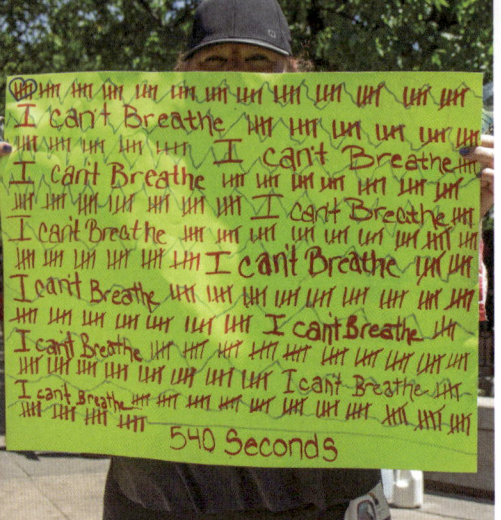

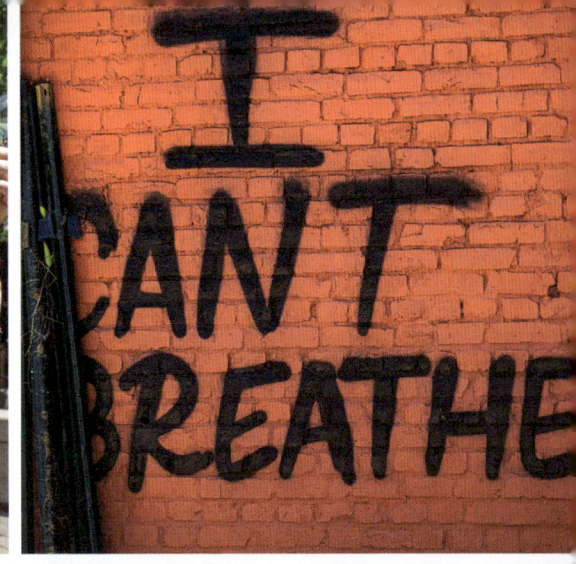

I CANT BREATHE

I CAN'T BREATHE

I Can't Breathe

I CANT BREATHE MOMMA

I CANT BREATHE

WE ALL CAN'T BREATHE

"

Even when you might not feel like you're in the position of greatest power…I think you can advocate, and you can be centered in what your ethics are at any age, right? You don't have to be the name-on-the-door architect to have a position. So… recognize your own agency.

Jennifer Newsom
architect and educator

Othering

Othering is a process of stereotyping and social exclusion based on a perception of what is normal, desirable, or comfortable, as opposed to what is unfamiliar, undesirable, or uncomfortable. Every social group, regardless of whether they are members of a majority or minority, engages in othering—defining an "us" (those on the inside who belong) and a "them" (those on the outside who don't belong). Othering is based on power relationships and is deployed to cast suspicion on, discriminate against, devalue, insult, or exclude groups due to race, ethnicity, socioeconomic status, age, gender identity, etc.

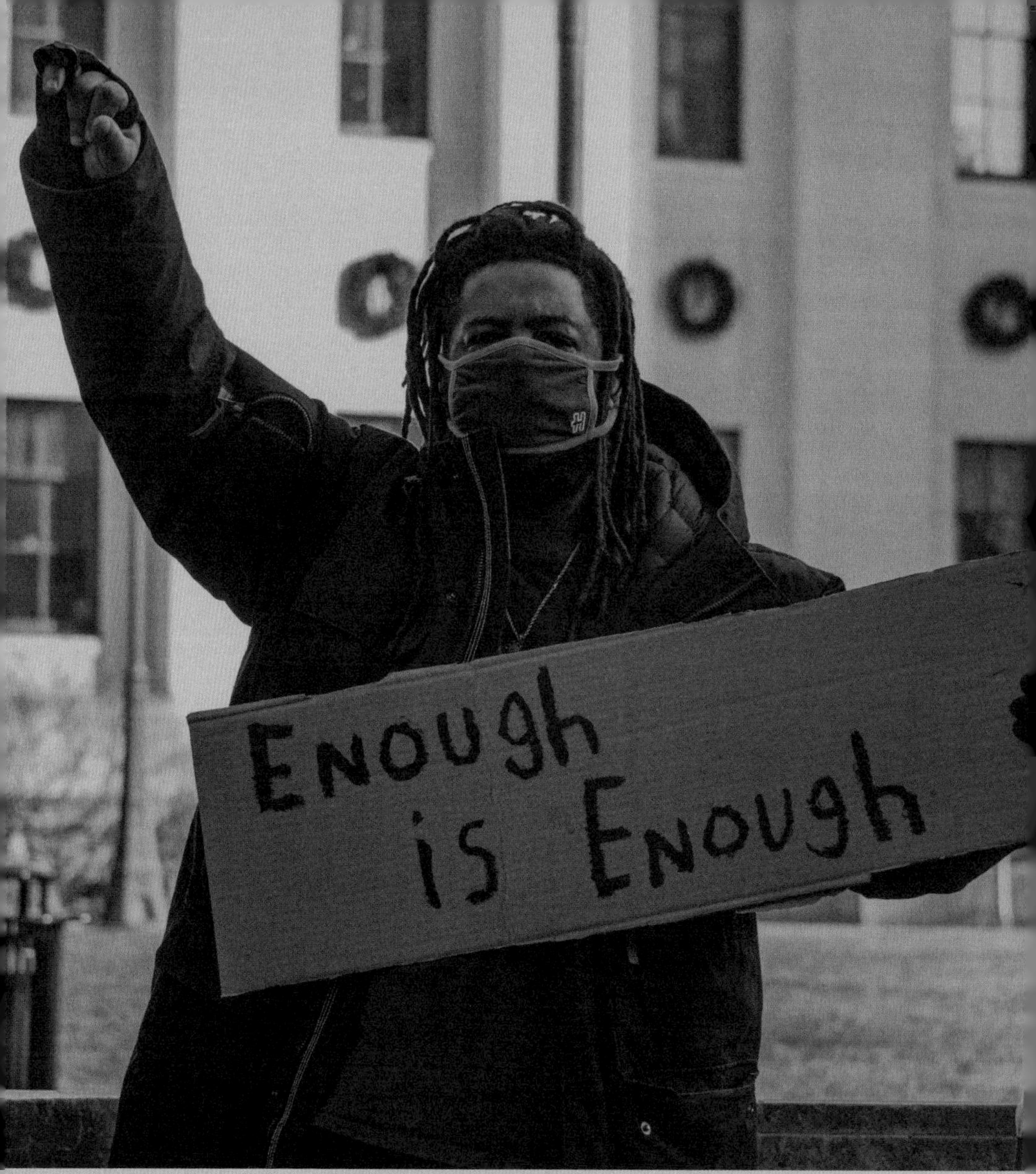
Enough
is Enough

[SNAPSHOT]

STANDING IN SOLIDARITY

Pascale Sablan

In my second week of school, in an architecture history class, a professor asked me and another student to stand. As the two of us rose, I assumed I was being volunteered for something. But he said, "Okay, these two will never become architects because they're Black and because they're women."

I call that "I was asked to stand" moment the moment when I started to understand my purpose—that I couldn't just be Pascale when I walk into a space. That I would always be representing my gender and my race, so therefore I had this responsibility to always show up and show out. This particular moment stands out for me because it was the singular moment that I can recall being outed in that way.

When sharing my story with audiences, I ask people to stand if they've also been told at some point that they were not adequate to be a designer in this profession because of their gender or race. And people stand. People are standing in schools of architecture; people are standing in schools of design; and people are standing in professional settings, which means that what happened to me hasn't happened only to me.

Erasure

Erasure is the removal of all traces of something or someone by ignoring them, rewriting history as if they had never existed or as if their role was or is unimportant, and/or removing references to them from history books (or social media). Erasure is a means of silencing ideas or presences that make a dominant or more powerful group feel uncomfortable or accused, often because they cast their past or present actions in an unfavorable light.

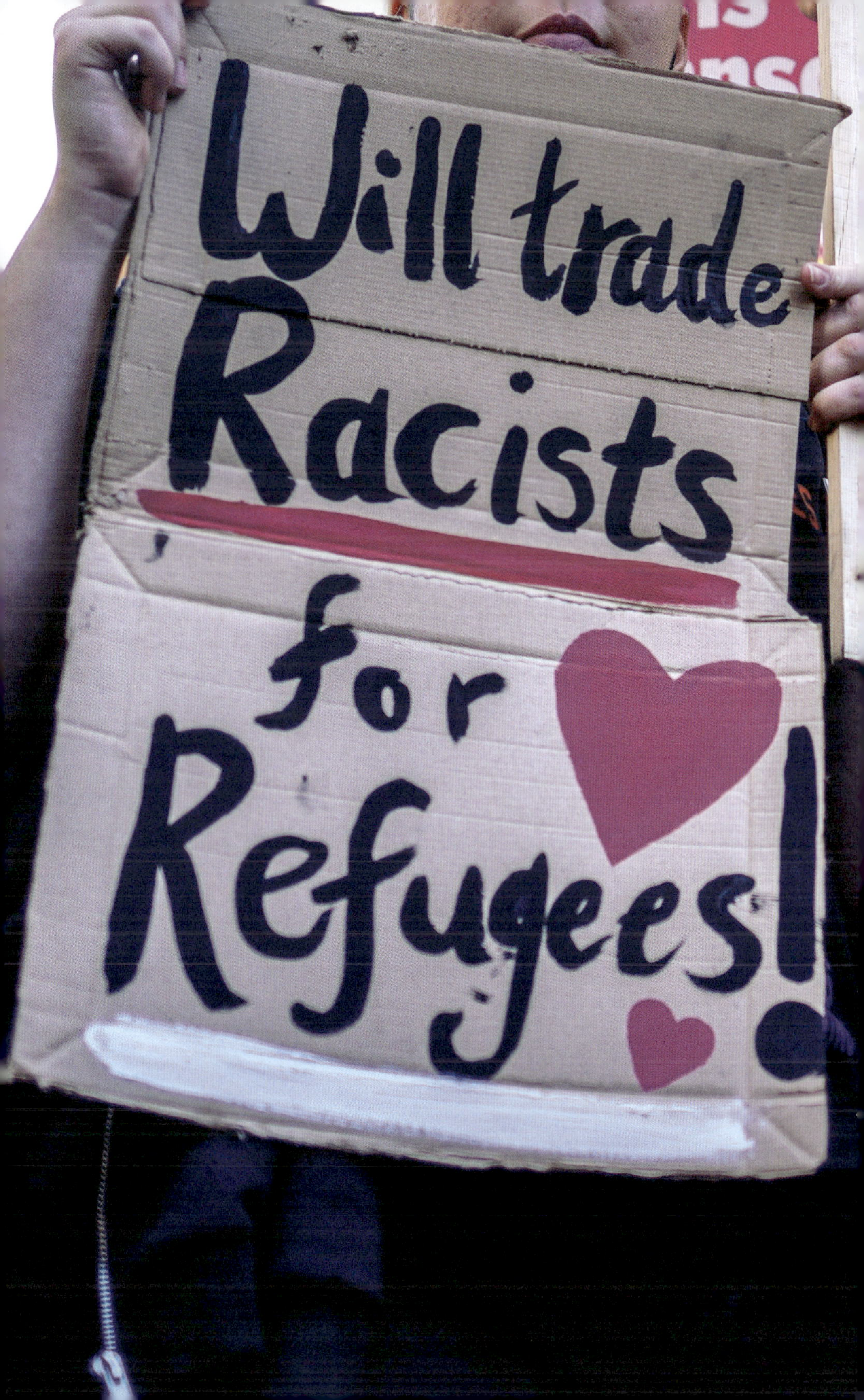
Will trade
Racists
for
Refugees!

[BENCHMARK]

ERASED

Katy Gerfen

On June 12, 2020, Architect *magazine editor in chief Katy Gerfen issued the following apology regarding the literal erasure of Justin Garrett Moore, the only Black panel member, from the video of an AIA + ARCHITECT panel at the 2018 AIA Conference in New York.*[1]

Moore was edited out of a video posted on this website. His voice should have been celebrated. We must do better.

    Justin Garrett Moore is an urban designer, the executive director of the New York City Public Design Commission, and an adjunct associate professor of architecture in the urban design and planning programs of Columbia University's Graduate School of Architecture, Planning and Preservation. His influential work on the guidelines in *Designing New York: Quality Affordable Housing* revolutionized the approach to the critical—and consistently underserved—typology, creating better, more inclusive, and more holistic spaces to serve communities. Because of his expertise and design innovation, we were honored to have him speak on an AIA + ARCHITECT panel at the 2018 AIA Conference in New York. But when the video of that panel was posted to this website that August, Moore, the only Black voice on the panel, was (as he tweeted on June 9) "literally erased."

    And he was erased. The edited video erased his presence and participation completely, but left that of the other three panelists, who are white. It was a complete lapse in judgment in our events-content development process, and a breakdown of protocols.

---

1. The full text is available at https://www.architectmagazine.com/practice/architects-erasure-of-justin-garrett-moore_o.

Its creation and posting circumvented editorial staff review and the checkpoints intended to ensure the accuracy and completeness of *Architect*'s content.

The fact that Moore and his fellow panelists reached out following their viewing of the video and were ignored is indefensible, as is the fact that it took Moore's tweet, two years later, to make me aware of his erasure. **And while the intent behind the edits was not motivated by the desire to silence the voice of a Black designer, the impact and appearance are exactly that. It caused pain and trauma, and perpetuated the pervasive silencing of Black voices in our society and industry.** The video was *Architect*'s content entirely—AIA did not have a role in the creation or editing of it. *Architect* takes full responsibility for it, and I thank Moore for holding us accountable....

Equality vs. Equity

Equality means that each person has the same resources, rights, and opportunities as every other person. For example, a pie that serves eight can be divided into eight equal-sized pieces. Equity, on the other hand, recognizes that each person has different circumstances and allocates resources and opportunities as needed so each person can reach an equal outcome; it levels the playing field by identifying and addressing disparities to ensure that everyone has what they need to achieve success. An equitable cutting of the pie could mean that the slices are different sizes, allocated according to need and means.

> **Equity, if I boil it down to its most essential element, is making it right.**
>
> Kimberly Dowdell
> architect and AIA president 2024–25

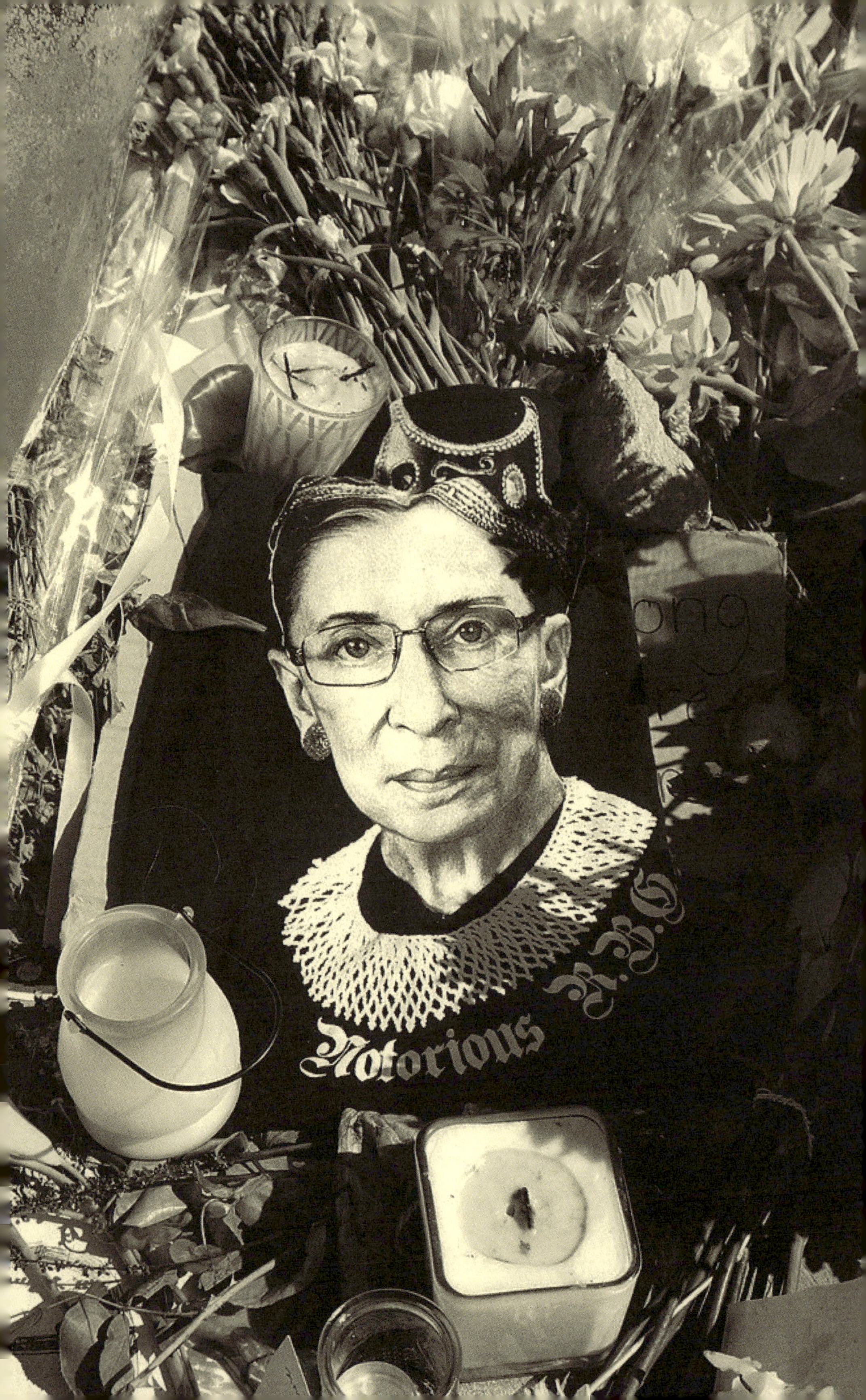
Notorious R.B.G.

[BENCHMARK]

PETITION TO THE PRITZKER PRIZE JURY REGARDING DENISE SCOTT BROWN

Women in Design at the Harvard Graduate School of Design

Despite the fact that Robert Venturi worked in equal partnership with his wife, Denise Scott Brown, for his whole career, he alone was awarded the 1991 Pritzker Prize, which honors an architect's entire oeuvre. In 2013, members of Women in Design at the Harvard Graduate School of Design launched a petition on Change.org to recognize Brown retroactively for her work.[1] As of October 2023, the petition has garnered 21,804 signatories, including many well-known architects worldwide, of whom nine are Pritzker Prize laureates. The Pritzker Prize jury declined to revise the award.

Women in architecture deserve the same recognition as their male counterparts. Denise Scott Brown's contributions were seminal to her partner Robert Venturi winning the Prize in 1991. It was an unfortunate oversight by the Pritzker Architecture Prize committee to deny her of the recognition she undoubtedly had earned.

We demand that Denise Scott Brown be retroactively acknowledged for her work deserving of a joint Pritzker Prize.

Brown had been a co-partner for over 22 years in their practice Venturi Scott Brown and Associates and played a critical role in the evolution of architectural theory and design alongside Venturi for over 30 years. She co-authored the 1972 book *Learning from Las Vegas*, among others.

---

1. The petition resides at https://www.change.org/p/the-pritzker-architecture-prize-committee-recognize-denise-scott-brown-for-her-work-in-robert-venturi-s-1991-prize.

However, her role as "wife" seemed to have trumped her role as an equal partner when the Pritzker jury chose to only honor her husband....

For women's equality to become a reality today, we need to rectify the mistakes of the past. Help change history by demanding equal recognition for equal work.

On June 14, 2013, Lord Peter Palumbo, jury chair of the 2013 Pritzker Architecture Prize, responded with a letter[2] on behalf of the jury:

Dear Arielle Assouline-Lichten and Caroline James,

Thank you for sending your petitions and letters, and those of others, about Ms. Denise Scott Brown and the Pritzker Architecture Prize. Insofar as you have in mind a retroactive award of the prize to Ms. Scott Brown, the present jury cannot do so. Pritzker juries, over time, are made up of different individuals, each of whom does his or her best to find the most highly qualified candidate. A later jury cannot reopen, or second guess the work of an earlier jury, and none has ever done so.

Let us assure you, however, that Ms. Scott Brown remains eligible for the Pritzker Award. That award is given on the basis of an architect's total body of built work. Ms. Scott Brown has a long and distinguished career of architectural accomplishment. It will be up to present and future juries to determine who among the many architects practicing throughout the world receives future awards. Not every knowledgeable observer always agrees with the jury's selection....

That said, we should like to thank you for calling directly to our attention a more general problem, namely that of assuring women a fair and equal place within the profession. To provide that assurance is, of course, an obligation embraced by every part of the profession, from the schools that might first

---

2. The full letter can be found at https://www.dezeen.com/2013/06/14/pritzker-jury-rejects-denise-scott-brown-petition/.

encourage students to enter the profession to the architectural firms that must facilitate the ability of women to fulfill their potential as architects. We believe that one particular role that the Pritzker Jury must fulfill, in this respect, is that of keeping in mind the fact that **certain recommendations or discussions relating to architectural creation are often a reflection of particular times or places, which may reflect cultural biases that underplay a woman's role in the creative process.** Where this occurs, we must, and we do, take such matters into account.

Your communications remind us of this obligation, and we appreciate your sending them. Insofar, however, as they ask us to reopen the decision-making process of a previous jury, we cannot do so.

Yours sincerely,
Lord Peter Palumbo, chair of the Pritzker
Architecture Prize jury, 2005–16

TWO

BUILDING OTHER "AMERICAN" DREAMS

Essays by
Chris Cornelius
Indians of All Tribes
Dahlia Nduom
Ronald Rael
Michelle Magalong
Ghazal Jafari
Architect's Newspaper editors

> My advice for young people… would be: believe in something that is larger than yourself that connects you to your genealogy, culture, and locality. Then build relationships around that larger something.

Dr. Sharon Egretta Sutton
architect and educator

INTRODUCTION
José L.S. Gámez

The authors included in chapter 2 confront legacies of colonization and injustice by engaging specific histories, identities, and practices in their approaches to architecture and design. Their work thus ruptures conventional categories of technique, technology, or tradition. In many ways, the collection of texts points both to the destructive power of settler colonialism and to the resilient power of imagination as a critical form of resistance. By figuratively and literally reorienting our vantage points, the authors demonstrate that practices, objects, technologies, and materials can exist simultaneously as both high and low art, as simple and sophisticated material application, or as metaphors for the cultural achievements of a people or place.

Past and recent histories remind us of the necessity for such resistant practices. Through means articulated in a US government treaty, the 1969 Alcatraz Proclamation started a nearly two-year occupation of Alcatraz Island in an attempt to reclaim lands previously promised to Native peoples; the rejection of their claim highlighted the persistent and continuing failure of the federal government to uphold its commitments to Indigenous peoples. Nearly fifty years later, in 2016, #NotMyAIA was born from opposition to a twenty-first-century version of the legacy of dispossession and the complicity of mainstream organizations with misguided federal policies. The experiences shared by Dahlia Nduom and Michelle Magalong in their snapshots point out that colonial legacies continue to produce and reproduce difference through a range of systems that include design education.

For Chris Cornelius and Ronald Rael, indigeneity links their work to specific places and lands. Both cultivate architectural practices and techniques that recover knowledge deeply rooted in the past and redeployed with powerful urgency in the present. Each expands the discipline to create a more diverse space of empowerment, of remembrance and resistance, embracing a broader sensibility of practice that aims to decolonize the academy and the profession.

Ghazal Jafari echoes the themes of Cornelius and Rael in her approach to spatial histories, providing a deep understanding of the forces that systemically dispossess people of their lands. She outlines a fundamental cultural project that identifies imperial projects even in the present—a condition that designers must engage through new and creative counter-practices and activist agendas. Through such struggles, new arenas for cultural translation emerge both as spaces of refuge and as transcultural spatial expressions.

Thus, while the consequences of colonialism may persist in many familiar forms, when viewed through the lenses provided by these authors, they come into focus as common landscapes now rebuilt and reimagined outside the restrictions in which they have been trapped for far too long.

NOT YOUR FETISH
NOT YOUR SCAPEGOAT
NOT YOUR MODEL MINORITY

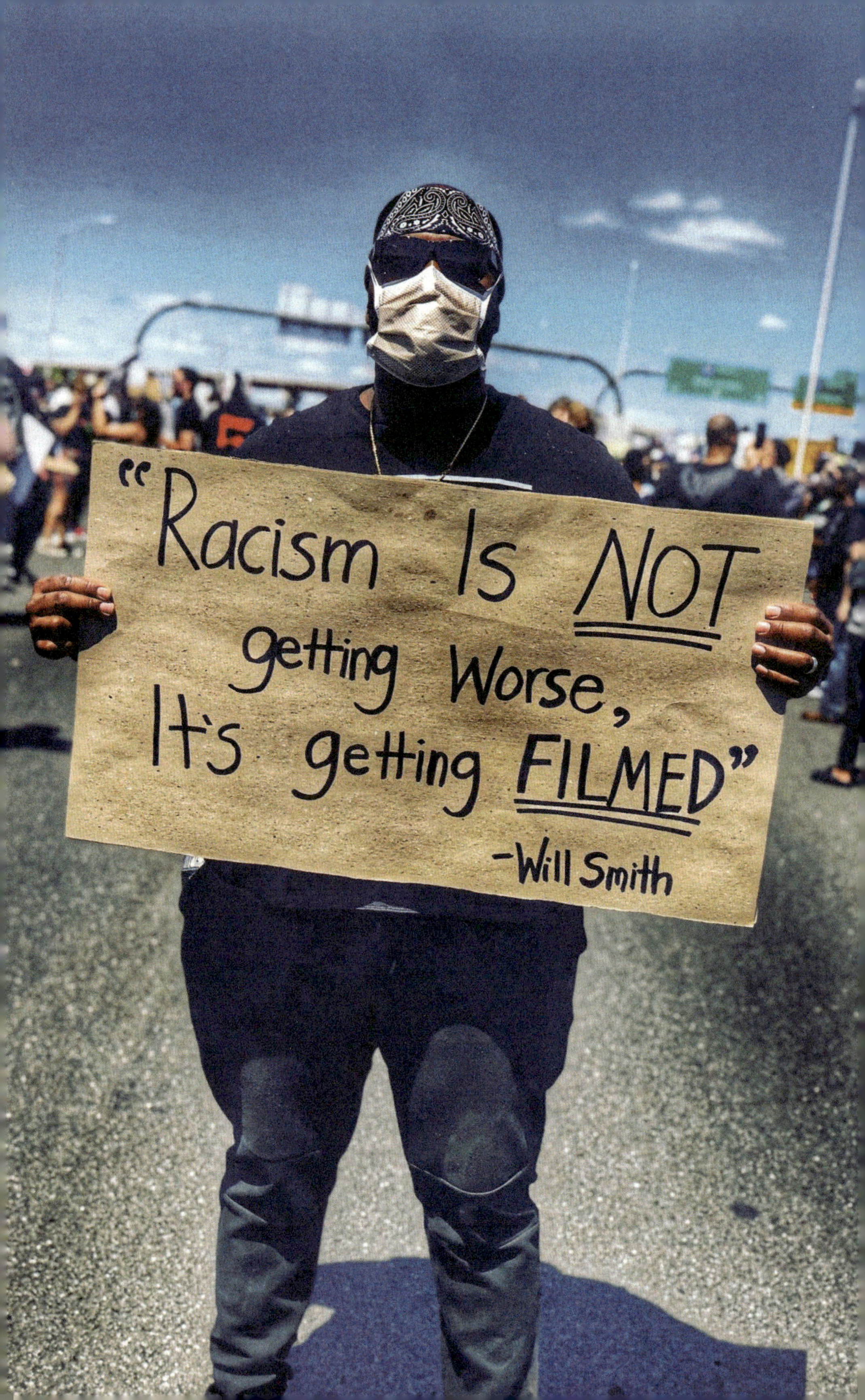
"Racism Is NOT
getting Worse,
It's getting FILMED"
-Will Smith

Identity

Identity refers to the way a person perceives or defines themselves in relation to social and cultural categories such as race, ethnicity, gender, sexual orientation, nationality, religion, socioeconomic status, disability, or intersectional combinations thereof. Some aspects are factual, while others refer to beliefs or personality traits that characterize a person's sense of self. Identity is nurtured and framed by environment, and consciously or unconsciously can change over time. No two people's identities are exactly the same. Sometimes stereotypical identities, usually negative, are assigned to groups of people by other groups. These include things such as having lower intelligence, being lazy, having a tendency to be violent, and even having less ability to feel emotional or physical pain. Reducing the identity of any person or group to a small set of stereotypical traits allows extremists to demonize them more easily. Being poor or ill or elderly is not a condition of identity but a condition of circumstance, even though other people may attach value judgments to these circumstances.

THE TRICKSTER: STORIES OF INDIGENOUS PLACE AND SPACE

Chris Cornelius

Chris Cornelius is a citizen of the Oneida Nation of Wisconsin and professor and chair of the architecture department at the University of New Mexico. He is the founding principal of studio:indigenous and creates architecture and artifacts that dismantle stereotypes surrounding Indigenous design and offer a distinct vision of contemporary Indigenous culture. His search for a new architectural language through drawing and making absorbs, embeds, and ultimately obscures direct references to Indigenous forms. Cornelius was born in Milwaukee, Wisconsin, and raised on the Oneida Reservation. He holds a bachelor of science in architectural studies from the University of Wisconsin-Milwaukee and a master of architecture from the University of Virginia. His awards include the inaugural Miller Prize from Exhibit Columbus, a 2018 and 2022 Architect's Newspaper Best of Design Award, and an artist residency at the National Museum of the American Indian. Cornelius has exhibited widely, including at the 2018 International Architecture Exhibition in Venice. He was the spring 2021 Louis I. Kahn Visiting Assistant Professor at Yale University.

I am Chris Cornelius of the Wolf Clan, and People of the Standing Stone is the earth that I come from. As an Indigenous architect, I have framed my design processes and my built and speculative projects through constant reference to Indigenous values, culture, and meanings, and have rendered those evident in architecture that serves Indigenous and non-Indigenous people.[1]

What does it mean to me to practice this way? My academic and professional architecture work is informed by practices that allow me to think about architecture differently, including key recognitions that

Design is ceremony;
Drawing is medicine;
Decolonization entails remembering and resistance.

* * *

DESIGN IS CEREMONY

Design is a ceremony, not just a professional discipline or an activity. As a ceremony, it includes rituals that guide the project's "worldview" and influence the processes of both creativity and putting things into the world.

Design Rituals: Observing, Naming, Rendering Evident

Indigenous people see the natural world differently, and this is reflected in the names they give to things and to the land. A national monument in Utah was named in the four different Indigenous languages of the people who inhabited the area—Hoon'Naqvut, Shash Jáa, Kwiyagatu Nukavachi, and Ansh An Lashokdiwe—with each of these names essentially translating as "bear's ears." The landscape looks like the ears of a bear that is partly submerged in the earth. There are many examples like this, where we relate the land to animals or other entities. These names are gateways into understanding and explaining scientific things, geological things, and natural things. How Indigenous people see the land—how their culture is connected to building, inhabitation, and rituals—embodies a series of reciprocities rather than simple cause-and-effect relationships.

[1]. Interested readers might seek out Shawn Wilson, *Research Is Ceremony: Indigenous Research Methods* (Halifax and Winnipeg: Fernwood, 2008); Linda Tuhiwai Smith, *Decolonizing Methodologies: Research and Indigenous Peoples* (London and New York: Zed Books, 1999).

COMMUNITY SCHOOL, MILWAUKEE

Observing, Values, and Culture

In 2003, I was a cultural consultant and collaborating designer with Antoine Predock on the Indian Community School in Milwaukee—a private school serving 340 students from kindergarten to eighth grade from all the tribes of Wisconsin. The students came mostly from urban areas in Milwaukee, and many were disconnected from their home reservations, so we endeavored to instill Indigenous values throughout the project. We studied the various tribes of the eastern woodland region, seeking inspirations. We discovered many cultural similarities and shared values among the tribes, and chose thirty for deeper study and inspiration.

Among these values, the building's connection to nature was crucial. The large interior public spaces are occupied by massive white pine columns from the Menominee Nation. Many of the trees are more than three hundred years old and existed prior to European contact. These ancient trees hold stories. Other shared values included dance, the cycles of the moon, and the communal role of fire. The values were graphically illustrated on large three-by-four-foot illuminated transparencies containing superimposed images that allowed us to visualize potential interactions, overlaps, and reciprocities. Through this we created a culturally specific vocabulary for naming the programmatic elements and communicating the design and spatial intentions.

Language and Naming

Naming things is of greater importance than their simple identification; it imbues them with meaning and begins building spatial stories. We rejected typical architectural labels for the spaces in favor of value-laden names like "animal," "feast," and "drum." The students, staff, and teachers pass on these names and stories to this day.

kályo?[2]	"animal": how we spoke of the building itself
atekhwah(e)l	"feast": the place of eating
kwʌhlal	"community": the place of entry
ka?náhkwa?	"drum": the gathering theater
atnʌhlineht	"migration": the space of approach and departure, recognizing the daily ritual of coming and going

[2]. Oneida words were translated in the Wisconsin dialect using the translator at https://www.uwgb.edu/dictionary/EnglishToOneida.aspx.

Architects Antoine Predock and Chris Cornelius, Indian Community School, Milwaukee, a K-4 through eighth grade school serving students with Indigenous ancestry from the eastern woodland tribes of Wisconsin. The transparency collage is a visualization of selected and overlapping values consistent among the tribes.

REAL AND IMAGINED PROJECTS: BUILDING ARCHITECTURAL STORIES

The ritual of storytelling in Indigenous cultures passes traditions, history, and beliefs from one generation to the next. Investing architecture with stories allows it to participate in this profound cultural tradition. In Indigenous lore, a Trickster is a character, usually a coyote or a rabbit, who teaches us lessons about human nature—greed, vanity, folly, envy. The animals never lose their animal-ness, yet they are also somewhat human. I wanted to build architectural Tricksters—playful beings with big personalities. The projects could be like animals, not in their appearance but rather in their ability to inhabit and animate a place and suggest imagined circumstances that might speak to me and to others.

Design Rituals: Storytelling

Architecture often reflects and communicates cultural and aesthetic values; when addressing Indigenous themes, it can be a vehicle for storytelling. Structures as storytellers take on a life of their own. The Trickster projects began as a set of small-scale speculative models, allowing great creative latitude regarding their stories, purposes, and imagined circumstances. Musing upon fictional programs that were not driven by clients or pragmatic requirements allowed the structures to probe alternative architectural realities.

- *Were they created by an animal or a supernatural being possessing a tacit understanding of nature?*
- *Were they occupied by animals instead of humans? (Scale figures were bears, deer, and other creatures.)*
- *Could their purpose be driven by their connection to nature—perhaps a place to sit and look at the moon?*

opposite: Chris Cornelius, series of imagined projects created for an exhibit at the University of Arkansas. Design as ceremony allows consideration of alternative narratives of the authorship and purpose. It is an architectural exercise akin to running drills before a race.

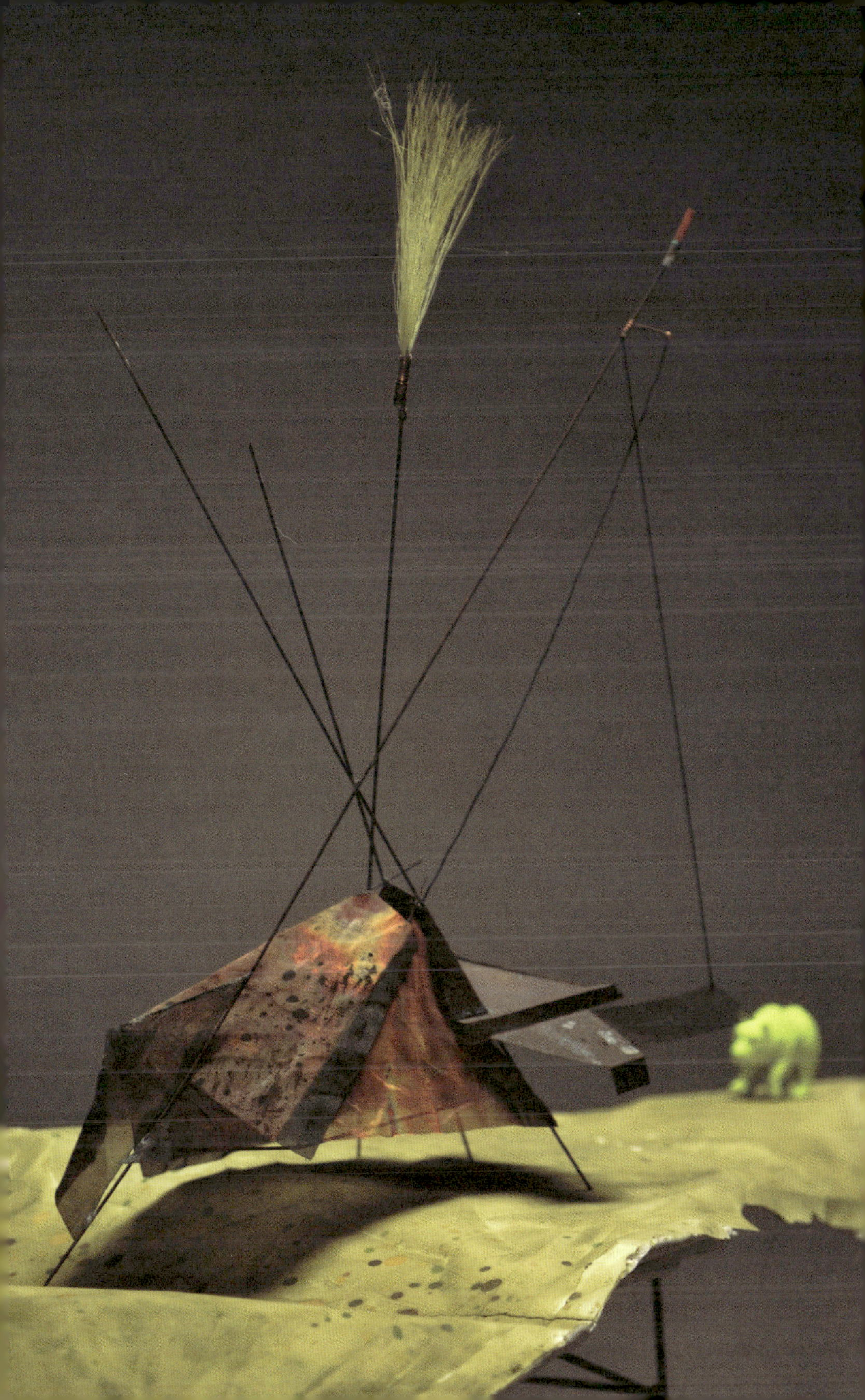

Chris Cornelius, *Trickster 1 (itsnotatipi)* in a children's literature garden in Sheboygan, Wisconsin, built as part of an artist's residency and inspired by small speculative exercises

- **Could the constructs themselves be like animals, with personalities and animal characteristics such as eagle feather claddings?**

The small models evolved spontaneously. Brass, bronze, and copper forms were joined with solder, patinated, and then cast into plaster "landscapes" or set into the confines of a found-object box that served as a proxy site. Like a site, each box began with a history and unique contingencies. Paradoxically, once the box was opened as a site, it could never be closed again. Making these models was a form of design ritual. They were like athletic conditioning, running a series of drills before a race. Sometimes they evolved into full-scale projects.

TRICKSTER 1 (ITSNOTATIPI), SHEBOYGAN, WISCONSIN

The first full-scale Trickster was made directly on site, based on inspiration from the speculative models. Sapling trees were harvested and loosely lashed together into a simple tripod structure that could be easily lifted and moved around. It was clad with patinated copper mesh, and at the top was the Trickster's "regalia." It became an animal-like entity living among the trees, and children can make up their own stories about why it is there and where it came from.

Regalia: *a cultural hyper-ornament, inspired by Indigenous dress. Regalia is not just adornment; it acts as a trophy that signifies the wearer's origin, clan, battles, or awards.*

TRICKSTER 2 (ITSNOTAWIGWAM), MARQUETTE UNIVERSITY, MILWAUKEE

A second Trickster was built to live indoors in a gallery space. Its structure was made with trees twenty-six to twenty-eight feet tall, copper mesh, and elaborate antler regalia. The copper mesh cladding was like a garment—a shirt for a giant bear. The Trickster wore a tag to remind the viewer: "You're on Indigenous land."

DRAWING IS MEDICINE

In Indigenous culture, medicine is a thing that not only makes you feel better but addresses all of who you are. Drawing and making are medicine for me. They allow me to create in ways that are informed by Indigenous values. Through creative acts of drawing, I am healing and being healed. I am thinking about making a place better, myself better, and the discipline better.

Design Rituals: Speculative Drawing and Modeling

Conventional architecture drawings and models are made to represent a design, the specifics of which are often known at the outset. Speculative drawing and modeling are fundamentally different. They allow for the discovery of questions and the excavation of findings that are not predicted or fully formed from the start. They invite reflection on subjects that are less concrete and not specifically architectural. The process and its outcomes create an evolving story as they progress and speak to the architect. The design gains specificity and a potential to be brought into the physical material world.

Early provisional lines, made when thoughts are uncertain, are drawn lighter but never erased. The act of drawing reveals the right questions. As ideas become clearer, the drawing gains intensity; I darken the lines, develop them, and add highlights or watercolor to amplify the design that is taking form and shape. The early marks gradually fade or are absorbed. As a designer who makes things and is interested in materials, I practice speculative sketching, modeling, and mapping to examine Indigenous design themes and methods. Drawing freely removes risk and allows me to challenge my own preconceptions and think outside the box. Through speculative drawing, questions are sparked:

- *Can I create a structure that is not static and regular, but just a densely packed bundle of sticks?*
- *Could the construct have an apparatus at the top to hear the thunder, like a deer's ear?*

MOON CALENDAR DOMICILES

The Moon Calendar Domiciles are imagined sites that arose through speculative drawing. The moon guides important Indigenous rituals, and moon calendars relate each new moon to something that is happening in the environment at a particular time of year. The third moon is about maple syruping. The fourth moon is about hearing the first claps of thunder. Other moons relate to planting, harvesting, and hunting.

The project aimed to translate the moon calendar architecturally in a set of small structures. I didn't want to make architecture that was a metaphor for the moon. Instead, I made an architecture based on its relationship to time. Speculative drawing allowed me to hone a set of essential shared parameters for the domiciles—their height above the ground, their size and volume, and the inclusion of antennae for communication. The speculative process also revealed each domicile's distinctions, such as the way it addressed the sky in relation to the monthly pattern.

overleaf: Chris Cornelius, Moon Calendar Domiciles, a project inspired by the Oneida moon calendar, which celebrates changes in the environment during different months of the year, like planting, gathering, hunting, or collecting maple syrup. The projects are not metaphors for the moon, but domiciles to celebrate the themes of these changes and corresponding cultural practices.

POS N/W TRANS

I ROLL OUT
TO MAKE

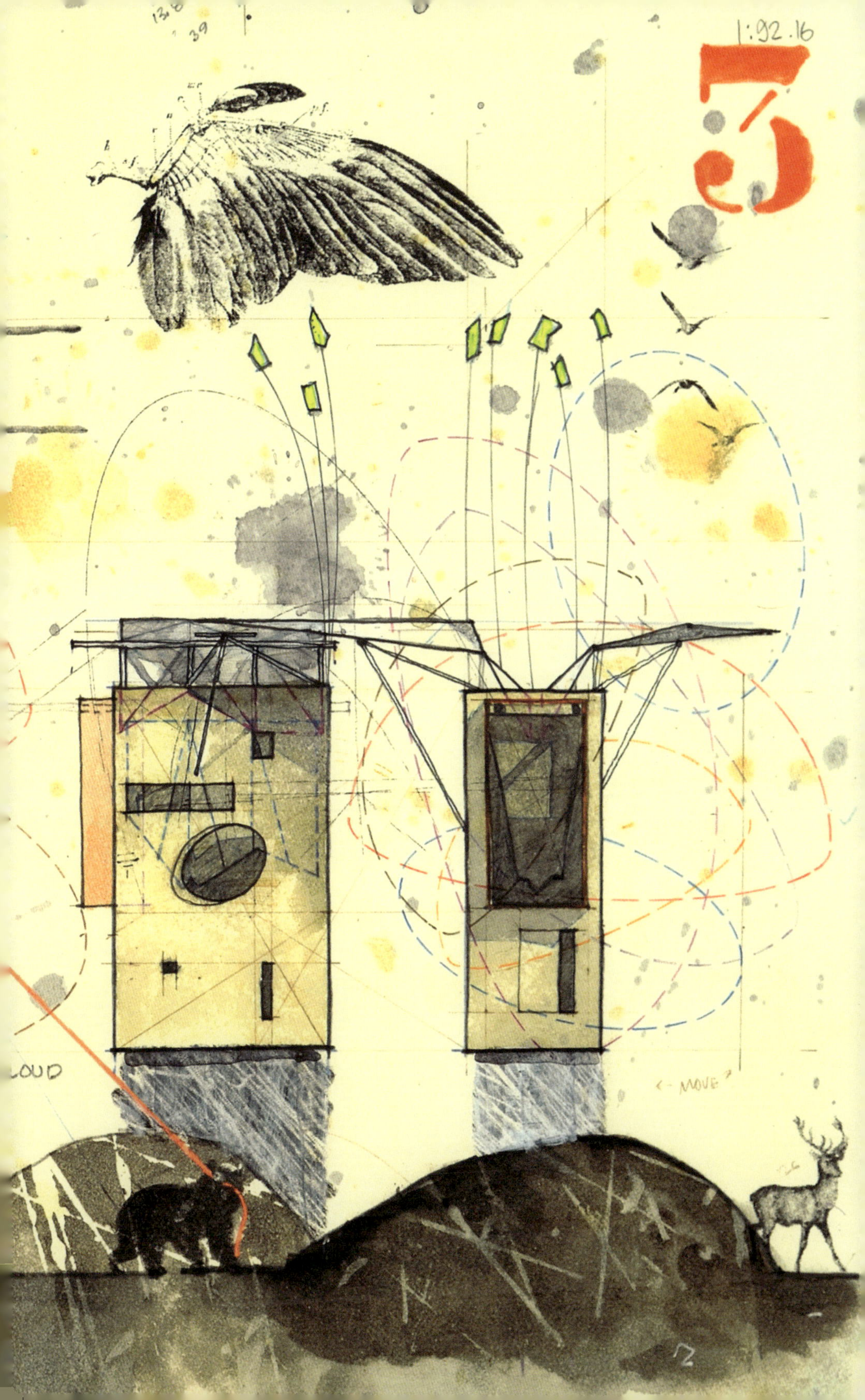
3
← MOVE →

NATURE IS MINE OR NATURE IS ME

We tend to think that the architectural history of the Americas began around 1492 with the arrival of European colonizers. This oversight fails to recognize the preceding history—the tens of thousands of years of Indigenous people's practices of inhabitation and building. In this context it is fundamentally instructive to compare the historically sanctioned but fictional Eurocentric "origin story" of architecture with actual examples of early Indigenous architecture that expose fundamentally different ideals about architecture and nature. In Marc-Antoine Laugier's idealized primitive hut, the classicist "architect" points at a proto-natural temple made of trees, essentially saying, "Look what I did." It conveys an idea of nature as a set of resources to use, to dominate, to build with, and to own—"nature is mine." By contrast, the worldview reflected in Indigenous architecture is that "nature is me"—it is us. We, and the architecture that we build, are related to nature—the trees and every living thing.

There is much to learn from this perspective. If we thought about nature and buildings as parts of ourselves, like family, we would show care for the people who make buildings and craft materials, their families, and everyone who uses the buildings, including those who administrate and maintain them. We would assume greater responsibility for every single material put into the buildings. This extends to the deep political, socioeconomic, and environmental implications of making architecture. This value system and culture of care is at the heart of Indigenous architecture.

Design Rituals: Remembering Cultural Practices

My practice is inspired by the ways that Native people see and occupy the world, nature, and buildings, as seen in Indigenous structures and cities that were built long before colonization. Some, such as the Acoma Pueblos, had multistory buildings. The Anasazi had complex masonry structures rivaling Roman technologies. Architects need to learn what Indigenous people were doing in their landscapes, not just in the United States, but all over the world. I am careful not to directly replicate Indigenous forms—mimicking the appearance of a wigwam, for example. Inspiration comes from discovering the logic and the meaning that influenced these forms, which then can be translated and transformed in a contemporary way using modern materials.

WIIKIAAMI, COLUMBUS, INDIANA

Wiikiaami *is the Miyaamia people's word for wigwam—a traditional dwelling type that is characteristic of several Indigenous cultures around the Great Lakes. Its constituent elements include a domed structure framed with bent tree saplings that are anchored in the ground and a cladding of shingled layers of reed or bark mats. The traditional* wiikiaami *were technologically advanced, well suited to the weather, and made for interior fires, having two sources of air to vent the smoke. The contemporary Wiikiaami was an opportunity to call attention to the Indigenous Miyaamia people of Indiana, whose history has been largely erased. It sought to translate lessons of the traditional* wiikiaami *in a contemporary expression.*

- **Structure:** *The pliable lashed saplings of the structure were translated into sticks of flexible steel rebar that were lashed by hand. Instead of bending*

the curved structure over into a dome, the structural bands bent in and up.
- ***Fire and light:*** *The installation could not contain a fire, so the ceiling hole was reinterpreted as an aperture oriented to capture the sun at the fall equinox.*
- ***Cladding:*** *Traditional bark and reed mat claddings were translated into an expanded steel skin to allow for transparency.*
- ***Program:*** *The installation does not have a specific purpose or program—it acts as a place of gathering, storytelling, and choreographed dance. It is like an animal that lives on the site. It sits comfortably nestled within the shelter of a dense tree canopy. It sleeps at night.*

opposite: Chris Cornelius, Wiikiaami, a project created for a site near Eliel Saarinen's First Christian Church in Columbus, Indiana, inspired by the environmental sophistication of the domed wigwam structures of the Indigenous Miyaamia people. The structure of the skin reflects cultural and natural patterns.

THE TRICKSTER

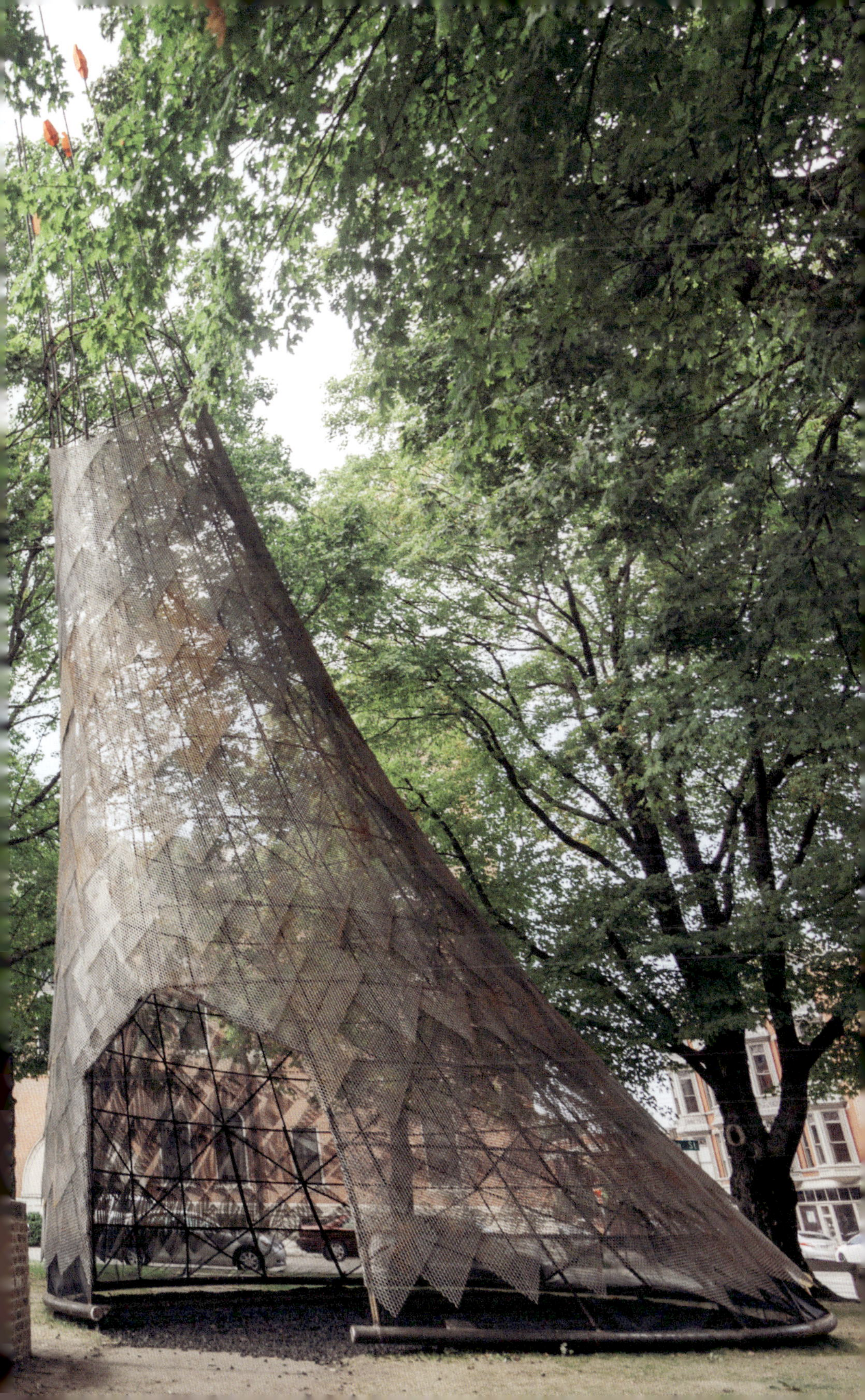

DECOLONIZATION ENTAILS REMEMBERING AND RESISTANCE

Colonize: *to send a group of settlers to a place to establish political control over it; to settle among and establish political control over the Indigenous people of an area; to appropriate a place or domain and its resources for one's own use*

Colonization relies on various systems and apparatuses of control, some of which are fundamentally architectural. In *Decolonizing Methodologies* (1999), Linda Smith offers an essential vocabulary of colonization, including some primary spatial concepts and devices:

- **Line:** Colonization lines relate to the construction of maps, surveys of territory, and boundaries—often a defining first move of colonization.
- **Centers and outsides:** A colonizing power uses architecture to establish physical manifestations of power, often buildings such as churches or seats of government. The center is a spatial position that establishes proximal and distant territories. We are inside; you are outside. We belong and have authority; you do not.

The United States was colonized using these devices. Colonizers measured and surveyed and created power centers of religion and state, increasingly pushing Indigenous populations west into the terra nullius, or no-man's-land. These remote landscapes were harsh, difficult to farm and cultivate, hard for people to survive within. Maintaining the inside-outside relationship reflects a fundamental lack of empathy, allowing the erasure of peoples and cultures who inhabited the land before.

Design Rituals: Remembering and Resistance

The RADIOFREEALCATRAZ project built upon a specific historical event to bring greater awareness to wider historical conditions of colonizing, domination, and forced migration.

RADIOFREEALCATRAZ: AN ARCHITECTURAL SPECULATION

From November 1969 to June 1971, Alcatraz Island in San Francisco Bay, home to a decommissioned federal penitentiary, was occupied by an Indigenous protest group under the name Indians of All Tribes. Under the 1868 Treaty of Fort Laramie, the US government had promised that unused "surplus" land could be used by Indigenous peoples. The group did not seek to reclaim the unused land for political or financial gain, but instead to create a new Native cultural center and Indigenous university. My RADIOFREEALCATRAZ project sought to translate data related to the Alcatraz occupation as well as the long history of Indigenous displacement and forced migration, making it visible in drawings and models.

The drawing entitled "Trajectories" juxtaposes maps showing how colonized territories were claimed. It includes Indigenous forced migration routes such as the Trail of Tears, where people were marched from the Carolinas, Florida, Georgia, and Mississippi to Oklahoma, and the path taken by the Oneida people from New York State to Wisconsin. Other Indigenous themes are mapped on multiple layers of translucent film to reflect a sense of condensed history. Graffiti from the Alcatraz occupation created a visual and spatial rhetoric for reclaiming the territory, and some of these marks are superimposed in the drawings.

The drawing entitled "Territories" superimposes geological, vegetative, and aeronautical maps. The accumulated layers reflect processes of land secession—the shrinking Lakota Nation of South Dakota and the Oneida's purchase of the Wisconsin territory that was retaken by the US government by the 1830s. Territorial petroglyphs are also mapped in the layers.

overleaf: Chris Cornelius, RADIOFREEALCATRAZ, a project inspired by the 1969–71 Native American occupation of Alcatraz Island. The project involved both imagined structures for a future Indigenous university and collaged maps combining rhetorical graffiti from the occupation with other cultural imagery, such as land succession maps showing shrinking Indigenous territory and maps of forced migration.

taos

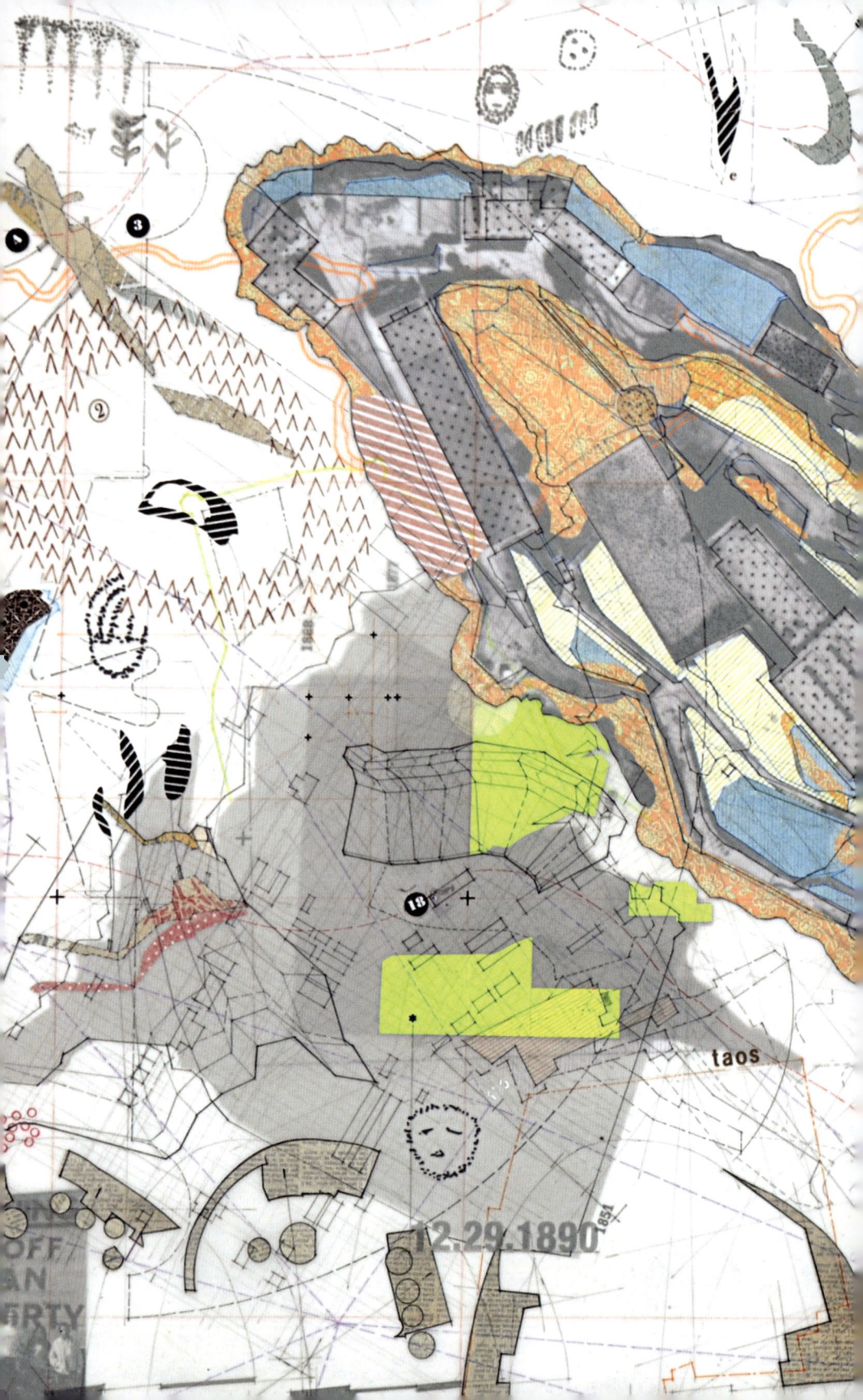

12.29.1890

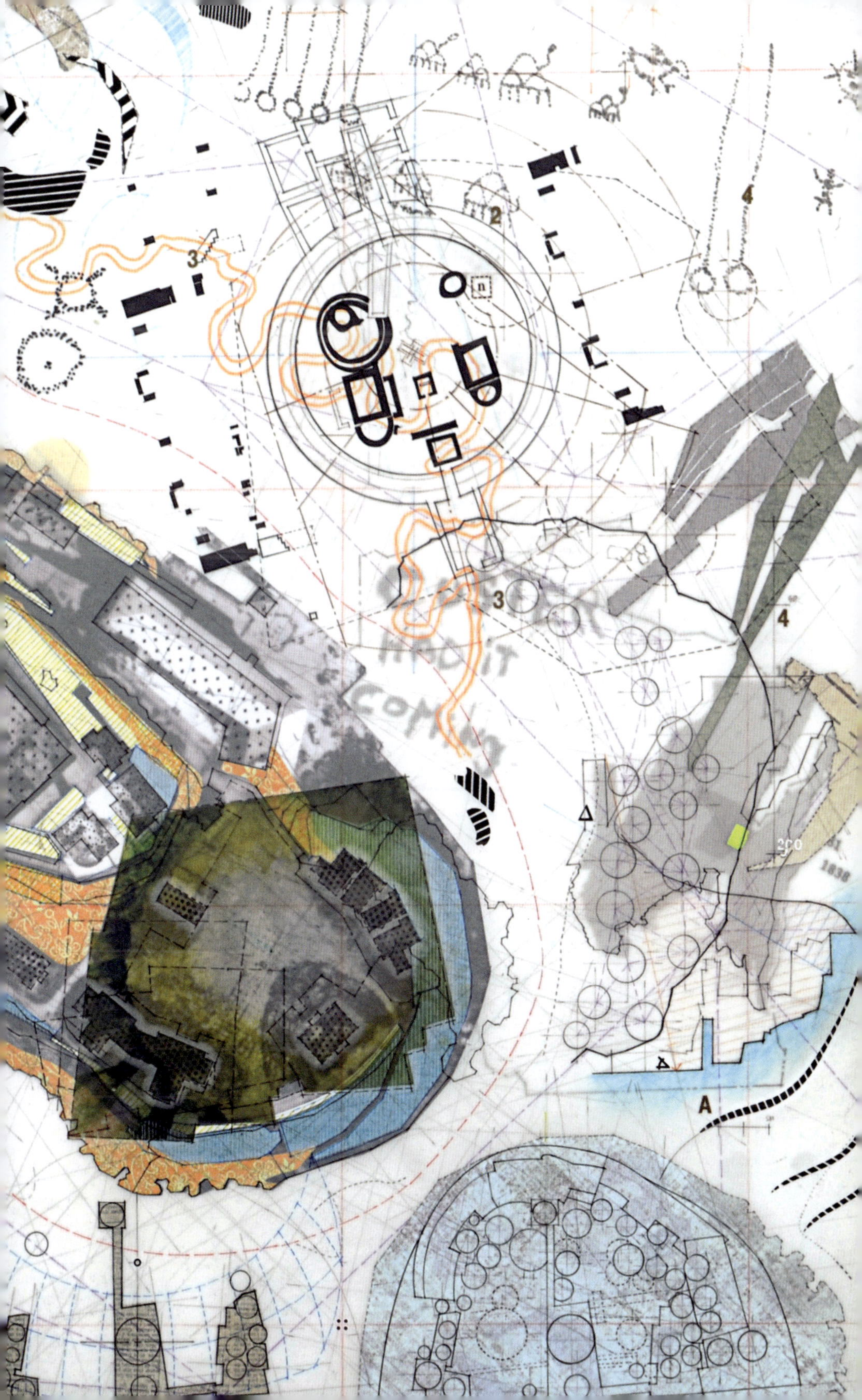

2
3
3
4
4
A

CONCLUSION

My architectural education was an emancipation—it got me off the reservation—but I had to learn to negotiate and eventually challenge the Eurocentric biases that dominate practice and academia. When you ask me about architecture, I can say, "I love Corbusier. I love the golden section." But that's not the only answer; it's not the end. I take conventions and use them, almost twist them, to create a dialogue between Western and Indigenous syntaxes. My Indigenous identity and culture have led me to embrace the fundamental ideas that design is ceremony, drawing is medicine, and decolonization entails remembering and resistance. This way of thinking is essential to my life as an architect; it enables me to see architecture differently and influences how and what I put into the world. It is not a recipe for Indigenous design, but a set of guiding principles that can make all design better.

> **Indigenous thinking can be for everyone, not just for Indigenous people or the fifteen to twenty Indigenous licensed architects in the United States—that's a colonizing mentality.**

Indigenous thinking can be for everyone, not just for Indigenous people or the fifteen to twenty Indigenous licensed architects in the United States—that's a colonizing mentality. We can all learn from the wisdom of people who have been stewards of this land for thousands and thousands of years. Shifts in the way we think about architecture can't be generated from somewhere or someone on the outside. Change must come from within practice and academia, and that's where I position myself as an architect and an educator—inside the system, where I can begin to dismantle it. Building by building, studio by studio, conversation by conversation, we can make architecture Indigenous again.

Disenfranchise

To disenfranchise an individual or group is to deprive them of rights or privileges to which they are due as citizens. To be disenfranchised is to lose one's power or ability to make choices, effect change, or have one's voice heard. Disfranchisement may be accomplished explicitly by law or policy, or implicitly through exclusion, marginalization, or intimidation.

INDIANS
WELCOME

UNITED STATES PENITENTIARY

ALCATRAZ ISLAND   AREA 12 ACRES
$1\frac{1}{2}$ MILES TO TRANSPORT DOCK
ONLY GOVERNMENT BOATS PERMITTED
OTHERS MUST KEEP OFF 200 YARDS
NO ONE ALLOWED ASHORE
WITHOUT A PASS

[BENCHMARK]

THE ALCATRAZ PROCLAMATION

Indians of All Tribes

From November 20, 1969, to June 11, 1971, Native Americans took over and held Alcatraz Island as Indian land, citing the 1868 Treaty of Fort Laramie between the United States and the Sioux that returned all retired, abandoned, and out-of-use federal lands to Native peoples. Alcatraz penitentiary had closed in 1963, and the US government had declared the island "surplus federal property." The dissidents announced their wish to build a center for Native American studies, an American Indian spiritual center, an Indian center of ecology, and an Indian training center on the island. The occupation lasted nineteen months. It ended when the Native Americans were forcibly removed by the federal government. During the occupation, The Movement *newspaper published the satirical Alcatraz Proclamation, excerpted below, to increase the visibility of the occupation and the issues surrounding it.*[1]

Proclamation to the Great White Father and All His People

We, the native Americans, re-claim the land known as Alcatraz Island in the name of all American Indians by right of discovery. We wish to be fair and honorable in our dealings with the Caucasian inhabitants of this land, and hereby offer the following treaty:

We will purchase said Alcatraz Island for twenty-four dollars ($24) in glass beads and red cloth, a precedent set by the white man's purchase of a similar island about 300 years ago.

---

[1]. The full text is available at https://muscarelle.wm.edu/rising/alcatraz/proclamation/.

We know that $24 in trade goods for these 16 acres is more than was paid when Manhattan Island was sold, but we know that land values have risen over the years....

We will further guide the inhabitants in the proper way of living. We will offer them our religion, our education, our life-ways, in order to help them achieve our level of civilization and thus raise them and all their white brothers up from their savage and unhappy state....

We feel that this so-called Alcatraz Island is more than suitable for an Indian Reservation, as determined by the white man's own standards. By this we mean that this place resembles most Indian reservations in that:

1. It is isolated from modern facilities, and without adequate means of transportation.
2. It has no fresh running water.
3. It has inadequate sanitation facilities.
4. There are no oil or mineral rights.
5. There is no industry and so unemployment is very great.
6. There are no health care facilities.
7. The soil is rocky and non-productive; and the land does not support game.
8. There are no educational facilities.
9. The population has always exceeded the land base.
10. The population has always been held as prisoners and kept dependent upon others.

Further, it would be fitting and symbolic that ships from all over the world, entering the Golden Gate, would first see Indian land, and thus be reminded of the true history of this nation....

Assimilation

Assimilation—whether compelled through force or undertaken voluntarily—is when a minority social group conforms to the dominant social group's customs, attitudes, beliefs, language, etc. Assimilation most often affects immigrants and Indigenous peoples and can result not only in the loss of knowledge and skills, but also the eradication of entire cultures. An example of assimilation is the forced reeducation of Native Americans. Starting in the mid-1900s, approximately four hundred boarding schools were built in the United States to reeducate more than one hundred thousand Native American children, some of whom were kidnapped at gunpoint. The children were forbidden to speak their Native languages, their hair was cut, and they were forced to renounce Native beliefs and their Native American identities, even their names.

[SNAPSHOT]

THE "EXOTIC" PRIMITIVE HUT

Dahlia Nduom

I was first confronted with the stereotypical narrative of island life in primary school in Antigua. The Caribbean has often been associated with the "exotic," and the mud hut has been one of the most prominent signifiers of this trope. A pen pal from England conveyed this narrative to me, asking if I went barefoot and lived in a mud hut. While I am proud to be Antiguan and celebrate our rich culture at every opportunity, as a child, questions like these made me feel "less than" and baffled that this was how Antigua was perceived.

While earth construction was pivotal to the Indigenous and freed African populations in Antigua, this construction technique (along with thatch) has since been co-opted to represent an exotic other. This exotification of traditional building practices was part of a narrative crafted during colonization, when the idea of primitiveness was celebrated in photographs, paintings, and literature—*Robinson Crusoe* (1719) being the paradigmatic example—to signify colonial progress and sustain colonial power dynamics. Tropicalized representations, including plantation paintings, in early-twentieth-century photographs and postcards were used as propaganda to encourage the burgeoning tourism industry.

This colonial legacy of local traditions being seen as inferior has been perpetuated ever since. When I moved to Ghana from New York, several people couldn't understand why I would want to move there for architectural opportunities. With a note of disdain in her voice, someone even asked if I would work on mud huts. Having been to Ghana several times before moving, I shrugged off comments like these, knowing the rich architectural legacy and experience awaiting me. Being in Ghana, surrounded by people who looked like me with a shared cultural history, was truly rewarding. As an architect, it was also professionally gratifying to explore diverse cultures, architectural traditions, and practices, and to work with notable architects striving to push previously marginalized African architecture to the forefront of critical discourse. Investigating the nuances of construction techniques, spatio-cultural practices, and climatic, social, and political influences strengthened my resolve to celebrate the richness of the architecture of the African diaspora.

Now that I teach at Howard University, it is my mission to shed light on locales that have been underrepresented in architecture and alleviate some of the stereotypes and othering through critical discourse on the architectures of the African diaspora.

> In this process of being a designer, my inner world becomes the outer world of the other. My human warmth, thoughts, clarity, inner mobility, originality, and liveliness will potentially become someone else's habitat.

Vaibhavi Chirra
architecture graduate student

White Gaze

White gaze refers to the tendency to consciously or unconsciously represent things from the perspective of whiteness, and to assume that one's audience shares that perspective. Such representations bias white experiences, aesthetics, culture, values, and attitudes. White dominance in the media space reinforces stereotypes and racialized power imbalances, and implies authority of white norms or preferences.

FRONTIERS OF DESIGN

Ronald Rael

Ronald Rael's creative endeavors blur the borders between architecture, art, technology, land-based practices, and social justice. Rael writes books, forms start-up companies, advocates for human rights at the US-Mexico border, creates software, invents novel materials and new forms of construction, and designs buildings as an applied research enterprise. His studio is known globally for the project Teeter-Totter Wall, a forty-minute guerilla event that took place on both sides of the US-Mexico border wall to bring families and communities together. He cofounded the start-up company FORUST, which rematerializes wood waste via 3D printing to produce beautiful end-use products, and has innovated processes for the robotic construction of raw earthen buildings. His work can be found in the permanent collections of the Museum of Modern Art, New York; the Cooper Hewitt, Smithsonian Design Museum, New York; the London Design Museum; the Los Angeles County Museum of Art; the San Francisco Museum of Modern Art; and the Renwick Smithsonian American Art Museum, Washington, DC. He is the chair of the department of art practice and Eval Li Memorial Chair in Architecture at the University of California at Berkeley, and divides his time between Oakland and La Florida, Colorado.

> **These territories are not simply a barren desert landscape comprised of 'bad hombres,' but an ecologically rich and socially diverse set of communities filled with intelligent and caring families who live with their children in communities where they laugh, play, and take pictures with their cell phones despite the hardships of poverty, xenophobia, and the oppression reflected in the construction of walls.**

On July 28, 2019, my studio gathered a team of collaborators, friends, and community members along the eighteen-foot-high steel wall that divides El Paso and Ciudad Juárez, just to the west of those two cities—a desolate stretch between Sunland Park, New Mexico, and the Mexican *colonia* of Anapra. Over the course of a few hours, we installed three pink teeter-totters that used the fence as a fulcrum (pink was chosen to pay respect to the hundreds of women and girls killed since 1993 in Juárez). That afternoon, at our humble border gathering, mothers, children, artists, designers, and curators from both sides of the divide congregated and shared a moment of *convivencia*. This word doesn't have a direct translation in English; "coexistence" or "fellowship" might come close, although the former seems too scientific, and the other too religious. In this context, the closest translation would probably be simply "hanging out and having fun."

Unexpectedly, this event was shared by millions across social media. Many called it an important moment of release from the tensions fueled by continued media coverage of family separations at the border and from the ceaseless quest by the Trump administration to acquire funds for more border wall construction. For me, the work also demonstrated that there is another borderland that exists outside the surficial one defined by the white gaze of "sanctioned" news outlets and political propaganda—the primary vehicles through which the people and ecologies of the border are represented. The event communicated something that one does not often hear about or see when learning about the "realities" of the borderlands. These territories are not simply a barren desert landscape comprised of "bad hombres," but an ecologically rich and socially diverse set of communities filled with intelligent and caring families who live with their children in communities where they laugh, play, and take pictures with their cell phones despite the hardships of poverty, xenophobia, and the oppression reflected in the construction of walls.

My creative practice has worked on projects near the US-Mexico border since 2001, but my ancestors have lived along the Rio Grande watershed for millennia. This region extends from where the Rio Grande currently ends in El Paso and Ciudad Juárez to where it begins in the San Luis Valley in southern Colorado, which prior to 1848 was the northernmost borderland of the Mexican territory, known as Santa Fe de Nuevo Méjico. As a designer, I recognize that my own work, in my own land, does not have to contort to a view of the borderlands as defined from the vantage point of the white gaze. Instead, I can demonstrate who borderland people actually are.

Working outside the lens of the white gaze has been an increasing focus of my studio's borderland work. Seen together, it questions the limited range of processes, materials, agendas, and technologies that architectural institutions uniformly agree upon as relevant. This emphasis is particularly true for those institutions that reflect a Eurocentric, modernist perspective that has traditionally dominated architectural discourse, as well as the "-isms" pervading the recent history of our profession: deconstructionism, postmodernism, parametricism. That moment of *convivencia* on the Teeter-Totter Wall demonstrated that play and design can be forms of activism.

MUD FRONTIERS

Using a similar approach, during that same summer of 2019 my studio concluded a project called Mud Frontiers. In 2010, on the fortieth anniversary of *Smithsonian Magazine*, the publication announced "40 Things You Need to Know about the Next 40 Years." Number one proclaimed that "sophisticated buildings will be made of mud"—a bold, even controversial prognostication at a time when digital fabrication and computer-aided design were seen as the avant-garde in architecture. Long before the Smithsonian put its prediction in print, I believed in the power of mud, having grown up in the same adobe house that I currently live in today—the house of my mother, her mother, and her mother before her.

Mud Frontiers was a two-part research project to better understand the capacities and potentials of the pottery and earthen construction traditions that guided our ancestors for centuries. Over the course of the investigations, I journeyed from the contemporary borderlands along the Rio Grande watershed in El Paso to the ancient borderlands and headwaters of the Rio Grande in the San Luis Valley.

Each phase of Mud Frontiers consisted of on-site research and a set of built explorations that posed new possibilities for architecture, expanding the range of the most traditional of materials—clay, water, wheat straw—with new robotic tools. Within our profession today, these materials would be categorized under the unfortunate term "alternative," implicitly connoting other-ness. The othering of materials, by which some materials are demoted and defined as not fitting within professional norms, goes hand in hand with the othering of people, particularly those whose cultural heritage practices employ earthen building materials. In

> **The othering of materials, by which some materials are demoted and defined as not fitting within professional norms, goes hand in hand with the othering of people, particularly those whose cultural heritage practices employ earthen building materials.**

RONALD RAEL **155**

opposition to this xenophobic practice, I use these materials to push the boundaries of sustainable and ecological construction in a project that explores traditional clay craft in the contexts of both architecture and pottery. The end goal of this endeavor was to demonstrate that low-cost and low-labor construction should not be relegated to an "alternative" but instead be embraced as an intuitive choice that is simultaneously accessible and economical for audiences outside of the white gaze and typical notions of technological progress.

The first phase of the project analyzed the earthen architecture and clay pottery of the Mogollon culture (200–1450 CE). These artifacts are part of the archaeological history of the Jornada Mogollon, the region where the borderland cities of El Paso and Juárez are currently situated. Excavated pit houses and aboveground adobe structures characterize Mogollon architecture. By 400 CE, this region witnessed the development of a distinctive indigenous coil-and-scrape pottery technique known as El Paso brownware.

In the project's second phase, my studio, working with the University of Texas El Paso departments of ceramics and geology and twenty-five potters from El Paso and Juárez, explored the earthen architecture and clay pottery traditions of ancestral Pueblo cultures (700 CE–present) and both the Indigenous and colonized cultures of northern New Mexico and southern Colorado (1598 CE–present). Collectively these region-defining architectures tell a story of an evolving set of craft traditions centered on earthen materials. Subsequent scaled-up spatial explorations were inspired by numerous related contemporary techniques recently used to make large-scale 3D printed structures. The spatial experiments were conceptualized under four themes: Hearth, Beacon, Lookout, and Kiln.[1]

Hearth explores how thin mud-wall construction can be reinforced using local, rot-resistant juniper wood. The wood holds the walls together, but it also extends beyond the walls of the structure on the outside, while remaining flush on the inside. This dynamic form of construction references the cultural differences between the architectural traditions of Pueblo and Indigenous *mejicano* buildings. The interior contains a 3D-printed adobe bench (also known as *tarima* in the local dialect) surrounding a *fogón* (fireplace), which burns the aromatic juniper.

[1] To gather samples for the research, I worked with an industry partner, 3D Potter, codesigning and deploying customized but low-cost and portable robots into the environments where we worked. The robots were engineered to be carried into a site where local soils could be harvested and tested.

top: Hearth
bottom: Beacon

RONALD RAEL

Lookout

Beacon tests how the texture and undulation of 3D-printed mud coils can produce the thinnest possible structural enclosures. These coils are then illuminated at night, contrasting the luminous difference between the concave and convex curves that form the mud walls.

Lookout is an exploration in structure—a 3D-printed staircase made entirely of adobe. A dense network of undulating mud coils is laid out to create a structure strong enough to be walked upon. This method also demonstrates how wide, airy walls can create interior enclosures that represent new possibilities for insulation, especially in the

Kiln

harsh climate of the San Luis Valley, which can drop below -20°F in the winter.

Kiln iterates several techniques, including undulating or interlocking mud deposition, to create structural and insulative walls. Kiln is also used to enclose an area that draws in oxygen while building radiant heat to fire locally sourced clay with burning juniper wood. The products of the kiln—fired micaceous clay derived from the traditions of Taos and Picuris Pueblos—are new hybrids of Indigenous technology and technique.

BORDER SEPARATION SIGN

While developing these projects, I was incensed by the news that nearly two thousand children had been separated from their families at the US border. In response, I created an open-source, downloadable sign that anyone could use to protest these horrific and inhumane acts. The new image was adapted from an earlier design created in the late 1980s by the Navajo graphic artist John Hood, a Vietnam War veteran from New Mexico who worked for the California Department of Transportation. Hood was tasked with creating a sign in response to the sharp rise in immigrant traffic deaths. Because people immigrating from Mexico without documents were not able to cross through official ports of entry, they were being dropped off on the side of the highway by coyotes (smugglers), leaving them with no choice but to run across the dangerous roads.

Hood's image was meant to elicit human empathy as well as the immediate recognition of a potential traffic hazard. A little girl's flowing pigtails evoke the motion of a child running. She is accompanied by a father who has a profile similar to Cesar E. Chavez. This iconic sign was a functional warning as well as a subversive work of design activism. Hood believed that drivers would be more cautious if a little girl was the face of the campaign; he felt that they "are dear to the heart, especially for fathers." Hood also likened the immigrants' plight to those endured—past and present—by the Navajo tribe, such as the 1864 Long Walk of the Navajo and the conditions of present-day reservations in northeastern New Mexico.

To build upon the genius of Hood's original work in a contemporary protest against family separation, I made one simple design move: I turned the family to face each other—a child running to the arms of a parent.

In 2017, the last of Hood's original signs was removed from the Southern California county where they were first placed. But there was an unexpected reaction. Our open-source, downloadable sign found itself returning to the highway in the form of a massive billboard, seen by hundreds of thousands of motorists. The sign had been mounted by the For Freedoms campaign—a set of programs, exhibitions, and public art installations led by the artists Hank Willis Thomas and Eric Gottesman. The campaign's intent was to deepen public discussions on civic issues and core values in order to advocate for equality, dialogue, and civic participation.[2]

This design act became a profound catalyst. For me, it demonstrated the power architects possess to reconsider the topics, landscapes, and "clients" in which we choose to invest our time and energy, even if such an approach does not fit neatly within the dogmas of the discipline.

[2]. Read more at https://forfreedoms.org/about/.

Reunite

ACTIVISM

As a body of work, the Teeter-Totter Wall, Mud Frontiers, and the adapted immigration sign explore contemporary possibilities for sustainability, accessibility, and open-source technology through the lens of local traditions. Yet the work is also a form of activism, standing as physical manifestations of the belief that design is an integral component of the activist agenda. This form of power can be transformative and demonstrates that our relevance as a profession can emerge from materials that are often not considered—like mud or a highway sign—and from landscapes that are unfamiliar to the majority—like the borderlands—that exist beyond the white gaze and white-adjacent audiences that are often assumed to be the only consumers of and participants in creative work. Instead, these projects lean toward the voices of the least represented—the participants in the built environment that the profession very rarely hears from.

Toni Morrison, in her 2019 documentary *The Pieces I Am*, said: "The little white man that sits on your shoulder and checks out everything you do or say…you sort of knock him off and you're free." As designers of color, we must seek the freedoms found by abandoning the hegemonic pressures of intractable canons that have long shaped decisions in narrow halls of power. Instead, we must return to the essential issues that have shaped our heterogeneous becoming and define the broad spectra of who we are.

* * *

LAS FRONTERAS DEL DISEÑO (SPANISH VERSION)
RONALD RAEL

> **Estos territorios no son simplemente un paisaje desértico y árido compuesto por 'bad hombres,' hombres malos cómo el ex presidente Trump describió a los migrantes, sino más bien un conjunto de comunidades ecológicamente ricas y socialmente diversas llenas de familias inteligentes y solidarias, que viven con sus hijos en comunidades donde ríen, juegan y disfrutan y que toman fotografías con sus celulares a pesar de las penurias de la pobreza, la xenofobia y la opresión reflejada en la construcción de muros.**

Durante el día 28 de julio de 2019, mi estudio reunió un equipo de colaboradores, amigos, y miembros de la comunidad a lo largo del muro (18 pies de altura) que divide las ciudades de El Paso y Ciudad Juárez, justo al oeste de esas dos ciudades, un tramo desolado entre Sunland Park, Nuevo México[3], y la colonia mexicana de Anapra. En el transcurso de unas horas, instalamos tres balancines rosados que utilizaron la valla fronteriza como punto de apoyo.[4] Esa tarde, en nuestra humilde reunión a lo largo de la frontera, madres, niños, artistas, diseñadores y curadores de ambos lados de la frontera se congregaron y compartieron un momento de convivencia. Esta palabra, convivir, no tiene traducción directa en inglés. "Coexistir" o "comunidad" podrían acercarse; sin embargo, una traducción parece demasiado científica, mientras que la otra suena demasiado religiosa. En este contexto, la traducción más cercana probablemente sería simplemente "pasar el tiempo divirtiédonos."

Inesperadamente, este evento fue compartido por millones en las redes sociales. Muchos lo llamaron un momento importante de liberación de las tensiones alimentadas por la continua cobertura mediática de las separaciones familiares en la frontera y de la búsqueda incesante de la administración Trump para adquirir fondos para continuar construyendo el muro fronterizo. Para mí, el trabajo también demostró que existe otra zona fronteriza fuera de la superficial definida por una Mirada racialmente privilegiada, de los medios de comunicación "autorizados" y la propaganda política, que son los vehículos principales a través de los cuales se representan las personas y las ecologías

[3]. Sunland Park es una ciudad en el sur de Nuevo México, inmediatamente al este de El Paso, en la frontera de Texas y el estado mexicano de Chihuahua.

[4]. Los balancines son de color rosa, un color utilizado para rendir homenaje a los cientos de mujeres y niñas asesinadas desde 1993 en Ciudad Juárez.

de la frontera. Más bien, el evento comunicó algo que uno no oye ni ve cuando aprende sobre las "realidades" de las zonas fronterizas. Estos territorios no son simplemente un paisaje desértico y árido compuesto por "bad hombres," hombres malos cómo el ex presidente Trump describió a los migrantes, sino más bien un conjunto de comunidades ecológicamente ricas y socialmente diversas llenas de familias inteligentes y solidarias, que viven con sus hijos en comunidades donde ríen, juegan y disfrutan y que toman fotografías con sus celulares a pesar de las penurias de la pobreza, la xenofobia y la opresión reflejada en la construcción de muros.

Mi práctica creativa ha trabajado en proyectos cerca de la frontera entre los Estados Unidos y México desde el año 2001, pero mis antepasados han vivido a lo largo de la cuenca del Río Grande durante milenios. Esta región se extiende desde donde actualmente termina el Río Grande en El Paso, Texas y Juárez, Chihuahua, hasta donde comienza en el Valle de San Luis en el sur de Colorado, lo que era la zona fronteriza más al norte del territorio mexicano, conocida como Santa Fe de Nuevo Méjico, antes de 1848. Como diseñador, reconocí que mi propio trabajo, en mi propia tierra, no tenía por qué contorsionarse con una visión de las tierras fronterizas definidas desde el punto de vista de la mirada blanca. En cambio, podría demostrar quiénes son realmente las personas de las zonas fronterizas.

Trabajar fuera del lente de una mirada privilegiada ha sido un foco cada vez mayor de nuestro trabajo en la zona fronteriza. Visto en conjunto, cuestiona la gama limitada de procesos, materiales, agendas y tecnologías que las instituciones arquitectónicas acuerdan uniformemente como relevantes. Este énfasis es particularmente cierto para aquellas instituciones que reflejan una perspectiva eurocéntrica y modernista que tradicionalmente ha dominado el discurso arquitectónico, así como los "-ismos" que han impregnado la historia reciente del discurso en nuestra profesión, incluido el deconstruccionismo, el posmodernismo y parametricismo. Ese momento de convivencia en las subibajas rosados (el Teeter-Totter Wall) demostró que el juego y el diseño pueden ser formas de activismo.

MUD FRONTIERS

Utilizando un enfoque similar, durante ese mismo verano de 2019, mi estudio concluyó un proyecto llamado, en Inglés, Mud Frontiers (fronteras de barro). En 2010, en el cuadragésimo aniversario de la revista Smithsonian, la publicación anunció "40 cosas que uno necesita saber sobre los próximos 40 años." El número uno proclamó que "Los edificios sofisticados estarán hechos de barro," un pronóstico audaz, incluso controvertido, en una época en la que fabricación digital y el diseño asistido por computadora se consideraban la vanguardia en arquitectura. Mucho antes de que el Smithsonian publicara su predicción, yo creía en el poder del barro, ya que crecí en la misma lugar de adobe en la que vivo actualmente: la casa de mi madre, su madre, y su madre antes que ella.

Mud Frontiers fue un proyecto de investigación de dos partes para comprender mejor las capacidades y el potencial de la cerámica tradicional y las tradiciones de construcción con tierra que guiaron a nuestros antepasados durante siglos. En el transcurso de las investigaciones, viajé desde las zonas fronterizas contemporáneas a lo largo de la cuenca del Río Grande en El Paso hasta las antiguas zonas fronterizas y las cabeceras del Río Grande en el Valle de San Luis, en el sur del estado de Colorado en los estados unidos.

Cada fase de Mud Frontiers consistió en investigaciones in situ y un conjunto de exploraciones construidas que plantearon nuevas posibilidades para la arquitectura, ampliando la gama de los materiales más tradicionales de arcilla, agua y paja de trigo con nuevas herramientas robóticas. Dentro de nuestra profesión hoy, estos materiales se clasificarían bajo el desafortunado término alternativo, que implícitamente connota una sensación de alteridad. La otredad de los materiales, es decir el fenómeno por el cual algunos materiales son degradados, definido como no encajar dentro de las normas profesionales; esto va de la mano con la alteridad de las personas, en particular de aquellas cuya

> **La otredad de los materiales, es decir el fenómeno por el cual algunos materiales son degradados, definido como no encajar dentro de las normas profesionales; esto va de la mano con la alteridad de las personas, en particular de aquellas cuya práctica del patrimonio cultural emplea materiales de construcción de tierra.**

RONALD RAEL

práctica del patrimonio cultural emplea materiales de construcción de tierra. En oposición a esta práctica xenófoba, utilizo estos materiales para ampliar los límites de la construcción sostenible y ecológica en un proyecto que explora la artesanía tradicional de arcilla en los contextos tanto de la arquitectura como de la cerámica. El objetivo final de este esfuerzo fue demostrar que la construcción de bajo costo y mano de obra no debe relegarse a una opción alternativa, sino adoptarse como una opción intuitiva que sea a la vez accesible, económica y para audiencias fuera del grupo blanco. mirada y nociones típicas del progreso tecnológico.

La primera fase del proyecto analizó la arquitectura de tierra y la cerámica de barro de la cultura Mogollón (200 d.C.- 1450). Estos artefactos son parte de la historia arqueológica de la Jornada Mogollón, la región donde actualmente se encuentran las ciudades fronterizas de El Paso y Juárez. Las casas excavadas y las estructuras de adobe sobre el suelo caracterizan la arquitectura mogollón. Hacia el año 400 d.C., esta región fue testigo del desarrollo de una técnica de alfarería indígena distintiva de enrollar y raspar, conocida como El Paso brownware.

En la segunda fase del proyecto, mi estudio, en colaboración con los departamentos de Cerámica y Geología de la Universidad de Texas en El Paso y veinticinco alfareros de El Paso y Juárez, exploró la arquitectura de tierra y las tradiciones de cerámica de arcilla de las culturas ancestrales Pueblo (700 d.C.–presente) y las culturas indígenas del norte de Nuevo México y el sur de Colorado (1598 E.C.– presente). En conjunto, estas arquitecturas que definen la región cuentan la historia de un conjunto en evolución de tradiciones artesanales centradas en materiales de tierra. Las exploraciones espaciales posteriores a mayor escala se inspiraron en numerosas técnicas contemporáneas relacionadas utilizadas recientemente para crear estructuras impresas en 3D a gran escala. Los experimentos espaciales se conceptualizaron bajo cuatro temas: Hogar, Baliza, Mirador y Horno.[5]

El hogar explora cómo se pueden reforzar las construcciones de paredes delgadas de barro, o adobe, utilizando madera de enebro local resistente a la putrefacción. La madera mantiene unidas las paredes, pero también se extiende más allá de las paredes de la estructura en el exterior, mientras permanece al mismo nivel en el interior. Esta

5. Para recolectar muestras para la investigación, trabajé con un socio de la industria, 3D Potter, codiseñando e implementando robots personalizados pero de bajo costo y portátiles en los entornos donde trabajábamos. Los robots fueron diseñados para ser transportados a un sitio donde se pudieran cosechar y analizar los suelos locales.

forma dinámica de construcción hace referencia a las diferencias culturales entre las tradiciones arquitectónicas de los Pueblo y los edificios indígenas-méjicanos. El interior contiene un banco de adobe impreso en 3D (también conocido como tarima en el dialecto local), que rodea un fogón, en el que se quema el aromático enebro.

Faro prueba cómo la textura y la ondulación de las bobinas de lodo impresas en 3D pueden producir los recintos estructurales más delgados posibles. Estas bobinas luego se iluminan por la noche, contrastando la diferencia luminosa entre las curvas cóncavas y convexas que forman las paredes de barro.

Mirador, o el puesto de observación, es una exploración de la estructura: una escalera impresa en 3D hecha enteramente de adobe. Se dispone una densa red de espirales de lodo ondulantes para crear una estructura lo suficientemente fuerte como para caminar sobre ella. Este método también demuestra cómo las paredes anchas y aireadas pueden crear recintos interiores que representan nuevas posibilidades de aislamiento, especialmente en el duro clima del Valle de San Luis, que puede caer por debajo de -20° F en el invierno.

El horno repite varias técnicas, incluida la deposición de barro ondulada o entrelazada para crear paredes estructurales y aislantes. El horno también se utiliza para encerrar un área que aspira oxígeno mientras genera calor radiante para cocer arcilla de origen local con madera de enebro quemada. Los productos del horno (arcilla micácea cocida derivada de las tradiciones de los pueblos Taos y Picuris) son nuevos híbridos de tecnología y técnica indígenas.

CARTEL DE INMIGRACIÓN ADAPTADO

Mientras desarrollaba estos proyectos, me indignó la noticia de que casi 2.000 niños habían sido separados de sus familias en la frontera de Estados Unidos. En respuesta, creé un cartel descargable de código abierto que cualquiera podría usar para protestar contra estos actos horribles e inhumanos. La nueva imagen fue adaptada de un diseño anterior creado a finales de los años 1980 por el artista gráfico navajo John Hood - un cartel de inmigración. Hood, un veterano de la guerra de Vietnam de Nuevo México, trabajó para el Departamento de Transporte de California y a el se encomendó la tarea de crear un letrero en respuesta al fuerte aumento de las muertes de inmigrantes en accidentes de tránsito. Debido a que las personas que emigraron de México sin documentos no podían cruzar por los puertos de entrada oficiales, los coyotes (contrabandistas) los dejaban al costado de la carretera, dejándolos sin otra opción que correr a través de las peligrosas carreteras.

La imagen creada por Hood estaba destinada a provocar la empatía humana, así como el reconocimiento inmediato de un posible peligro de tráfico. Las coletas sueltas de una niña evocan el movimiento de un niño corriendo. La acompaña un padre que tiene un perfil similar al de César E. Chávez. Este letrero icónico fue una advertencia funcional, también un trabajo subversivo de activismo del diseño. Hood creía que los conductores serían más cautelosos si una niña fuera el rostro de la campaña; consideró que ellos "son queridos en el corazón, especialmente para los padres." Hood también comparó la difícil situación de los inmigrantes con las que padeció—pasado y presente—la tribu navajo, como la Larga Caminata de los Navajo de 1864 y las condiciones de las reservas actuales en el noreste de Nuevo México.

Para aprovechar la genialidad del trabajo original de Hood en una protesta contemporánea contra la separación familiar, hice un movimiento de diseño simple: giré a la familia para que se enfrentaran: un niño corriendo hacia los brazos de uno de sus padres. En 2017, el ultimo de los carteles originales de Hood fue retirado del condado del sur de California donde se colocaron por primera vez. Pero hubo una reacción inesperada. Nuestro letrero descargable de código abierto regresó a la carretera en forma de un enorme cartel publicitario, visto por cientos de miles de automovilistas. El cartel había sido montado por la campaña Por las Libertades: un conjunto de programas, exposiciones e instalaciones de arte público dirigidas por los artistas Hank Willis Thomas y Eric Gottesman. La intención de la campaña era profundizar los debates públicos sobre cuestiones cívicas y valores fundamentales para abogar por la igualdad, el diálogo y la participación cívica.[6]

Este acto de diseño se convirtió en un profundo catalizador. Para mí, demostró el poder que tienen arquitectos para reconsiderar los temas, paisajes y "clientes" con los

6. https://forfreedoms.org/about/.

> **Este acto de diseño se convirtió en un profundo catalizador. Para mí, demostró el poder que tienen arquitectos para reconsiderar los temas, paisajes y 'clientes' con los que elegimos invertir nuestro tiempo y energía, incluso si ese enfoque no encaja perfectamente dentro de los dogmas de la disciplina.**

que elegimos invertir nuestro tiempo y energía, incluso si ese enfoque no encaja perfectamente dentro de los dogmas de la disciplina.

ACTIVISMO

Como conjunto de trabajos, las subibajas rosados (The Teeter-Totter Wall), fronteras de barro (Mud Frontiers) y el cartel de inmigración adaptado exploran las posibilidades contemporáneas de sostenibilidad, accesibilidad y tecnología de código abierto a través de la lente de las tradiciones locales. Sin embargo, el trabajo es también una forma de activismo, y se presenta como manifestaciones físicas de la creencia de que el diseño es un componente integral de la agenda activista. Esta forma de poder puede ser transformadora y demuestra que nuestra relevancia como profesión puede surgir de materiales normalmente no se consideran, como el barro o una señal de carretera, y de paisajes desconocidos para la mayoría, como las zonas fronterizas, que existen más allá de la frontera y de una mirada privilegiada, o audiencias eurocéntricas, que a menudo se supone que son los únicos consumidores y participantes en trabajo creativo. En cambio, estos proyectos se inclinan hacia las voces de los menos representados: los participantes en el entorno construido que la profesión escucha menos.

Toni Morrison, en su documental de 2019 *The Pieces I Am*, dijo: "El gringuito que se sienta en tu hombro y observa todo lo que haces o dices…lo derrotas y eres libre." Para los diseñadores de color, debemos buscar las libertades que se encuentran al abandonar las presiones hegemónicas de los cánones intratables que durante mucho tiempo han dado forma a nuestras decisiones en los estrechos pasillos del poder. En lugar de ello, deberíamos volver a las cuestiones esenciales que han dado forma a nuestro devenir heterogéneo y definir el amplio espectro de quiénes somos.

"

For while we have our eyes on the future, history has its eyes on us, this is the era of just redemption we feared in its inception we did not feel prepared to be the heirs of such a terrifying hour but within it we found the power to author a new chapter, to offer hope and laughter to ourselves, so while once we asked how can we possibly prevail over catastrophe, now we assert how could catastrophe possibly prevail over us.

Amanda Gorman
poet and activist
"The Hill We Climb," spoken word poem recited at the inauguration of Joe Biden as President, January 20, 2021

Activism vs. Advocacy

Though sometimes used interchangeably, activism and advocacy are different. Activism typically involves taking direct and sometimes confrontational action to bring about change. It might include marches, protests, or speeches. Advocacy likewise encompasses a range of activities aimed at addressing a specific issue, but advocates typically work within established systems and institutions over extended periods to shape policy, change laws, and cultivate resources in order to advance their cause.

YOU ARE WELCOME HERE

MINNEAPOLIS = SANCTUARY

antiwarcommittee.org

[SNAPSHOT]

UNCLE ROY

Michelle Magalong

As a college student and intern at a nonprofit organization in Los Angeles in 1999, I met a community elder named Royal Morales (aka Uncle Roy) as he gave a tour of his life through four places in and near downtown. His story of migration and movement through urban renewal and displacement, and how he had sought to preserve his history, was compelling. He spoke of growing up in the neighborhood and how he was seeking a National Register of Historic Places nomination for the Filipino Christian Church where his father had served as a pastor.

Captivated by his story, I asked, "How can I help?" Uncle Roy responded, "I have two dreams: I want the church to receive the highest historic landmark designation in the nation, and I want to name this neighborhood 'P-town' to recognize the historical contributions of Filipino Americans in Los Angeles." With those two aims, I was hooked.

Uncle Roy passed away soon after, and I went on to pursue my master's and doctoral degrees in urban planning at UCLA. In Uncle Roy's memory, I wrote my thesis based on his tour, and in 2002 the neighborhood was renamed Historic Filipinotown by the City of Los Angeles.

Years later, I worked on garnering support for the National Register landmark designation of the church. The support was undisputed by the congregation, given Uncle Roy's groundwork done years prior in teaching the importance of historic preservation. In 2019, I went to a community event at the church in Historic Filipinotown, and it was then that I learned that the National Park Service had approved the nomination of the church—it was now listed on the National Register of Historic Places.

In that moment I realized I had helped achieve Uncle Roy's two wishes. It is incredible to reflect on his legacy and how it has inspired and informed my work as a practitioner, activist, and scholar in historic preservation.

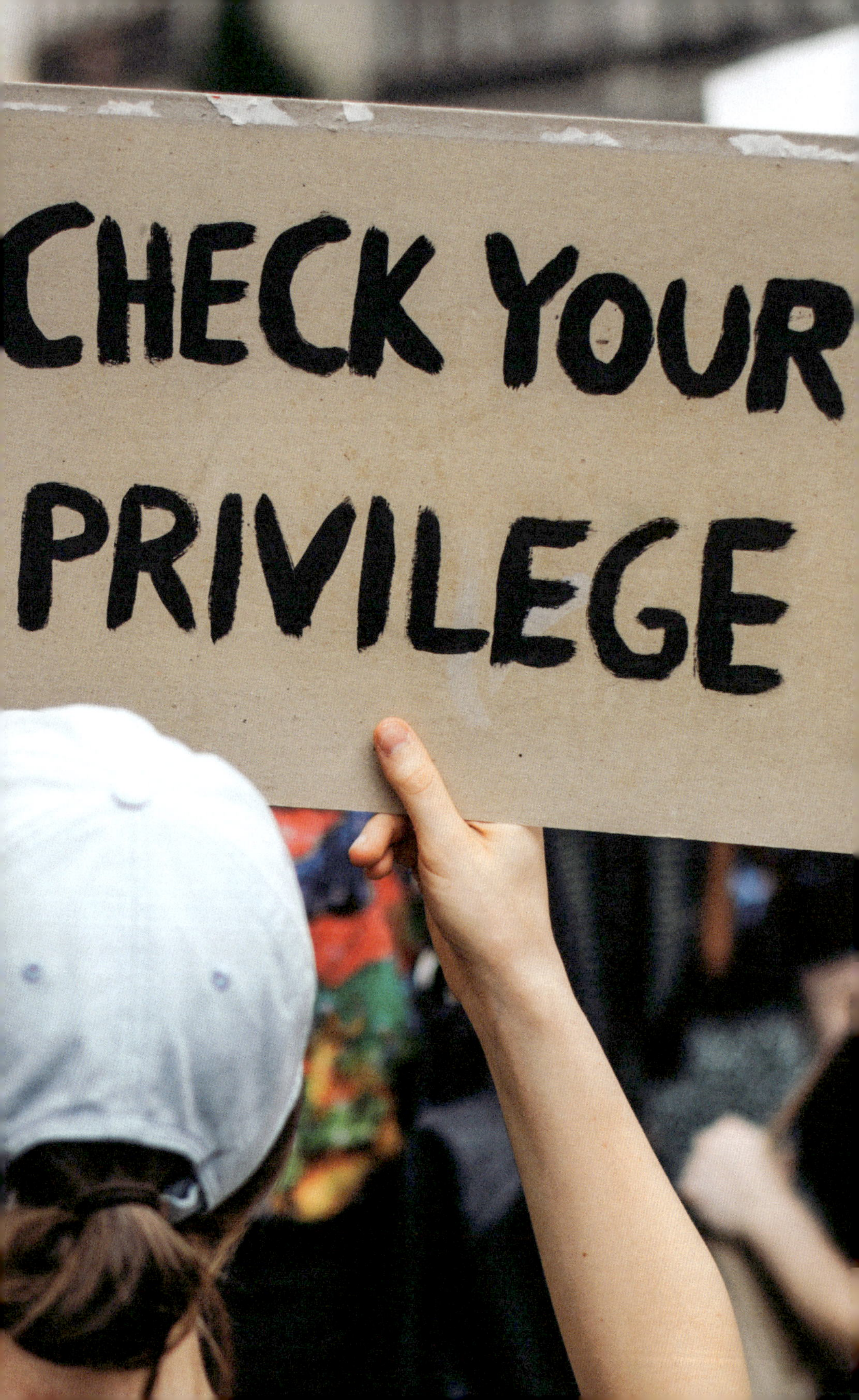
CHECK YOUR
PRIVILEGE

> The world in which you were born is just one model of reality. Other cultures are not failed attempts at being you; they are unique manifestations of the human spirit.

Wade Davis
cultural anthropologist

Colonization/ Decolonization

Colonization refers to processes by which a foreign group settles or occupies the sovereign lands of another, seeking to subjugate the people, exploit the land and resources, and impose foreign customs, culture, or religion. By physical means—violence, occupation, displacement—and/or sociocultural or political domination, colonizers assume control over Native peoples. Colonization involves sociocultural injustice through the suppression of Indigenous religions, language, and customs, and political oppression, denying self-rule and basic human rights and liberties. Much of the world has been colonized at one time or another. The legacies of colonization continue to shape today's social and political structures well beyond the past physical occupation of place.

Decolonization refers to complex processes of correction—both dismantling and rebuilding. Over time, colonially imposed legal, political, economic, and social systems that enable oppression become structurally entrenched, and so dismantling them can be critical. Recovery of lost languages, knowledge, and customs is indispensable to reestablishing culture and strengthening authentic heritage. Restoration of political autonomy and self-determination, taking measures toward economic justice and redress, and returning control over and ownership of land and resources are all paramount.

EXPULSION BY DESIGN

Ghazal Jafari

Ghazal Jafari is a territorial scholar, weaver, and educator, professionally trained as an architect and urban designer. Originally of Persian and Azeri descent and currently living in the United States, Ghazal focuses her research on spatial and environmental justice, landscape infrastructure, plant knowledge, feminist liberation, immigrant narratives, and non-Western spatial discourses. She is a founding director of OPEN SYSTEMS / Landscape Infrastructure Lab, a nonprofit organization dedicated to opening knowledge of complex ecological challenges and raising awareness about geopolitical conflicts at the intersection of spatial inequality, climate justice, and community self-determination. Recent projects and publications include A Botany of Violence: Across 529 Years of Resistance and Resurgence *(ORO Editions, 2022). Ghazal is an assistant professor of urban and environmental planning at the University of Virginia.*

اگر بنا بر این باشد که معماری و تخصصهای دیگر حرفه ای که سر و کارشان با طراحی و تنظیم فضایی زمین است دیدگاهی مسئولانه به بی عدالتی های اجتماعی و زیست محیطی امروز داشته باشند، شاید بهتر است این دیدگاه از نقد خود در تخصص ها و نقش حرفه ای شان در به بی عدالتی باشد. در این رابطه، متنی که در اینجا میخوانید نیم نگاهی است خلاصه به تاریخی بسیار وسیع و پیچیده که جای بسی کار و تأمل دارد. با اینکه این نوشته رویکردی است چند تخصصی به متن معاصر طراحی و برنامه ریزی فضایی در آمریکای شمالی، دانستن این تاریخ برای دانشجویان به اصطلاح جهان سومی همان قدر مهم است که دانستن تاریخ و فرهنگ بومی، چرا که سرزمینهای ما از قرن ۱۹ و همچنین تخصصهای حرفه ای دانشگاهی ما از اواسط قرن ۲۰ به بعد، تحت تاثیر و نفوذ سیستمهای دانش غربی بوده است که خود ریشه در استعمار و استثمار دارند. تجدید راه و رسم همزیستی عادلانه قبل از هر چیز وابسته است به امتناع از آنچه دانسته یا ندانسته از تاریخ استعمار به ارث برده ایم

* * *

Architecture's contemporary encounter with systemic injustices should perhaps begin with the central and rather controversial question about the relationship between the professional trajectory of the field and historical systems of dispossession and exploitation. While the self-serving separation of the technical and the political still shapes neoliberal architecture's predictably irresponsible approach to current social and environmental injustices, attention to the central role of representation, particularly representation of *Others*, confronts the elitists and white supremacist predispositions underlying this separation. The technical and the political cannot be separated. Design and planning, while deeply instrumental in altering ecological relations and reorganization of the inhabited ground, are also deeply political. The following text takes a transdisciplinary turn to create a small opening to a larger and much deeper inquiry about the politics of representation and methods of *othering* in geospatial fields of expertise, which are collectively responsible for how the land on which we live is traced, projected, and shaped.[1]

THE CULTURAL PRODUCTION OF POWER

Observing the United States' military invasion of Iraq in the aftermath of 9/11, geographer Derek Gregory explains that current imperialist structures on which colonial relations are constantly renewed are not merely geopolitical or

1. Here "land" refers to the lived multispecies ground where there is no separation between soil, water, and air. Land in many Indigenous cultures encompasses interspecies relations, ecologies, cultures, spiritualities, and laws.

geo-economic phenomena. Imperialism has always also been a cultural project that involves "production, circulation, and legitimation of meanings through representations, practices, and performances."[2] When used in Euro-American expansionist missions, representation has historically emerged as a weapon, rendering other ethnicities and cultures as "irredeemable *Other*" to "license the unleashing of exemplary violence against them."[3] Imperialism thus needs what Edward Said has called *imaginative geographies*, produced not only by nation-state lines on the map but also by the multiplicity of partitions and enclaves constantly dividing "us" and "them." The "universal practice of designating in one's mind a familiar space which is 'ours' and an unfamiliar space beyond 'ours' which is 'theirs' is a way of making geographic distinctions that can be entirely *arbitrary*."[4] It is arbitrary precisely because it does not depend on recognition or consent on behalf of those represented. The act of othering through representation by the oppressor regime never occurs on mutual grounds. Its main goal is domination, and it almost always involves some form of violence—beginning most likely with the elimination of the Natives.[5]

> "Imperialism has always also been a cultural project that involves 'production, circulation, and legitimation of meanings through representations, practices, and performances.'"

EXPULSION BY PARTITIONS

Critical reflections in geospatial fields of expertise about their role in the cultural production of imperialism are certainly rare, but incredibly valuable when done well. For instance, an inquiry into the establishment of urban planning's professional structure, as brilliantly elucidated by landscape architect Pierre Bélanger and his colleagues, reveals a close relationship between the planning's bureaucratic structures and the expansion of settler colonial spaces across the Canadian colony starting in the eighteenth century. The authors note:

> Embedded with colonial motivations of land domination through territorial acquisitions, the practice of planning is thus captured in the organizational geometries of the grid, the uncontested hegemony of the plan, the political

2. Derek Gregory, *The Colonial Present* (Malden, MA: Blackwell, 2004), 8. I am referring to imperialism as defined by Edward Said as "thinking about, settling on, and controlling land that you do not possess, that is distant, that is lived on and owned by others." Edward W. Said, *Culture and Imperialism* (New York: Vintage Books, 1994), 7. Therefore, imperialism as used in this text does not limit itself to the historical period of European expansion in the nineteenth century.

3. Gregory, *The Colonial Present*, 16.

4. Edward Said, *Orientalism* (New York: Pantheon Books, 1987), 54.

5. See Patrick Wolfe, "Settler Colonialism and the Elimination of the Native," *Journal of Genocide Research* 8, no. 4 (December 2006): 387–409.

erasure of the ground, and the simplification of complex ecological processes through land use controls. More precisely, its attendant roles were located in property development at one end and resource management at the other, between the city and the countryside. Often touted under the benevolent intentions of economy, health, or conservation, the practice of planning—whether by land survey, land use zoning, or property development—was originally conceived and today remains a politicized practice consisting in resource management, hierarchical bureaucracy, and population control with ideological foundations deeply and firmly rooted in class, gender, race, and religion.[6]

Accordingly, the cultural agency of planning, placed between the paper space of maps and the lived space of the material ground, becomes a double-edged sword. First, it erases what is seen as external or an impediment to the expansion of the colonial state through survey maps, for instance Indigenous sovereignties and cultural landscapes. Second, when projected colonial plans and policies are concretized in gridded patterns of spatial order, they become impossible to remove. Elimination through politics of representation is at work in both interpretive abstraction and selective register on the map, and futuristic projection by plan. The representational media are thus not limited to drawings and maps but also include standards and conventions of the field as expressed in such normalized spatial technologies as dividing lines, partitions, zoning, and systems of land use. Cultural reproduction of the land through technical language does not simply read or follow colonial rules; it shapes colonial sociopolitical relations and inscribes them in space.

Redefining land as resource—whether by classification of species and mineral tables or by property divisions—and its management by administrative zones has operated in tandem with the elimination of other lifeways and modes of stewardship. Built on the back of broken treaties, the extractive definition of land as resource has been followed by the unquestioned centrality of private property systems in the capitalist economy and the organization of urban environments today.[7] The close tie between design practices and the private property system is impossible to deny because every single building site in the current political economy benefits from this system. In other words, a

6. Pierre Bélanger, Christopher Alton, and Nina-Marie Lister, "Decolonization of Planning," in *Extraction Empire: Undermining the Systems, States, and Scales of Canada's Global Resource Empire*, ed. Pierre Bélanger (Cambridge, MA: MIT Press, 2018), 429.

7. Nicholas Blomley, "Law, Property, and the Geography of Violence: The Frontier, the Survey, and the Grid," *Annals of the Association of American Geographers* 93, no. 1 (2003): 121–41.

great portion of development projects, from buildings to parks, would cease to exist if they were not part of the profit-generating projects of global capitalism or spatial affirmation of the ruling class and race.[8]

From the scale of neighborhoods to entire regions, spatial segregation and the architecture of enclaves cause othering and marginalization, whether by distancing the commercial metropole from the rural, industrial periphery; under-servicing Indigenous reservations that are already removed from regional biodiversity on which their livelihoods and identities depend; propping up urban apartheids that racially and economically divide populations of towns and cities; or casting national parks and forests as the anthropocentric invention of Nature whose picturesque image fails to mask the rapidly vanishing biodiversity everywhere else. These enclaves built by land acquisition, property systems, and bureaucratic administration are central to the spatial and cultural reproduction of the colonial present. This constructed ground is a medium through which law, policy, state programs, and private capital have constantly activated various forms of oppression and violence against people of color.

* * *

در زمره شاخصه های معماری و شهرسازی که در به حاشیه راندن گروههای مختلف مردمی نقش دارند محدوده های محصور را میتوان دید که نقش جدا سازی فضایی را در جغرافی امروزی آمریکا را به عهده دارند ــ چه جداسازی مناطق اغلب ثروتمند اقتصادی شهری از حاشیه های محروم صنعتی و روستایی باشد، چه جدا سازی مناطق تحت کنترل مردم بومی از امکانات سازه ای حداقل، چه گسل بین همسایگی های شهری مردم سفید پوست و غیر سفید پوست باشد، و چه ابداع مناطق حفاظت شده طبیعی که بکری ظاهری شان نمیتواند از بین رفتن تنوع گونه ای و زوال محیط زیست را در کل قاره پنهان کند. این جدا سازی فضایی که بر آمده از اکتساب به زور زمین های بومی، سیستم مالکیت خصوصی، و مدیریت تحکم آمیز بوروکراسی است، در به وجود آمدن شرایط استعماری امروزی نقش مرکزی دارد. این جداسازی زمینه را برای تبعیض و به حاشیه رانده شدن مردم (اغلب غیر سفید) توسط قانون، تبصره، برنامه دولت، و سرمایه خصوصی فراهم میکند

* * *

Urban apartheid or segregated neighborhoods in the United States, for instance, have targeted Black and Brown populations and deprived them of upward mobility for decades.

8. For more, see Pierre Bélanger, Ghazal Jafari, Hernan Bianchi Benguria, Alexander Arroyo, and Tiffany Dang, "No Design on Stolen Land: Dismantling Design's Dehumanising White Supremacy," *Architectural Design* 90, no. 1 (January 2020): 120–27.

Gilpin Court and Jackson Ward, once thriving Black neighborhoods in Richmond, Virginia, have been decimated by decades of systemically racist urban policies, including the construction of Interstate 64, which displaced hundreds of families. The banality of the images reminds us how routine scenes of inequity and oppression can be.

GHAZAL JAFARI

above and opposite: Jackson Ward, once known as the Harlem of the South, is now mainly a scene of boarded-up shop windows, empty commercial buildings, and vast parking lots where grass grows uninterrupted. But murals remind us of the transgenerational sense of belonging and the Black right to this place, and local efforts are underway to revive the neighborhood.

The tools and techniques of this spatial marginalization have included the exclusionary zoning ordinances of the 1920s, redlining in the Federal Housing Administration's risk assessment maps of the 1930s, urban renewal projects in the 1940s and 1970s, erasure of entire neighborhoods by infrastructure, and continued urban gentrification today.

The current urban apartheid is not only at the heart of the uneven distribution of wealth and services, but indivisible from state violence exercised, for instance, in over-policing neighborhoods with higher POC populations and over-incarceration of Black and Brown bodies to fill up the prison-industrial complex with cheap or free labor—prison as the new plantation.[9] If erasure, oppression, dispossession, and exploitation have not been enough, strategic allocation of industrial dump sites completes the task of expulsion by slow environmental violence that manifests itself in shortening life expectancy and death by pollution.[10] Expulsion of others by design and planning is thus political—involving loss of voice, agency, sovereignty, and

9. See Richard Rothstein, *The Color of Law: A Forgotten History of How Our Government Segregated America* (New York and London: Liveright, 2018); Kelly Lytle Hernández, Khalil Gibran Muhammad, and Heather Ann Thompson. "Introduction: Constructing the Carceral State." *Journal of American History* 102, no. 1 (2015): 18–24.

10. Dina Gilio-Whitaker, *As Long as Grass Grows: The Indigenous Fight for Environmental Justice, from Colonization to Standing Rock* (Boston: Beacon Press, 2019); Daniel R. Wildcat, *Red Alert: Saving the Planet with Indigenous Knowledge* (Arvada, Colorado: Fulcrum, 2009).

EXPULSION BY DESIGN

self-determination—and corporeal, which is to say it is physical, emotional, and psychological.

ERASURE BY EDUCATIONAL AND CULTURAL INSTITUTIONS

Othering is also carried out by academia and other educational-cultural institutions such as museums, exhibitions, and publishing houses. This occurs through formation of knowledge systems based on a selective approach to legitimization of knowledge by which (knowingly or unknowingly) white privilege is guaranteed. After all, "knowledge and the power to define what counts as real knowledge lie at the epistemic core of colonialism."[11] Design and planning are not exceptions in this regard. To understand what is externalized, how, and why, a non-Western critical interrogation begins with historical examination of the significance of colonialism in the production of Western knowledge. We cannot overlook the "contributions of geographically situated knowledge made by colonial subjects in the formation and practice of modern sciences and social theory" as well as art and humanities.[12] In short, legitimized knowledge systems at the core of current Western educational institutions have been at least partly developed within the colonial socioeconomic realm that fostered and condoned theft and appropriation of Indigenous knowledge, while simultaneously externalizing from formal education other ways of knowing that do not fit in the cadre of what has been culturally, ideologically, and strategically aligned with the purpose of colonialism. By erasing other ways of knowing, this system also erases other worlds, humanities, and sovereignties.

> After all, 'knowledge and the power to define what counts as real knowledge lie at the epistemic core of colonialism.'

* * *

ورای طراحی فضایی که پیشتر مطرح شد، نهادهای دانشگاهی و فرهنگی نقش به سزایی در به حاشیه رانده شدن مردم محروم بازی میکنند. این به حاشیه رانده شدن توسط ساختار انتخابی دانش اتفاق می افتد و تصمیم گیری اینکه چه دانشی دارای ارزش و مشروعیت علمی در سیستم دانشگاهی است. خود این پروسه تحت تاثیر ارزشهای استعماری بوده است. برای آنکه بهتر بفهمیم چه دانشی بیرون انداخته شده و چرا، ابتدا باید یاد آور شویم که بخش بزرگی از آنچه به عنوان دانش غرب از آن یاد میشود شکل گرفته در سیستم استعمار و بر گرفته از دانش بومی مردمان مستعمره ها بوده است که علی رغم نقش مهم شان در تمدن غرب، هیچگاه به رسمیت شناخته نشده اند. به علاوه، آن دانشی که در جهت منافع و همراستا با سیاست و اقتصاد استعمار و سرمایه داری نبوده، چه دانش فنی باشد، چه فرهنگی، عقیدتی، یا راهبردی باید حذف میشده. با حذف این دانشها و راههای متفاوت شناخت که اغلب با زندگی های غیر استعماری و غیر سرمایه داری همخوانی داشته اند، سیستم استعماری در واقع گونه های دیگر زندگی، جهان بینی، انسانیت، و مدیریت سیاسی را حذف کرده اند، یا حد اقل سعی کرده اند که حذف کنند

* * *

11. Linda Tuhiwai Smith, "Introduction to the Third Edition," in *Decolonizing Methodologies: Research and Indigenous Peoples* (London: Zed Books, 1999), digital copy.

12. Smith, "Introduction."

Māori scholar Linda Tuhiwai Smith observes: "It appalls us that the West can desire, extract and claim ownership of our ways of knowing, our imagery, the things we create and produce, and then simultaneously reject the people who created and developed those ideas and seek to deny them further opportunities to be creators of their own culture and their own nations."[13] With sensibility to colonial processes of knowledge production, the critique of Western disciplinary trajectories in design and planning can take a cross-cultural and transformative stance today. This position at one level is concerned with interrogation of the past and alternative histories that reveal the agency of externalized Others. This approach is evident in Kofi Boone's 2020 essay "Black Landscapes Matter," which retraces the agency of Black people in landscape history through Black struggles in the United States and landscape knowledge rooted in African cultures.[14]

At another level, this critical lens confronts the continuous dispossession and erasure of Others by ongoing cultural appropriation that is evident, for instance, in the self-indigenization and race-shifting characteristics of Rem Koolhaas's exhibition *Countryside, The Future* (2020–21) at the Guggenheim Museum in New York. In an open letter addressed to Koolhaas and the museum's board of trustees published in January 2022, a group of concerned designers, educators, Indigenous elders, and activists warn, "Widespread throughout the exhibition [*Countryside*] and accompanying publication are several strategies of dispossession premised on extraction, erasure, and race-shifting.... Nowhere are these strategies made clearer than in the exhibition's platforming of self-indigenization. The language of the exhibition's Preservation section is especially egregious: 'The second [model] proposes a more intensive sharing/mixing of all our territories, as if we moderns could become 'indigenous' again.'"[15] The exhibition then regurgitates the romanticized images of Alexander von Humboldt's botanical expeditions as an archetype of colonial cartographies that "uncritically reproduce the historical myth of the dominance of European imperial science… at the expense of Indigenous knowledge."[16] In its failure to diverge from architecture's compliance to capitalist exploitation and environmental destruction, *Countryside* now romanticizes Indigenous knowledge and lifeways;

13. Smith, "Introduction."

14. Kofi Boone, "Black Landscapes Matter," *World Landscape Architect*, June 3, 2020.

15. "Re: The Writing on the Wall," January 17, 2022, http://whiteskinwhitewallswhiteli.es.

16. "Re: The Writing on the Wall."

GHAZAL JAFARI **187**

it claims them while erasing Indigenous territorial sovereignties and histories of resistance.

This widespread trend is also exemplified in Julia Watson's compendium of Indigenous technics in *Low-Tek: Design by Radical Indigenism* (2019) published by Taschen. This book, far from engaging cross-cultural dialogue, is a feminist renewal of the colonial gaze, which can be traced in the the trajectory of vernacular architecture's romanticized narratives, such as Bernard Rudofsky's *Architecture Without Architects* (1964).[17] In her rather superficial catalog and under the auspices of rebuilding "an understanding of indigenous philosophy and vernacular architecture," Watson dispossesses Indigenous peoples of agency precisely by avoiding deeper questions about the territorial and political impediments of Indigenous material and environmental praxis, as if what's at stake for documented people is recognition by the white academy.

Dispossession also happens through robbing Others of narrating their histories, for instance, in the twentieth-century frenzy of historicizing professional lineages by Western historians (often in conjunction with civilization histories), in which the non-Western cultural landscapes are placed in an antiquated and pre-modern stage and thus rendered as relics without futures or present relevance. This type of erasure by antiquation is exemplified in Norman Newton's widely circulated textbook, *Design on the Land* (1971).[18] These few examples point to an incredibly pervasive epidemic of cultural appropriation and misrepresentation at the center of the colonial process of disabling.

Such condescending and predatory behavior should not come as a surprise. If academic and cultural institutions are best understood through their relationships and allegiances to other major institutions, namely corporations and professions, then in the current hyper-commercialization of education and culture it should not be surprising if values are highly influenced by the predatory nature of capitalism.[19] Likewise, when it comes to institutional change, it would not be shocking if current inclusion and equity campaigns prefer a cosmetic approach to diversity by recruiting visibly nonwhite faculty without much interest in their embodied knowledge. This institutional tokenism prefers people of color who do not challenge structures of domination. When it comes to transformative change through decentering the

17. Julia Watson, *Low-Tek: Design by Radical Indigenism* (Cologne: Taschen, 2020); Bernard Rudofsky, *Architecture Without Architects* (NYC: The Museum of Modern Art, 1964).

18. Norman T. Newton, *Design on the Land: The Development of Landscape Architecture* (Cambridge: Harvard University Press, 1971).

19. For institutional relations of academia and how they shape the missions of academic institutions, see Donncha Kavanagh, "The University as Fool," in *The Future University: Ideas and Possibilities*, ed. Ronald Barnett (London: Taylor & Francis Group, 2011), 101–11.

mission and content of education, institutions show far less tolerance. In this condition many POC faculty who are hired find themselves deceived by false promises and captive in conservative, white supremacist institutional structures.[20] Exclusion of other geographies, worldviews, and knowledge systems continues to be essential in the reproduction of disciplinary canons and the safeguarding of key positions in academia.[21] By externalizing Others, institutions not only control knowledge and power but they also hide the real cost and extended imprint of urban economies.

If we consider different means of othering and expulsion that were briefly described in this text as part of the larger cultural setting and ground preparation necessary for maintaining the current colonial condition, then it should be clear that without reckoning with the role of design and planning, no meaningful professional response to shared contemporary struggles would be possible. Complex social and environmental problems—from climate change and loss of biodiversity to widening economic disparities and breakouts of violence—are not unintended consequences but a priori conditions of capitalism. One may begin to think that breaking off from this history is contingent on cultural and political change, starting perhaps with counter-representations, with identifying geospatial tools of othering and expulsion in order to un-build them and approaching the land as a living home to which and on which one must rebuild new relations based on consent and mutual respect. A genuine break off from this history, however, demands decolonization that is not a metaphor for professional reform and academic posturing, but deeply rooted in politics of land.[22] Alas, amid current world affairs, as long as there are authorities with the means and the will to apply violence to gain access to land by all means necessary—as we witness around the world, from Brazilian Amazon forests to Wet'suwet'en Territory, from Palestine to Iran—speaking of cultural change in design and by design may not be more than wishful thinking.

20. Menna Agha and Jess Myers, "The Cluster Hires Will Not Be Silenced," *Places Journal: Field Notes on Design Activism* 7 (November 2012); Editors, "Lesley Lokko Explains Her Resignation from City College of New York's Spitzer School of Architecture," *Architectural Record*, October 5, 2020.

21. Kendall A. Nicholson, "Where Are My People? Middle Eastern and North African in Architecture," ACSA, July 9, 2021.

22. Eve Tuck and K. Wayne Yang, "Decolonization Is Not a Metaphor," *Decolonization: Indigeneity, Education and Society* 1, no. 1 (2012): 1–40.

> We swim in an ocean of racism. Racism is the system of structuring opportunity and assigning value based on the social interpretation of how one looks (which is what we call 'race'), that unfairly disadvantages some individuals and communities, unfairly advantages other individuals and communities, and saps the strength of the whole society through the waste of human resources.

Camara Phyllis Jones
physician and anti-racism activist
"Seeing the Water: Seven Values Targets for Anti-Racism Action," 2020

Implicit Bias and Unconscious Bias

Unconscious bias and implicit bias are often used interchangeably to refer to subconscious associations and perceptions of others based on race, gender, religion, age, or other differences. Unconscious bias can be shaped by societal influences, media, stereotypes, prejudices, or personal experiences, and can elicit unjustified, seemingly automatic responses to people or situations. Bias may unintentionally affect our judgment and behavior toward others in ways that include acts of discrimination.

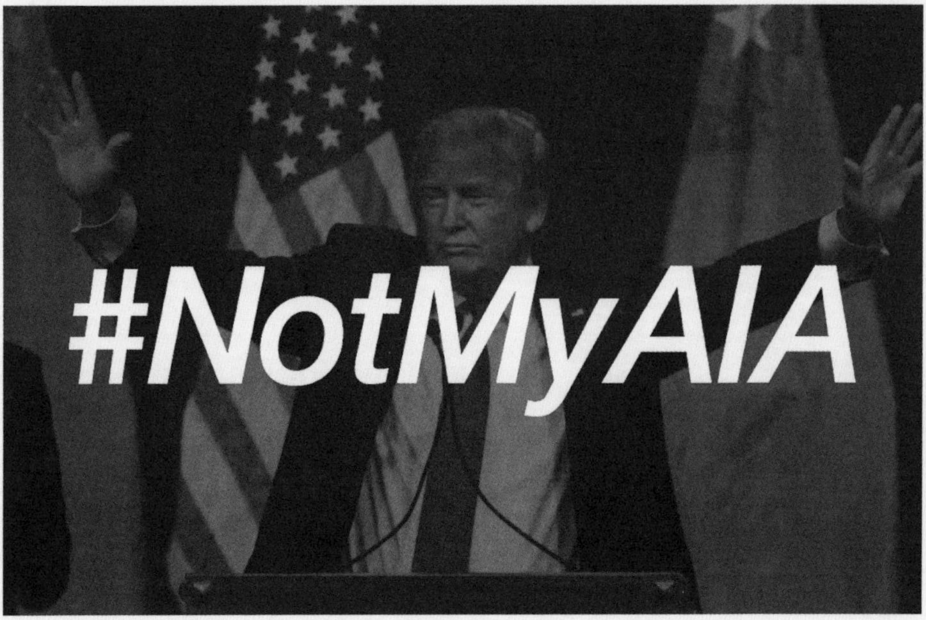
#NotMyAIA

[BENCHMARK]

#NOTMYAIA

Architect's Newspaper editors

The following is excerpted from the story "AIA Pledges to Work with Donald Trump, Membership Recoils," which ran in the Architect's Newspaper *on November 11, 2016.*[1]

The American Institute of Architects (AIA) is drawing ire from across the architectural profession after releasing a post-election memo containing conciliatory and supportive language for President-elect Donald Trump's campaign pledge to embark on a $500 billion infrastructure building program.

Following Tuesday's election results, Robert Ivy, AIA Executive Vice President and Chief Executive Officer, released the following statement on behalf of the national AIA apparatus and membership:

The AIA and its 89,000 members are committed to working with President-elect Trump to address the issues our country faces, particularly strengthening the nation's aging infrastructure. During the campaign, President-elect Trump called for committing at least $500 billion to infrastructure spending over five years. We stand ready to work with him and with the incoming 115th Congress to ensure that investments in schools, hospitals and other public infrastructure continue to be a major priority.... This has been a hard-fought, contentious election process. It is now time for all of us to work together to advance policies that help our country move forward.

---

1. The full text is available at https://www.archpaper.com/2016/11/aia-pledges-work-donald-trump-membership-recoils/.

While the editorial board agrees that a spirit of togetherness is vital for moving the country (and the architectural profession) forward, *The Architect's Newspaper* strongly disagrees with Ivy's conciliatory note....

It is plain to see that Donald Trump ran a racist, misogynist, and hateful campaign rooted in the forceful removal of undocumented immigrants, voter suppression targeting people of color, and xenophobic anti-Muslim profiling. The many hate crimes and acts of intimidation taking place across the country in the days since the election are a testament to the violence and racism his campaign has enlivened.

Though Trump's campaign was relatively anemic in terms of specific, actionable policy proposals and objectives, a clear plank of the Republican candidate's message was, Ivy correctly states, related to infrastructure, namely, the erection of a border wall separating Mexico from the United States.... **It is anathema to this editorial board to fathom the positive impact of such a work of infrastructure as the proposed border wall or its attendant detention centers, federal and private prisons, and militarized infrastructure that would be necessary in order to achieve the President-elect's stated deportation policy goals.** To ignore the role design and designers could play in instituting and perpetuating the inequality inherent in the racist patriarchy Trump's ideology embodies is irresponsible and reprehensible.

Archinect
@archinect · Follow

Do you agree w/ @robertivy's statement, on behalf of AIA's membership, to the election of @realDonaldTrump? #NotMyAIA

Yes	10%
No, but I will renew	18.9%
No, and I will not renew	53.3%
I don't care	17.8%

Archinect Twitter poll

THREE

MILES TO GO BEFORE WE SLEEP

Essays by

Teddy Cruz and Fonna Forman

The Johnson Study Group

Zena Howard and Lauren Neefe

Isabel Strauss

ACSA / CELA / ACSP / IDEC

Meejin Yoon and Betsy West

Lesley Lokko

AIA / AIAS / ACSA / NOMA

> **Radical simply means
'grasping things at the root.'**
>
> Angela Davis
> educator and political activist

INTRODUCTION
José L.S. Gámez

The authors in chapter 3 point to new avenues of collective action, even as the benchmarks remind us of the work that remains to be done. It is all too easy for mainstream organizations, if not vigilant, to fall prey to power structures that actively produce, reproduce, and maintain inequitable social and spatial distinctions. While progress has been made since the civil rights era, the path forward for architecture is by no means clear or clean-cut.

The apology from *Architect* magazine for erasing a prominent Black architect from its video recording of a panel event points out just how easily voices can be silenced. The joint statement from the American Institute of Architects (AIA), American Institute of Architecture Students (AIAS), Association of Collegiate Schools of Architecture (ACSA), and National Organization of Minority Architects (NOMA) following the Supreme Court's regressive ruling on university admissions policies suggests that progressive solidarity and decisive resistance are taking hold in architecture's professional institutions despite setbacks that arise. Snapshots from Isabel Strauss and Lesley Lokko remind us that communities of color have long been aware that the slow march toward equity takes a toll.

But connections exist across design practices and cultural politics that identify potential sites of resolution and negotiation. Zena Howard and Lauren Neefe, Teddy Cruz and Fonna Forman, and Meejin Yoon each explore how designers can engage with communities to transform the built environment, heal past harms, and engender a public sphere hospitable to multivalent forms of cultural expression. For Howard and Neefe, the act of designing is also an act of remembering, of nourishing, and of reparation. In this sense, cultural rifts that exist in specific places with specific histories become opportunities to form new arenas for meaning and representation. Migrant landscapes provide a

Harvey Gantt with reporters on the day in 1963 he entered Clemson University as its first Black student. He went on to found his own architecture firm, Gantt Huberman Architects, and served as Charlotte's first Black mayor for two terms, from 1983 through 1987.

similar terrain for Cruz and Forman, for whom the geospatial divisions of the borderland demand an encounter with new forms of cultural hybridity and transnational citizenship. For Yoon, past conditions give rise to present action and raise questions about our collective societal, disciplinary, and professional values.

In each essay, we see how contemporary landscapes have accrued meaning, often in uneven and unexpected ways. We also see how design practices can contribute to the creation of an inclusive public realm. The essays illustrate how constructs of nationality and visages of the past can be reappropriated, reinvented, and reinvigorated through design. As a result, we see that struggles over representation, visibility, and voice are very much struggles that exist across space and time.

> **The route to achieving equity will not be accomplished through treating everyone equally.
> It will be achieved by treating everyone justly according to their circumstances.**
>
> Paula Dressel
> educator and equity advocate

YOU CAN'T STAY HOME IF YOU DON'T HAVE A HOME
ON VA
EVICTE
#ReliefIsDue

Social Justice

Social justice refers to the equitable experience of all people in a society with regard to quality of life, such as access to resources, protection from harm, opportunities to advance, and guaranteed civil rights. For communities that have historically been denied services and resources or that have experienced the brunt of economic or environmental harm, social justice can refer to remediation that aims to create fair and equal provision, or even the return of fundamental rights. It begins with recognition and awareness of inequitable conditions through direct work with underrepresented communities. Awareness may become action through advocacy and social and spatial reinvestment in infrastructure, institutions, or environments. In the context of architecture and design, this might include advocating for the human right to housing that is affordable, culturally sensitive, universally accessible, and environmentally sustainable.

SPATIALIZING JUSTICE AT THE US-MEXICO BORDER

Teddy Cruz and Fonna Forman

Teddy Cruz is a professor of public culture and urbanism in the department of visual arts at the University of California, San Diego. He is known internationally for his urban research around the Tijuana–San Diego border, advancing border neighborhoods as sites of cultural production from which to rethink urban policy, affordable housing, and public space. He holds an MDes from Harvard Graduate School of Design.

Fonna Forman is a professor of political theory and founding director of the Center on Global Justice at the University of California, San Diego. A theorist of ethics and public culture, she focuses on poverty alleviation, climate justice, migration and borders, and participatory urbanization. She holds a PhD from the University of Chicago. Cruz and Forman are principals in Estudio Teddy Cruz + Fonna Forman, a research-based political and architectural practice in San Diego investigating issues of informal urbanization, civic infrastructure, climate adaptation, and public culture. It blurs conventional boundaries between theory and practice, and merges the fields of architecture and urbanism, political theory and urban policy, visual arts and public culture. Together, Cruz and Forman lead the UCSD Community Stations, a platform for community-engaged research and teaching on poverty and social equity in the border region. Their work has been exhibited in prestigious venues globally. In 2022 they published the coauthored two-volume monograph Spatializing Justice: Building Blocks *and* Socializing Architecture: Top-Down / Bottom-Up *(MIT Press and Hatje Cantz Verlag).*

We radicalize the local.

We resist the idea that global justice is something that happens "out there" in the world somewhere. Living and working where we do, we don't need to go far to engage with territorial conflict, migration, poverty, and climate injustice. We are minutes away from an international border in crisis, and this enables a critical proximity between studio and field, between theory and practice.

The San Diego–Tijuana region is a microcosm of all the injustices and indignities experienced by vulnerable people across the globe: political violence, climate disruption, accelerating migration, rising nationalism, border-building everywhere, deepening inequality, and the steady decay of public thinking. Climate change will inevitably intensify these regional stressors in the years to come. Conventional "wisdom" blames northward migration in this part of the world on poverty and violence, and certainly this is part of a larger truth. But for the vast number of people on this planet whose lives depend on agriculture, the economy and the environment are the same thing. Climate change is fundamentally a threat multiplier. It deepens human suffering and makes poverty and food insecurity worse. It aggravates violence, accelerates human displacement, and ultimately compounds the reasons why people walk north.

Such fundamental human struggles regularly attract artists and cultural producers from around the world to engage in gestures of performative protest. Reactionary upticks in ephemeral cultural action dip in and out of the conflict, extracting momentary attention, but most often lack any lasting awareness of or commitment to what happens after the "happening." We advocate for a longer view of ongoing resistance. We are deeply engaged in a decades-long project to build a cross-border citizenship culture in the San Diego–Tijuana region—a culture in which one's sense of belonging is defined not by the nation-state or the documents in one's pocket, but by shared interests and aspirations among people who inhabit a violently disrupted civic space.

> **" We are deeply engaged in a decades-long project to build a cross-border citizenship culture in the San Diego–Tijuana region—a culture in which one's sense of belonging is defined not by the nation-state or the documents in one's pocket, but by shared interests and aspirations among people who inhabit a violently disrupted civic space. "**

Estudio Teddy Cruz + Fonna Forman, *De-Bord(er)*, 2015

We think strategically about cultural, institutional, and spatial transformation in this border region, and reject ideas of citizenship that fragment and divide rather than unite us. Border regions are a natural laboratory for reimagining citizenship along these lines; San Ysidro has been our laboratory to research the positive impact of immigrants in the transformation of US neighborhoods.[1] We have documented how Tijuana's "confetti" of nonconforming mixed land uses migrate north, and how these "pixels of difference" transform both homogeneous swaths of exclusionary land uses of San Diego's sprawl and existing mono-use parcels across inner-city neighborhoods into more complex, sustainable, and plural social, economic, and cultural environments.

These are migrant urbanizations of retrofit, as older neighborhoods are adapted into alternative bottom-up spaces of socialization and economy. Such practices reflect the everyday survival strategies of migrant communities negotiating boundaries, spaces, and resources. Researching these cross-border migrant flows has been essential to

1. Teddy Cruz and Fonna Forman, *Socializing Architecture: Top-Down / Bottom-Up* (Cambridge, MA: MIT Press; Berlin: Hatje Cantz Verlag, 2023), chapter 3.

UCSD Community Stations, 2019

proposing new migrant housing paradigms and environmental infrastructures.

We condemn the economic forces that marginalize people into slums, but we are continually inspired by ingenious self-built logics, the vibrancy of informal market dynamics, and the solidarity of communities confronting marginalization, scarcity, and danger. The informal border neighborhoods where we work are typically denigrated by formal planners and policymakers as ugly, criminal, to be avoided, to be cleared, and to be cleaned up. Instead, we observe intensely creative urban agents who challenge the dominant paradigms of urban growth that exclude them. They demonstrate other, more inclusive and collective ways of inhabiting the city.

We are committed to learning from the bottom up.

Meaningful advances in social housing design cannot be achieved without advances in housing policy and the economy. This includes transformations in exclusionary land use and zoning policies, and a new political economy to support alternative social densities, transitional uses, and shared economies found within migrant neighborhoods. Key to this work has been the creation of a system that connects our design lab at the University of California, San Diego, with conditions in the field—a network of sanctuary spaces on both sides of the wall called the UCSD Community Stations.[2] We have built four UCSD Community Stations—two in San Diego and two in Tijuana. We designed this system as both a collaborative education platform and a model of shared urban intervention. Community Stations are sites where public universities, municipalities, and community organizations meet to share knowledge and resources, and collaborate on research, dialogue, cultural and educational activities, and urban design-build projects, including emergency and migrant housing as well as environmental infrastructure.[3] They are a model of urban co-development to create spaces of dignity in the city's periphery. Each station is designed, funded, built, programmed, and maintained collaboratively by the campus and the community.

COMMUNITY STATIONS: BUILDING BLOCKS OF A SPATIAL PRACTICE

We might begin to introduce the several core commitments, or "building blocks," that shape our work through a visit to the UCSD-CASA Community Station in San Diego. This Community Station is a partnership with the non-profit Casa Familiar, a thirty-year-old community-based social-service organization. It is located in the border neighborhood of San Ysidro, site of the busiest land crossing in the Western hemisphere. The community is 90 percent Latinx and has one of the highest unemployment rates, lowest median household incomes, and worst air quality indexes in San Diego County.

The UCSD-CASA Community Station began with the adaptive reuse of a beloved historic church that had sat for decades in disrepair. Its renovation was a catalyst that was followed by a process of aggregating small parcels into infrastructures for social, economic, and cultural production. Small lots were reorganized into linear public systems to strengthen and expand an existing network of old alleys used by migrant residents as informal pedestrian corridors.

2. Read more in Cruz and Forman, *Socializing Architecture*, chapter 6.

3. These building blocks are described in greater detail in Teddy Cruz and Fonna Forman, *Spatializing Justice: Building Blocks* (Cambridge, MA: MIT Press; Berlin: Hatje Cantz Verlag, 2022).

Living Rooms at the Border / UCSD-Casa Community Station, 2019

TEDDY CRUZ AND FONNA FORMAN

We renovated the historic church into a community theater with an outdoor stage. This performance space is flanked on one side by a series of small accessory buildings for Casa Familiar's social programming, and on the other side by an open-air civic classroom-pavilion. This social, educational, and cultural infrastructure anchors affordable housing at both ends of the parcel, all mediated by pedestrian walkways.

The UCSD-CASA Community Station is a double project: a parcel-size social infrastructure made of spaces for cultural and economic activity, and affordable housing. The organizational design of the parcel through a system of linear strips with a variety of small-scale buildings performing different roles was also a deliberate strategy to mobilize diverse financial streams to fund the different building typologies, synergizing university, community, and foundation economic resources. Through this process, our grassroots organization partner, Casa Familiar, became an alternative developer of affordable housing for its own community, and public space was the detonator.

The UCSD-Casa Community Station exemplifies several building blocks in our practice:

- **Housing beyond units:** In conditions of poverty, housing must be embedded in an infrastructure of social, economic, and cultural support. In other words, housing is public infrastructure.
- **Socialize density:** Density should be measured not as an abstract number of objects or people per area, but as the intensity of social and economic exchanges per area. Migrant neighborhoods have taught us that these exchanges mobilized by bottom-up urbanization are the DNA for democratizing the city.
- **Demand generative zoning:** Zoning must stop being punitive, preventing socialization, and instead be conceptualized as a generative tool that anticipates, stimulates, and organizes social and economic activity in neighborhoods.
- **Intervene into the developer's pro forma:** The developer's pro forma is architecture's financial plastic. Inside the mathematics of this spreadsheet, our services as architects amount to 15 percent of a project's

construction costs. This undercapitalized asset can be mobilized as collateral for development.
- Rethink ownership: The sweat equity of architects, cultural producers, and community leaders; the economic equity of public universities; and municipal protocols for accessing public parcels can all be bundled, aggregated, to enable communities to develop their own neighborhoods.

Across the border in Tijuana, the UCSD-Divina Community Station and the UCSD-Alacrán Community Station at Santuario Frontera are located in Los Laureles Canyon, an informal settlement adjacent to the border wall that is home to ninety-two thousand people. Over the past decade, fully 70 percent of the natural land in the canyon has been lost to irregular urban growth. Here, the topography of Tijuana's canyons clashes with the border wall before spilling northward into the environmentally protected San Diego River Estuary, now layered with security infrastructure. At this hot spot, the conflict between natural and jurisdictional systems and between ecological and political priorities is profound.

Los Laureles Canyon is impacted by dump sites as well as severe erosion, flooding, and landslides, all of which are exacerbated by drastic fluctuations of climate change. Because it lacks water and waste management infrastructure to mitigate these impacts, much of the trash and tons of sediment end up in the San Diego River Estuary, contaminating this ecologically diverse region, a shared binational asset. We have been identifying un-squatted lands that are still environmentally rescuable to shape an archipelago of conservation, advancing an ambitious regional project called the Cross-Border Commons. This is an environmental conservation initiative that links the San Diego River Estuary with informal settlements in Mexico, forming a continuous social and ecological envelope that transgresses the border wall and protects the shared environmental systems.

The UCSD-Alacrán station works in partnership with Embajadores de Jesús, a religious organization led by activist pastor Gustavo Banda Aceves that established a refugee camp to provide shelter, food, and basic services to thousands of

> **At this hot spot, the conflict between natural and jurisdictional systems and between ecological and political priorities is profound.**

Santuario Frontera / UCSD-Alacrán Community Station, 2023

Haitian and Central American refugees pouring into Tijuana. It is located in the most precarious and polluted subbasin of Los Laureles Canyon.

    Surrounding these informal settlements in Los Laureles Canyon are multinational maquiladoras that benefit from easy access to cheap labor. Over the years, we have experimented with factory-made materials and systems in collaboration with the maquiladoras both to structurally mediate the recycling of waste and to invest in emergency housing. One such collaboration has been with Mecalux, a Spanish maquiladora that produces lightweight metal shelving systems for global export. They have adapted their prefabricated systems into structural scaffolds for informal housing. We designed a catalog with the factory's engineers to test a variety of prototypes. As a result, we accelerated production of Mecalux frames to install them on vernacular post-and-beam concrete systems as housing infrastructure.

Together we are now building Santuario Frontera (Border Sanctuary), a live-work collective for homeless refugees designed to house 350 residents. In order to sustain the construction process over time, we are designing a "sanctuary economy," embedding housing in spaces of fabrication, training, and small-scale economic development. We have assembled a refugee cooperative, the Little Haiti Construction Company, with a tool library, wood and metal machines, and a couple of trucks and tractors. After the cooperative completes construction of this site, it will remain operational for future habitat restoration jobs across the canyon, to advance the cross-border commons. Santuario Frontera has advanced two important building blocks for our practice:

- **Temporalize infrastructure:** Urban informality decolonizes the meaning of infrastructure. For us, the informal is a praxis—a dynamic set of urban operations from below that transgress top-down political power and exclusionary economic models.
- **Transcend hospitality:** Hospitality is the first gesture when the immigrant arrives, but charity is not the appropriate model for building an inclusive society. We need to move from hospitality to inclusion. Thinking beyond shelter is a call for rethinking refugee camps everywhere, from places of short-term habitation and service provision to durable infrastructures for inclusion.

GLOBALIZING THE LOCAL

There is much more to say about the Community Stations, about our partners, and about what we do together in these spaces. While the stations focus on different issues reflecting the priorities of each community, they all aspire to foster solidarity and collective agency, and counter exploitation, dispossession, deportation, and environmental calamity. Ultimately, we want to cultivate an elastic civic identity here from the bottom up. To do this, we

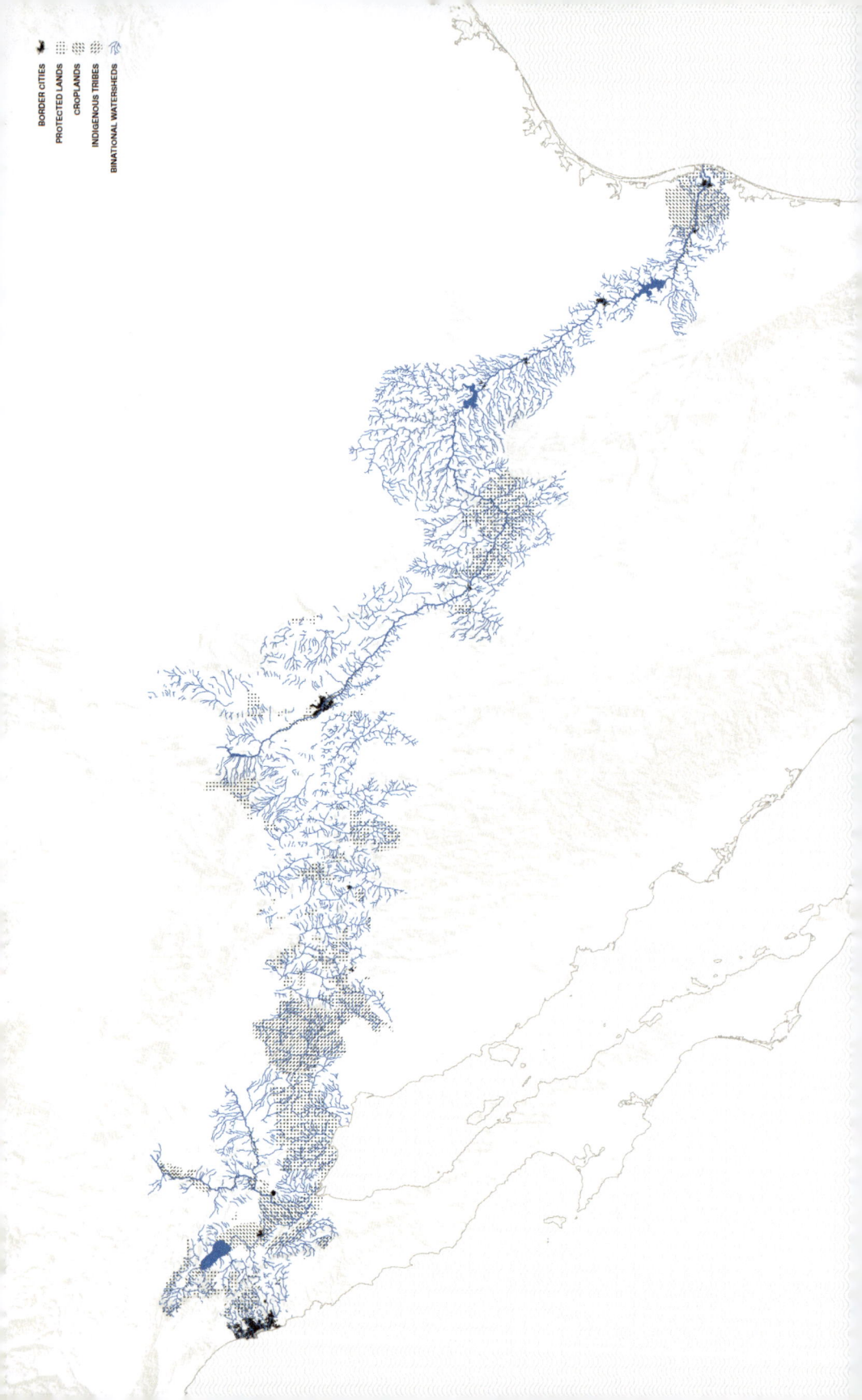

BORDER CITIES
PROTECTED LANDS
CROPLANDS
INDIGENOUS TRIBES
BINATIONAL WATERSHEDS

> **Ultimately, we want to cultivate an elastic civic identity here from the bottom up. To do this, we curate 'unwalling experiments' that dissolve the wall using visual tools like diagrams and radical cartographies to situate border neighborhoods within broader spatial ecologies of circulation and interdependence**

curate "unwalling experiments" that dissolve the wall using visual tools like diagrams and radical cartographies to situate border neighborhoods within broader spatial ecologies of circulation and interdependence, from local to regional to continental and global scales. We see elasticity as a civic skill—an ability to stretch and return between local and more expansive ways of thinking, and to envision opportunities for solidarity across walls.

The conflicts we experience here locally between nation and nature are reproduced again and again along the entire trajectory of the border between the United States and Mexico. Over the years, we have collected aerial photos that document precise moments when the jurisdictional line collided with natural systems, powerfully illustrating what dumb sovereignty looks like when it hits the ground in a complex bioregion.

Our MEXUS project dissolves the border into a bioregion whose shape is defined by the eight binational watershed systems bisected by the wall. MEXUS also exposes other systems and flows across this bioregional territory: tribal nations, protected lands, croplands, urban crossings, many more informal crossings, fifteen million people, and more. Ultimately MEXUS counters wall-building fantasies with more expansive imaginaries of citizenship and cooperation beyond the nation-state. Going local here means recognizing ourselves as a region of interdependence and cooperation. Despite the wall and the rhetoric designed to divide us, we are a binational ecology of flows and circulation, and our future is intertwined. Air, water, waste, health, culture, money, hope, love, justice—these things don't stop at walls. Border zones are unrelentingly porous, and these flows shape the transgressive, hybrid identities and everyday practices of this part of the world.

Here at the border, the idea of the bioregion has been a powerful imaginary for activating more elastic civic thinking.

opposite: Estudio Teddy Cruz + Fonna Forman, MEXUS: Geographies of Interdependence, 2019

White Supremacy

White supremacy is based on the false and toxic idea that white people are inherently superior to BIPOC, Jewish, and Muslim people as well as people who identify as nonbinary or LGBTQ+. White nationalism is a form of white supremacy that champions the creation of a whites-only homeland. White supremacy and nationalism are often based on a sense of righteousness and include violent right-wing movements and religious fundamentalist groups, but they also exist in more insidious forms in all corners of society–from politics and finance, to military and police forces, to legal and educational systems. Social media has made it easier for white supremacists to organize. As of 2018 there were more than six hundred known white supremacy organizations in the United States.

> **Remember: white supremacy is not a shark; it is the water.**
>
> Kyle "Guante" Tran Myhre
> spoken word artist
> "How To Explain White Supremacy to a White Supremacist," 2014

Dismantle White Supremacy

[BENCHMARK]

THE RACIST PAST OF PHILIP JOHNSON COMES HOME TO ROOST

The Johnson Study Group

In response to architect Philip Johnson's thoroughly documented fascist and racist views, the Johnson Study Group sent the following open letter, dated November 27, 2020, to the Museum of Modern Art and Harvard Graduate School of Design. More than 115 architects, designers, educators, and artists were signatories. Harvard responded swiftly, renaming a private residence Johnson built there as his graduate thesis project. A spokesperson from MoMA said the museum is undertaking research to gather and explore all available information. Johnson worked at MoMA and founded the museum's department of architecture, which dedicated its architectural exhibition space to him as a tribute in 1984. His name is also included in the title of one of the museum's curatorial positions—the Philip Johnson Chief Curator of Architecture and Design.

November 27, 2020

To whom it may concern:

As architects, designers, educators, and artists, we call on the Museum of Modern Art, Harvard Graduate School of Design, and any other public-facing nonprofit in the United States to remove the name of Philip Johnson from every leadership title, public space, and honorific of any form. Philip Johnson's widely documented white supremacist views and activities make him an inappropriate namesake within any educational or cultural institution that purports to serve a wide public.

This demand for removal relates specifically to the role that naming plays in public institutions. There is a role for Johnson's architectural work in archives and historic preservation. However, naming titles and spaces inevitably suggests that the honoree is a model for curators, administrators, students, and others who participate in these institutions.

Johnson's commitment to white supremacy was significant and consequential. He used his office at MoMA and his curatorial work as a pretense to collaborate with the German Nazi party, including personally translating propaganda, disseminating Nazi publications, and forming an affiliated fascist party in Louisiana. He effectively segregated the architectural collection at MoMA, where under his leadership (1933–1988) not a single work by any Black architect or designer was included in the collection. He not only acquiesced in but added to the persistent practice of racism in the field of architecture, a legacy that continues to do harm today.

We call on all members of MoMA, and all alumni of the Harvard Graduate School of Design [sic], to refrain from supporting either institution until Johnson's name is struck from all spaces and titles.

We call especially on white allies to do this work. Organize. Spread the word. Further the impact. We must not only speak of undoing the work of white supremacy, we must call it out by name and uproot it.

We call on other donors of both institutions, including philanthropist Agnes Gund and Peggy Rockefeller, to demand better of the institutions that they support.

In keeping with Design Justice Demands that have circulated from Design as Protest and in solidarity with the Black Reconstruction Collective, as well as the wider Movement for Black Lives, we cannot pretend that architectural institutions might work toward any dismantling of white supremacy when such work is presented under the name of Philip Johnson. This is a minor but clarifying step in making room for other legacies to come.

Signed, The Johnson Study Group

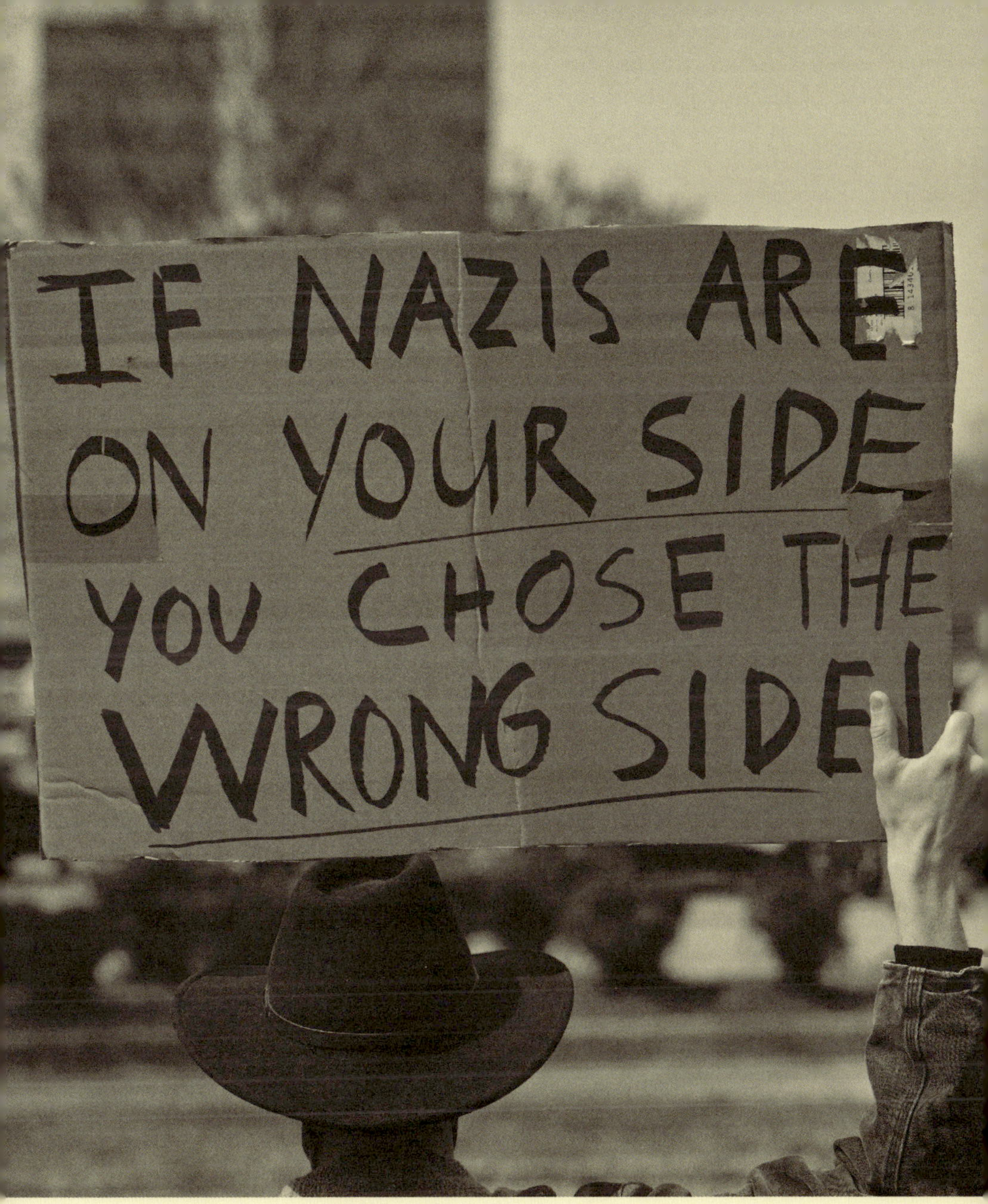
IF NAZIS ARE
ON YOUR SIDE
YOU CHOSE THE
WRONG SIDE!

> "I only went to my advisor [at Howard University] one time… because the first time I went, he said something like, 'You know, most of you would be better in home economics or something.' And I never went back; that was it. I did not need an advisor if that's how he felt, so I never saw him again.

Roberta Washington
architect

Access

Access refers to the opportunity to have, use, or benefit from resources, services, facilities, or people. It affects and encompasses human needs from essentials like safe housing, food, and health care to political representation to higher education and the pursuit of a career. Access, or lack thereof, has a compounding effect. For instance, good health and nutrition improve one's ability to learn. Success in K–12 education opens access to higher education, which in turn opens access to better jobs and upward mobility. Access can be limited or suppressed by individuals or by systemic barriers and discriminatory structures and practices. It is often facilitated or limited by where we live, the color of our skin, our gender identity, our level of education, our socioeconomic status, and the contacts we have who can help make crucial connections for us.

TOWARD FUTURES THAT SUSTAIN US: THE ARCHITECTURE OF REPAIR

Zena Howard and Lauren Neefe

Zena Howard, FAIA, is a principal and cultural and civic practice chair for the international architecture and design firm Perkins&Will. She is a founding member of their global Diversity and Inclusion Council and a member of the firm-wide board of directors. As an award-winning architect, strategist, and mentor, her career has been defined by culturally significant projects that navigate social issues of equity and justice and restore lost cultural connections by honoring history and memory. This work includes Destination Crenshaw in South Los Angeles, the nation's largest public project to celebrate African American contributions to world culture; the Smithsonian Institution's Bezos Learning Center in Washington, DC, a STEAM institution prioritizing access to underserved communities; and the expansion of the Motown Museum in Detroit. Previous projects include the Smithsonian Institution National Museum of African American History and Culture in Washington, DC.

Lauren Neefe is a writer, editor, and curator for Perkins&Will design leadership and research initiatives. She is the co-creator and executive producer of the Perkins&Will podcast Inhabit, a show about the power of design. She holds a PhD in English literature and a master's degree in poetry from the writing seminars at Johns Hopkins. She is an award-winning teacher, seasoned magazine and book editor, art and music lover, and audiophile and improviser.

Our profession slots memorializing kinds of work in the category of "cultural architecture." But history and culture do not stop where the National Mall ends or a curb cuts to the street or some parking lot marks a former paradise. Culture lives everywhere the public realm meets an incomplete history and the will to change the ending. Where a fortuitous meeting of realm, history, and will finds built expression, there lives the architecture of repair.

Several years ago, not long after the Freelon Group joined Perkins&Will and established the global firm's North Carolina practice, our design leadership took notice of something about our "cultural" projects. The places we had designed to be memorials were turning out to be stages for living history. When people needed to be in community, when they needed to be collectively seen and heard and move for change, they flooded into the way spaces of the places we helped create. We saw it, for example, at the National Center for Civil and Human Rights in Atlanta; Emancipation Park in Houston; the Route 9 Library & Innovation Center in New Castle, Delaware; and, to be sure, the National Museum of African American History and Culture in Washington, DC.

The "something" we observed was not a feature we necessarily anticipated in the plan or program of each design. It was not necessarily visible or perceptible in the architectural forms. Of course it had a lot to do with the proliferation of traumatic global events since the 2010s, or even since Hurricane Katrina in 2005. And in that political and cultural context, we saw that the organizing power of these places had become essential to the value of their designs. This new clarity about the stakes and purpose of our cultural work led us to formalize our design approach as a trademarked practice we call Remembrance Design.[1] In rapidly changing areas, the approach ensures that we build on the intergenerational assets that are already in place at a site. It prepares places to be agents of change, rather than merely delivering or perpetuating change on a place with unfit architecture.

From project pursuit to life-cycle impact, our approach leads with culture in every dimension and phase of design. That is, we work to infuse the design with culturally specific meaning for the communities served by the project, no matter its size. Public space takes priority over iconic, ego-driven object-buildings. Economic stability is a fundamental goal. Above all, Remembrance Design prioritizes

[1]. Remembrance Design is trademarked by Perkins&Will.

March for Our Lives rally at Atlanta's National Center for Civil and Human Rights, 2018

> **Put another way, our approach works to repair the historical failure to tell and retell the stories and experiences of those whose ancestors and cultures have been overlooked, marginalized, misrepresented, or even suppressed by official histories.**

incomplete histories as a framework to create places of social and cultural sustenance. By "sustenance," we mean dedicated spaces as well as resources, and story as a profound community resource. Therefore, we acknowledge the relevance of lived experience and the virtue in shared memories of conflict and loss, especially when we engage historically underserved communities.

Put another way, our approach works to repair the historical failure to tell and retell the stories and experiences of those whose ancestors and cultures have been overlooked, marginalized, misrepresented, or even suppressed by official histories. In the United States, these histories are most often those of racialized cultures—of Black and Brown peoples, peoples from throughout Asia, and the Native American nations. These communities' stories and lived experiences are largely absent from the archives promoted by conventional architectural training for studying the context of a site. And when our access to knowledge is compromised, so is our ability to design in a meaningful, responsible, responsive way.

It is audacious to ask traumatized communities to entrust their truth to our design teams. But history teaches us that the cost of any alternative is too high. When we neglect to ask for and build trust, our built environment remains a wound that never heals. When there is no provision for the past in the design, the past will overwhelm the built environment, as Toni Morrison observes in a final reflection from her influential essay "The Site of Memory": "You know, they straightened out the Mississippi River in places, to make room for houses and livable acreage. Occasionally the river floods these places. 'Floods' is the word they use, but in fact it is not flooding; it is remembering. Remembering where it used to be."[2] We dare to ask communities to trust us that we may grasp a truth not yet daylighted or dignified. When the truth of remembering is most fulsome, the opportunity afforded by Remembrance Design projects—and, more importantly, by the communities keeping watch over shared memory—is the chance to repair the historical record through built expression in public space.

2. Toni Morrison, "The Site of Memory," in *What Moves at the Margin: Selected Nonfiction* (Jackson: University Press of Mississippi, 2008), 77.

Not restricted to memorializing in Black communities, Remembrance Design nonetheless reflects a specific African American experience of the relationship between past and future, often represented by the Akan symbol of *sankofa*, a bird charging ahead while craning its neck around to retrieve an egg from its back: we remember the past to protect the future, sometimes translated as, "It is not taboo to go back and fetch what you forgot." This orientation to the future leads to place making that heals the past and empowers the future beyond the normative planning "vision." In short, sustaining futures are rooted in acknowledgment and anticipation, or remembrance and design.

Four projects at various scales and in different regions of the United States illustrate the significance of Remembrance Design. Each story of repair is unique, as one would expect. How each design evinces repair is also unique. Together they are a provocation to reexamine three imperatives of cultural architecture current to this historical moment: equity, the public realm, and community.

EQUITY IN SOUTH CENTRAL LOS ANGELES

When we work toward equity in the built environment, ownership has to be an objective, as well as fair access to infrastructure and amenities.

In 1948, the US Supreme Court struck down the redlining policies of the early twentieth century, igniting the transformation of South Central Los Angeles into the heart of Black LA.[3] In spite of systematic disinvestment, generations of African American artists and entrepreneurs have nurtured a culture that is exported and celebrated across the globe. The profits, however, have not returned to the community as equity. So when South LA's neighborhoods learned that the city's Crenshaw/LAX transit project was building a much-needed new metro line at street level through the largest Black business corridor on the West Coast, they clapped back with the vision for Destination Crenshaw. It is the first outdoor project of its kind in Los Angeles and the largest Black-centered public art project in the country. Stretching between the new K Line's 60th Street and Leimert Park stations, the 1.3-mile public art gallery, park, and streetscape design is monumental in its

[3]. For a general history, see Mike Sonksen, "The History of South Central Los Angeles and Its Struggle with Gentrification," KCET.org, September 13, 2017, https://www.pbssocal.org/shows/city-rising/the-history-of-south-central-los-angeles-and-its-struggle-with-gentrification. For scholarly studies of South Central's neighborhoods, see Darnell Hunt and Ana-Christina Ramon, eds., *Black Los Angeles: American Dreams, Racial Realities* (New York: NYU Press, 2010); Steven L. Isoardi, *The Dark Tree: Jazz and the Community Arts in Los Angeles* (Durham, NC: Duke University Press, 2023).

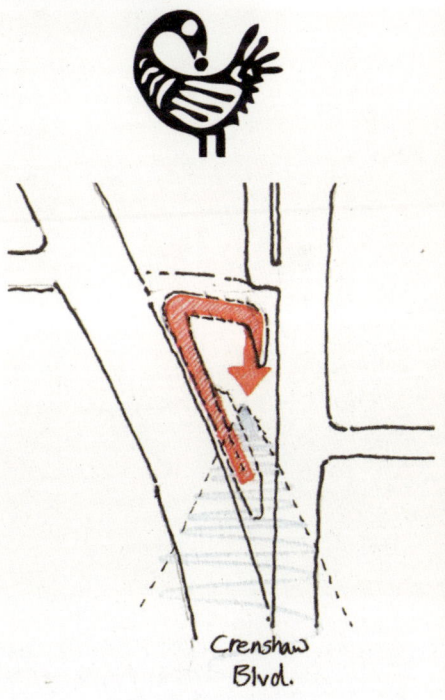

During a "visual listening" workshop with the South LA community, the *sankofa* bird symbol became the inspiration for the platform design at Sankofa Park at Destination Crenshaw. African American scholars coined the term to mean remembering our past to protect our future.

ZENA HOWARD AND LAUREN NEEFE

Perkins&Will's design for Destination Crenshaw is driven by a unifying theme: Grow Where You're Planted, inspired by the African giant star grass. Used by slavers as bedding in ships, the grass thrives in alien lands despite inhospitable conditions. Today it remains a profoundly resonant reminder of African American history, paths of global dispersion, and Black resilience in the face of violence and racism. Its form is reflected in the design of shade structures along Crenshaw Boulevard, and its root system provided inspiration for pavement patterns.

TOWARD FUTURES THAT SUSTAIN US

significance. Its form references the resilience of the giant star grass, a rhizomatic species of the African savanna that was used as bedding hay on slaving ships. Like the giant star grass, the African peoples who were forced to lie on it have thrived and spread their strengths throughout the diaspora, proving heroically resistant to even the most inhospitable conditions. As of this writing, the project has secured $100 million in capital investment.

The inaugural portion of the project is scheduled to open in 2024, and the impact will be tangible, not merely symbolic. When completed, the project will restore a disconnected place to the city ecosystem and promote economic independence for its residents. The pillars of the vision promote Black artists and Black-owned businesses, community-led development and design, and hiring preference for community members. As a model of repair, Destination Crenshaw was born of the understanding that a sustainable future is one in which the community that owns a place culturally accrues equity in the place it has created.

It shouldn't be radical, but it is.

PUBLIC REALM IN A CAROLINA CAPITAL

Publicly accessible spaces, even when not owned by the public, are where cultural values and norms are negotiated moment to moment. The public realm is where we make space for change.

On the other side of the country from Los Angeles, "lost cause" memorials and preserved plantation sites still glorify the slavery economy and claim space on threat of extrajudicial violence. This project carves out prominent public space for claiming the right to move freely and gather before a more complete history. Located on a one-acre corner parcel just a few blocks from the state capitol, North Carolina Freedom Park was conceived to broadcast the legacy and experience of the state's African American citizens in the municipal center of Raleigh. It would answer the history and legacy extolled on the capitol grounds, where until the summer of 2020, nine of thirteen plaques and statues commemorated the Confederacy and its apartheid afterlife.

The physical and social context of the "black codes"—instituted during Reconstruction to criminalize African

STATE ARCHIVES

GOVERNOR'S MANSION

NC FREEDOM PARK

GENERAL ASSEMBLY

MUSEUM OF HISTORY

MUSEUM OF NATURAL SCIENCES

STATE CAPITOL

● *Current Locations / Monuments*

● *Current Locations / Confederate Monuments*

● *Former Locations / Confederate Monuments*

Perkins&Will, North Carolina Freedom Park. Excavated pathways are inscribed with quotes by notable African Americans and converge at *Beacon of Freedom*, a memorial sculpture.

232 TOWARD FUTURES THAT SUSTAIN US

Perkins&Will, North Carolina Freedom Park

Americans' presence in public space—prompted us to assign greater meaning to the "action" for which the park's dedicated space could serve as a crucible. That is, we might be defining "action" too narrowly as collective social movement in times of civil unrest. In North Carolina Freedom Park, action could prove to be as basic as individual movement. Repair would be the affirmation of an African American's individual right simply to move safely, with pride, in whatever way, in the public realm. What is freedom, after all, without movement?

Centered on a flame-like sculpture called *Beacon of Freedom*, varied paths through the site create pedestrian connections among key civic destinations. As these paths signify the numerous routes to freedom, their excavated forms invite movement through the site. In contrast to the resolute neoclassicism of the surroundings, their irregular geometry expresses the counternarrative that is movement. And etched into the retaining walls are empowering statements excavated from the African American historical record, inviting the mind and spirit to be moved with the body toward a self-determined future.

It shouldn't be radical, but it is.

top: Sycamore Hill Baptist Church stood on a prominent corner in this Greenville, North Carolina, neighborhood before it burned in a suspected arson incident.
bottom: Perkins&Will, Sycamore Hill Gateway design, Greenville, North Carolina. Towering stained-glass walls rise from the ground on the original footprint of Sycamore Hill Baptist Church, and park benches recalling pews occupy the space that was once the church sanctuary.

COMMUNITY IN SYCAMORE HILL, COMMUNITY ON THE NATIONAL MALL

Every project is situated at the convergence of many communities, but community also emerges from harvesting the past together. Memory is a powerful bond for a community, but does its power scale up? South Central is a big-city district, and North Carolina is a state, but some communities are no bigger than a block. Two additional projects underscore the relationship between communal memory and learning in community that allows Remembrance Design to scale up from neighborhoods to the national stage.

When we designed Sycamore Hill Gateway Plaza in the town common of Greenville, North Carolina, the "community" served by the project was tight-knit and very clearly defined. An African American neighborhood, anchored by a thriving Baptist church, was razed by urban renewal in the 1960s, and the church felled by suspected arson. The residents were displaced, never to see any equity from the development for which their spiritual home was sacrificed. Remembrance Design facilitated a process of healing from the theft of their community, in turn generating the design of an outdoor memorial that reclaims their physical connection to a Carolina place of natural beauty, cultural nourishment, and spiritual grace.

But Sycamore Hill is a small-city neighborhood. How can a design team mine for shared values when the client is a huge institution such as the Smithsonian, catering to so many people that no one "community" can be singled out for engagement? Moreover, such institutions often select design teams through competitions in advance of any direct "community" engagement by the competitors. In the competition for the National Museum of African American History and Culture, the Smithsonian could select teams with affinities to the culture and history represented in the museum. Our team, a consortium of African American architects, drew on a shared ethos, our own lived experience, and our respective community networks to inform our entry's design approach.

> **How can a design team mine for shared values when the client is a huge institution such as the Smithsonian, catering to so many people that no one 'community' can be singled out for engagement?**

By contrast, the teams who competed for the Smithsonian's latest project, the Bezos Learning Center at the National Air and Space Museum, had little affinity with the project's intended community: children who have historically been excluded from the promise of the national space program. As such, all the teams were entering the design process largely in a vacuum of lived experience, without access to the remembrance that roots human connections to place. Ultimately, the Smithsonian selected our team for the sensitivity of our approach to the Mall context and our framework for design development. In keeping with the learning center's mission, the Smithsonian simultaneously undertook to break the competition mold. Concurrently with the design-team competition, it is conducting the Student Architecture and Design Challenge. Teams of two to three students who demonstrate eligibility participate in a two-phase competition to design an element of the building's exterior. Members of the winning team receive paid positions at the National Air and Space Museum and roles on the building project team, fully integrating an outlet for student representation and ownership in the design process.

At the Bezos Learning Center, education is reparation. Our approach invites learning in community by centering the public realm in the design. In this place dedicated to a future that is already light-years in the past, Remembrance Design brings the *sankofa* principle full circle at the national scale.

It shouldn't be radical, but it is.

FUTURE MEMORY

The past half-decade has given us a historic flood of conflict and loss in the form of disease, uprisings, mass shootings, police brutality, economic instability, climate devastation, and war. This trauma is both global and intensely local. In the United States, we have a growing shared consciousness of our political, cultural, and economic fault lines, even if the facts of our history have changed very little. How can we as architects, designers, and community members respond to this degree of change at this near-intolerable pace? How must Remembrance Design evolve to respond

> **In the United States, we have a growing shared consciousness of our political, cultural, and economic fault lines, even if the facts of our history have changed very little. How can we as architects, designers, and community members respond to this degree of change at this near-intolerable pace?**

in effective ways to the seismic shifts in our consciousness?

While Remembrance Design has to date focused largely on restorative work in disenfranchised and negatively impacted communities, there is a role for its approach in any place-making initiative. A project might be as intimate as the corner of a one-acre block or as spectacular as a public art gallery down a mile-long urban corridor. It might also be a community-embedded health district, or it might not be an urban environment at all. It could be a library or a park, a brownfield or a factory, a dorm, a stadium, a high-rise, or a storefront. It might very well be a national landmark. All projects hold the potential to mend physical, social, or economic rifts. If not in the strict sense of US House Resolution 40, we might regard each project as an opportunity to tender reparations. Our approach is Remembrance Design, but we urge everyone with a responsibility for the built environment to craft and manifest their own. The architecture of repair is urgent, because the only futures that can sustain us are the futures that make vivid sense of our pasts.

> Without having the wish to 'show them,' I developed a fierce desire to 'show myself.' I wanted to vindicate every ability I had. I wanted to acquire new abilities. I wanted to prove that I, as an individual, deserved a place in the world.

Paul Revere Williams
architect

Token

A token is a minority individual who is hired, included, consulted, etc., for the sake of appearance—to suggest an absence of discrimination based on race, gender, ethnicity, socioeconomic background, gender identity, or other minority status. The individual may be highly qualified or not qualified at all; the primary intent is what determines the tokenism.

> **It appears that my worst fears have been realized: we have made progress in everything, yet nothing has changed.**
>
> Derrick Bell
> attorney and American civil rights activist

[SNAPSHOT]

DERRICK BELL'S INTEREST CONVERGENCE THEORY

Isabel Strauss

In 2020, I was walking down the streets of Cambridge with a friend, telling stories about my master's program: How a manager of mine recently called reparations "the R-word." How a professor counters any mention of ancient pyramids with, "Architecture was invented in Europe—I know it's a hard pill to swallow." How the architecture chair weakly excused yet another all-white-male jury with, "We weren't able to get any Black critics this year because of scheduling." How professors whispered about diversity initiatives—"Why do we need this? What does this have to do with architecture?"—and then posed on the website with practitioners of color, their quotes of praise blinking bold, italicized, underlined.

My friend listened, then offered up Derrick Bell's interest convergence theory, which I knew in my bones though I didn't know it by name until that moment. It argues that the rights of Black people only advance when they converge with the interests of white people. This is a truth that people of color know intimately, a truth that follows us around. When we are accepted, "legacies" remind us that we were the affirmative action applicant. If we are not reminded explicitly, we wonder, "Am I the token? Did the school, the professor, the critic, pick me, choose me, compliment me publicly to prove they're not a racist?" We wonder this in stride, in class, at parties, at the podium.

Turning to my friend, I responded with, "Oh"—grateful to be validated in my experience, but embarrassed that I was not the one explaining the theory to him.

When I got home I googled Derrick Bell, thankful again for the theory that put words to my experience.

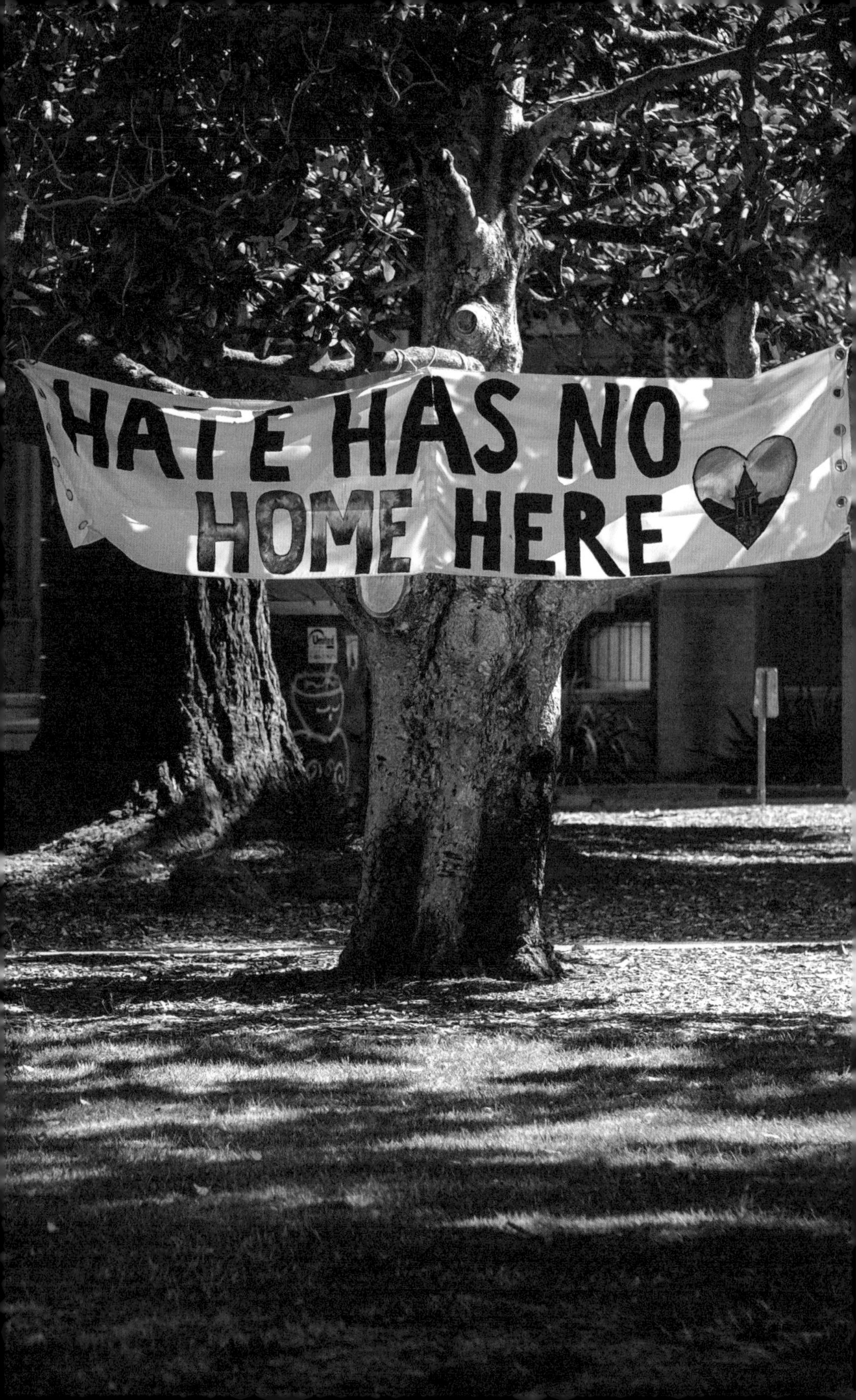
HATE HAS NO
HOME HERE

BIPOC

BIPOC is an acronym for Black, Indigenous, and people of color—including but not limited to Native Americans, Asian Americans, Alaska Natives, Latinx, Hispanics, Native Hawaiians, and other Pacific Islanders—and is used as an umbrella term for people who are in a racial or ethnic minority. Prior to the Black Lives Matter movement, the shorter acronym POC was often used, but in recognition of the specific nature of Native invisibility and anti-Black racism, the POC acronym was expanded to BIPOC.

[BENCHMARK]

JOINT STATEMENT REGARDING LAWS ENACTED TO PREVENT THE INCLUSION OF RACE AND RACISM IN SCHOOL CURRICULA

Association of Collegiate Schools of Architecture (ACSA)
Council of Educators in Landscape Architecture (CELA)
Association of Collegiate Schools of Planning (ACSP)
Interior Design Educators Council (IDEC)

For Immediate Release[1]

Washington, DC, September 21, 2023—The planning, design, and use of built and natural environments have direct and indirect impacts on people. Competent practitioners of architecture, landscape architecture, urban planning, and interior design must understand the histories of their profession and of the communities with which they will work. They must also be able to understand the impact of their work on people and communities as a result of practice today and in the future. Practitioners must understand the factors that affect vulnerable people and communities, including people of color, women, LGBTQIA people, and people with disabilities. No understanding is fully possible without access to educational information and discussion about social factors including privilege, bias, discrimination, sexism, and racism, among others.

"This united declaration stands as a strong objection to the legislation that silences educators from sharing the histories of the architectural profession. Practitioners, educators, and students must be granted access to the complete narrative. Being privy to only a portion of the story significantly disadvantages us all," Mo Zell, 2023–24 ACSA President.

---

1. Find the original post at https://www.acsa-arch.org/joint-statement-prohibitions-on-diversity-equity-and-inclusion-will-limit-the-professions/.

The boards of directors of the four organizations representing university programs and educators in architecture, landscape architecture, planning, and interior design—ACSA, CELA, ACSP, and IDEC—jointly communicate our opposition to any legislation that prevents educators from teaching and sharing complete and accurate knowledge about the built environment for the purpose of shielding students from "divisive" or "disagreeable" content related to the impact of race and racism in American and global society, as well as other pedagogy related to gender and LGBTQ+ identities. Such legislation has already been passed in Arkansas, Florida, Iowa, South Dakota, and Virginia, and other moves are underway. These laws serve to suppress student exploration of pressing issues that affect the country and that are essential to preparing future practitioners in the built environment disciplines.

The decisions to eliminate certain sectors of discourse in public institutions is [*sic*] especially concerning, because they impinge on students' right to free speech, on the basic principles of faculty's academic freedom, and on the ability of American citizens to participate fully in democratic use of our shared resources. Limited access to educational resources in K–12 education also impinges on students' access to future educational opportunities.

We call on federal, state, and local governments to respect the professional expertise of educators at all levels in preparing for the next generation of practitioners. We call on federal, state, and local governments to support educators as they provide students of all ages and backgrounds with the proper skills for emerging technologies.

STATISTICAL DATA DRAWN FROM "NCARB BY THE NUMBERS," 2022

THE PATH TO LICENSURE

The path to licensure in architecture is long, costly and strenuous. College and personal debt, the expense of study materials, the cost of sitting for the exam, and family obligations are obstacles along the path that disproportionally affect women and minority individuals.

It takes an average of five years to get a professional degree in architecture from an accredited architecture program.

Architecture graduates have to earn a minimum of 3,740 hours across six areas of experience while working for a licensed architect before they can sit for the Architecture Registration Exam (ARE). On average, this takes 4.8 years.

In order to become licensed, a candidate must pass all six sections of the ARE. This takes an average of 2.9 years.

From the point at which an individual begins a college degree program in architecture, it takes an average of 12.7 years to become a licensed architect.

A license is required to legally call yourself an "architect" and to practice independently.

UNIVERSITIES

In 2022...
The average accredited architecture program graduated only five Hispanic/Latinx students.

Black students made up only 5% of the student population at accredited architecture programs. This statistic had not changed in the past eleven years.

Black full-time faculty made up 5% of all full-time faculty, and Black full-time tenured faculty made up 3% of all tenured faculty.

Almost 45% of architecture schools did not have a Black faculty member in the department.

THE PROFESSION
In 2022 there were approximately 119,900 licensed architects in the US.

75% identified as men (approximately 65% as white men).
25% identified as women (approximately 18% as white women).

4% identified as Asian men.
2.5% identified as Asian women.

3.5% identified as Hispanic or Latinx men.
1.5% identified as Hispanic or Latinx women.

1.5% identified as Black or African American men.
0.5% identified as Black or African American women.

.04% identified as Native Americans.

> **Architects should be reaching out in every way possible to the general public. Because right now the profession basically talks to themselves.**
>
> Beverly Willis
> founder, Beverly Willis Architecture Foundation

Dominant Culture

Dominant culture refers to a perceived cultural hierarchy in which one group in a diverse society, by virtue of race, ethnicity, religion, language, politics, or some other identifiable characteristic, has more power than other groups. Being part of the dominant culture carries both obvious and subtle benefits in relation to social, educational, professional, political, and socioeconomic prospects. Benefits accrue to those in the dominant culture, who have greater representation in decision-making institutions that may protect and promote their interests over time, structurally codifying and controlling the narrative. Those outside the dominant culture experience barriers, and as a result are afforded less power and more limited access to social, educational, professional, political, and economic networks.

A CONVERSATION WITH MEEJIN YOON

Meejin Yoon and Betsy West

Meejin Yoon is the dean of the College of Architecture, Art, and Planning at Cornell University, and cofounding partner of Höweler+Yoon. An architect, designer, and educator, Yoon is committed to advancing creative and critical pedagogies, practices, scholarship, and research addressing the many urgent environmental and social challenges we face in our communities. Yoon's work and research examines intersections between architecture, urbanism, technology, and the public realm. Her professional projects include cultural buildings and public spaces, including the Karsh Institute of Democracy and the Memorial to Enslaved Laborers at the University of Virginia. Yoon has exhibited nationally and internationally, including at the Museum of Modern Art, New York; the Museum of Contemporary Art Chicago; the Museum of Contemporary Art, Los Angeles; and the International Architecture Exhibition in Venice. Her most recent book is Verify in Field: Projects and Conversations *(Park Books, 2021), which she co-authored with Eric Höweler. Yoon holds a bachelor of architecture degree from Cornell University and a master of architecture in urban design degree from Harvard. She served on the faculty of the department of architecture at MIT for seventeen years, and headed the department from 2014 to 2018. Recent honors include the Rome Prize, and election to the American Academy of Arts and Letters, the highest recognition of artistic merit in the United States.*

> **But now I'm very proud to say I'm a female architect or an Asian architect. I think owning one's identity is important. It's reflective of a more collective, shared understanding of race and the importance of striving for equity in the field. People were uncomfortable acknowledging these issues in the past.**

Betsy West — As an Asian American woman in a majority-white male field, no doubt you've faced tremendous challenges along the way. You cofounded your own firm, Höweler+Yoon, and now hold the position of dean at Cornell University's College of Architecture, Art, and Planning. When people look at you and your accomplishments, what do you want them to see?

Meejin Yoon — My perspective has changed incrementally over time. As a young architect, I wanted to be known as an architect first, and then maybe you could figure out what my gender and heritage are. I would be offended if someone called me a female architect, an Asian architect, a female Asian architect, as if these were qualifiers. I really just wanted to be an architect and be respected as such. But now I'm very proud to say I'm a female architect or an Asian architect. I think owning one's identity is important. It's reflective of a more collective, shared understanding of race and the importance of striving for equity in the field. People were uncomfortable acknowledging these issues in the past.

This moment is important. We are a multicultural profession in a multicultural democracy, and that democracy is being tested. We need to demonstrate that it can succeed. To do that, everybody needs to put energy and effort into articulating and advancing the principles of equality and democracy. We're seeing incredible movements toward awareness and solidarity, but these advancements exist alongside incredibly divisive politics. I'm surprised every day by new knowledge. That's a good thing. We're unlearning and relearning our individual histories, our nation's histories, our global histories, and that is going to be significant for our discipline.

BW — What should we be doing as a profession to engage these histories and move toward a more just and equitable future? What problems do we need to solve?

MY — In our contemporary moment, I think it's important that we ask, "What's the matter?" I'm referring to the term

> **Our age of information and big data is coinciding with an age of post-truth and the erosion of trust in things we once trusted, such as the news, institutions, government.**

"matter" as physical substance, sure, but really much more in terms of the essence of things, and specifically the essence of our problems. The problems of the moment are numerous and intersectional. They include racial violence, the COVID-19 pandemic, the overwhelming pervasiveness of technology that both advances and divides us, the breakdown of trust in social institutions, environmental crises that threaten humanity.

Racialized violence in the United States began with colonization and slavery and continues, affecting Indigenous communities, Black communities, and Asian communities to this day. Indigenous peoples suffer from ongoing economic and cultural oppression. There's religious violence. And structural racism extends racialized violence into economic and social inequalities. Our present moment is also characterized by a superabundance of information and digital collectivity, and simultaneously a lack of certainty. So our age of information and big data is coinciding with an age of post-truth and the erosion of trust in things we once trusted, such as the news, institutions, government.

The pandemic changed every aspect of life in terms of public health and how we interact with one another, calling into question public-ness and collectiveness. But data science, genomics, rapid prototyping, distributed manufacturing, machine learning, and AI have led to myriad technological advances that have enabled unprecedented innovations. At the same time, we recognize that technologies have both brought us together and pulled us apart. And we recognize that with devices, every interaction is mediated. Even in public, we use our devices to record events rather than focus on experiencing them; people are more engaged with their devices than with the world. This is a real problem, especially when it's set against the backdrop of a climate emergency, the need for environmental action to save our planet. We face layered urban crises, from climate change to economic imbalances to affordable housing shortages to declining infrastructure. All of these challenges are complex, multifaceted, and interconnected.

One of my favorite quotes about design comes from Charles Eames. When he was asked, "What are the limits of design?" he responded, "What are the limits of problems?"

Ray and Charles Eames, 1960

Design is defined by the many multilayered problems that need design attention. So, in taking stock of the present, when we ask "What's the matter?" we must question all of our values and beliefs and aspirations as a discipline. As architects, how do we materialize what we value? Essentially, how do we build what matters?

> **We should build our value systems into how we design and realize things in the world. And look to our value systems to determine how we build a practice.**

BW — As architects and designers, we are most often working with teams of people and multiple stakeholders. What are some of the challenges of that?

MY — I think one of our biggest challenges is owning our expertise. Architects are generalists to a large extent; we bring together experts, choreograph everything, and then synthesize it all. This is an incredible skill and knowledge base that not everybody has. I've seen people and companies who want to take on building. Their thinking is something like, "Why does construction take so long? The three-legged stool between architect, client, and contractor slows everything down. The policies, processes, and approvals make it very slow, very expensive." And some of those people are saying, "Well, you know, I'm a smart entrepreneur. Maybe I can do it better."

But architects are educated to do this and have a unique ability; we need to own that expertise. Our expertise is not purely problem solving. It's also a synthetic way of thinking about what creating and building in the world mean. And we have the ability to implement—we understand deeply the processes, the techniques. We should build our value systems into how we design and realize things in the world. And look to our value systems to determine how we build a practice.

I think the generations that follow—including our students—are doing an incredible job of making clear the values of their practices. For example, with the Memorial to Enslaved Laborers, we looked to the students to know where to go in order to shift the discipline. We get to do that through teaching; we get to do that through scholarship; and we get to do that through practice. And all of those things contribute in different ways to the field of architecture.

BW — How can designers begin to think about rehabilitating environments that grew out of racist ideologies?

MY — My expectation with that kind of project is that it is going to be very, very, very hard. Anything that deals with trauma or history or conflict will take an emotional toll and will require making space and time for that.

Recently we completed our work on the Memorial to Enslaved Laborers, which endeavors to tell the story of the approximately four thousand men, women, and children who built and sustained the University of Virginia from its founding in 1817 to the end of the Civil War. Many of their names and identities remain unknown today. The project was the work of many. It took a village and more than ten years of work before we as architects and designers arrived on the scene, relatively close to the end of the very important process that the university had gone through with its community.

The community came together in an unusual way. I think that was because it was students who pushed the beginning of the project. Then the faculty joined. They brought scholarship and knowledge. And we built upon that work to make the project a reality. We had an incredible design team that included the cultural historian and architect Mabel O. Wilson of Studio &, landscape architect Gregg Bleam, the incredible artist Eto Otitigbe, and Frank Dukes, whose expertise is in engagement and negotiation, and who had worked for many years on courses at UVA on race and repair.

While we were working on this project, Mabel once noted that "to tell the story of the United States requires a reckoning with hard truths, with those histories that have been silenced in the nation's archives and in the public spaces of our shared landscape." This is evident when you look at the first historical marker at UVA, which tells the story of the university's founding with no mention of slavery. In point of fact, the University of Virginia was founded by Thomas Jefferson, signer of the Declaration of Independence and third president of the United States—a man closely associated with the ideals of democracy. Yet he owned six hundred enslaved men, women, and children during his lifetime. Both the university and his home, Monticello, were built on the backbreaking labor of the enslaved.

The first recognition of this history at UVA was in the form of a plaque installed in 2007, and it had the unintended consequence of sparking outrage among the students. They were dismayed by the limits of this recognition, especially the wording—that enslaved people "helped to realize

Muntu Dance Theatre, ring shout, 2011

Thomas Jefferson's design for the University of Virginia." That same year, Frank Dukes founded UCARE—University and Community Action for Racial Equity—and in 2009 one of the student interns in that organization created an advocacy group called the Memorial to Enslaved Laborers. That's where the name of the memorial comes from.

In 2012, the university's troubled history became even more tangible when archaeologists discovered seventy unmarked graves behind the university's official cemetery. That same year, the president of UVA commissioned a study on this new piece of history and the possibility of creating a memorial. So, in 2016, when we were commissioned to design the memorial, almost a decade had already gone into the historical research.

The community shared that the memorial had to extend the work and ideas of the students and faculty, the local community, and the descendants' community. It should not only honor the lives of the enslaved people at UVA, but also be tied to the larger commemorative landscape

> **So we decided it would be a space inspired by both the ring shout—a dance from West Africa where the participants form a circle—and a kind of clearing in the woods like a hush harbor—a place enslaved people would gather in secret to practice religious traditions and organize resistance.**

in Charlottesville and at the university, where there had already been significant efforts to identify specific structures that address the history of enslavement. The community wanted it to be a living memorial, and in that way also a living archive. The memorial also had to express dualities—not only pain and suffering, but also resilience and dignity. It had to record the true humanity of those who were enslaved—both their strengths and their struggles.

We were given multiple possible sites. Initially, we didn't have a budget. We didn't have a scale. And our client group was, in a way, everyone. So we created a process to bring all our early concepts to the community early on to get input. During this outreach process, we learned there are people who are very uncomfortable coming to the University of Virginia. Some even refer to it as The Plantation. So we created a way to have ambassadors—students, faculty, and members of UCARE—go out into the community to listen and learn. Eto, Mabel, and I also met with the community. We gathered in local churches and schools. So many things we had assumed—from language to styling—were incorrect, and it really required dialogue and conversation and time to find the right approach.

What we heard in terms of reactions to some of our early sketches was that the memorial had to create a space in and of itself, a place for the community of the present to learn from the past. So we decided it would be a space inspired by both the ring shout—a dance from West Africa where the participants form a circle—and a kind of clearing in the woods like a hush harbor—a place enslaved people would gather in secret to practice religious traditions and organize resistance. We located the memorial in proximity to the Rotunda, but whereas the Rotunda is an enclosed dome, the memorial is open and conical, to reveal and invite. It's made of Virginia mist granite, and we introduced a kind of horizon line that sweeps around the memorial, expressing a duality between the rough and uneven texture on the exterior and the honed-smooth interior.

Of the estimated four thousand enslaved persons the memorial commemorates, many of their identities

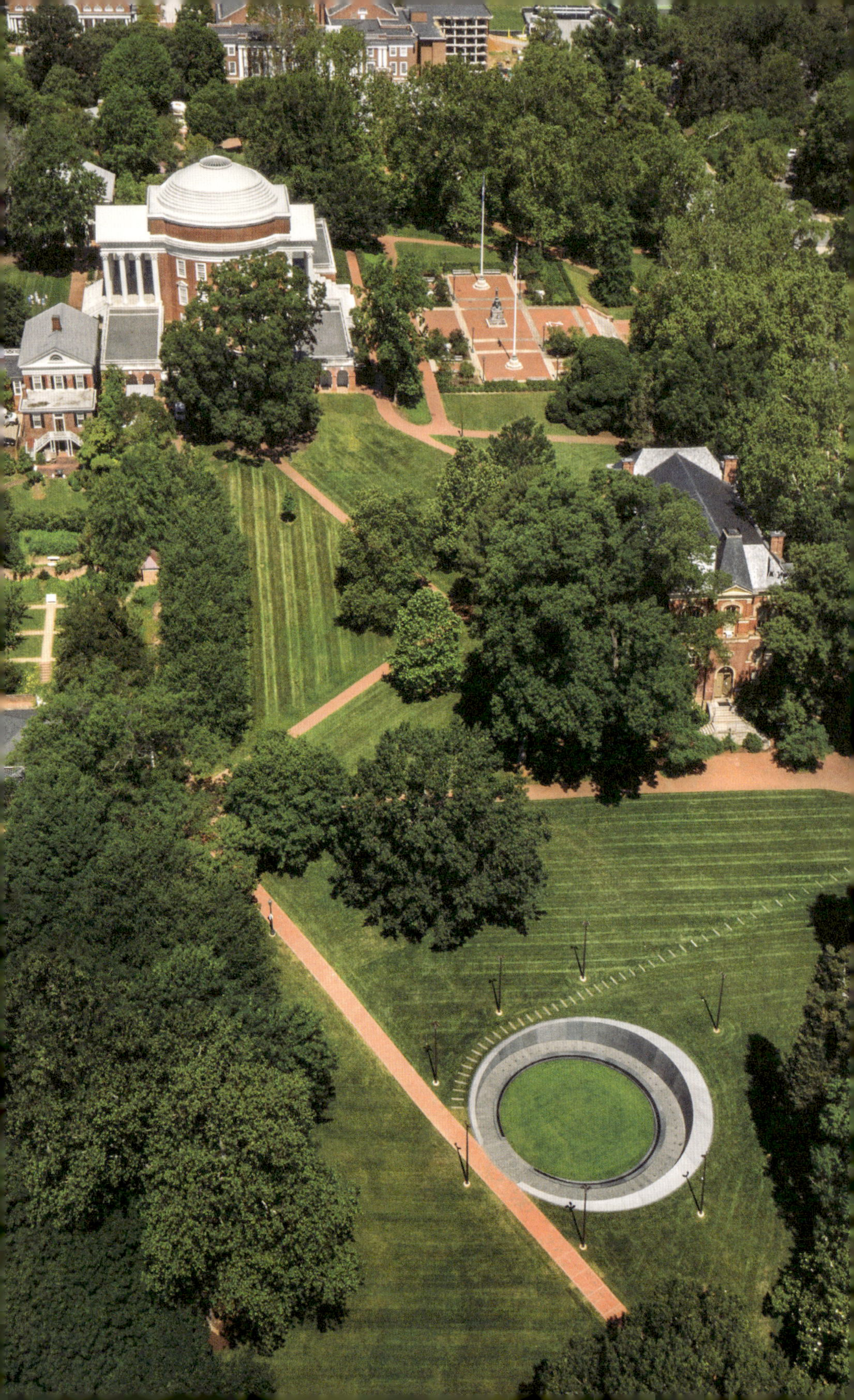

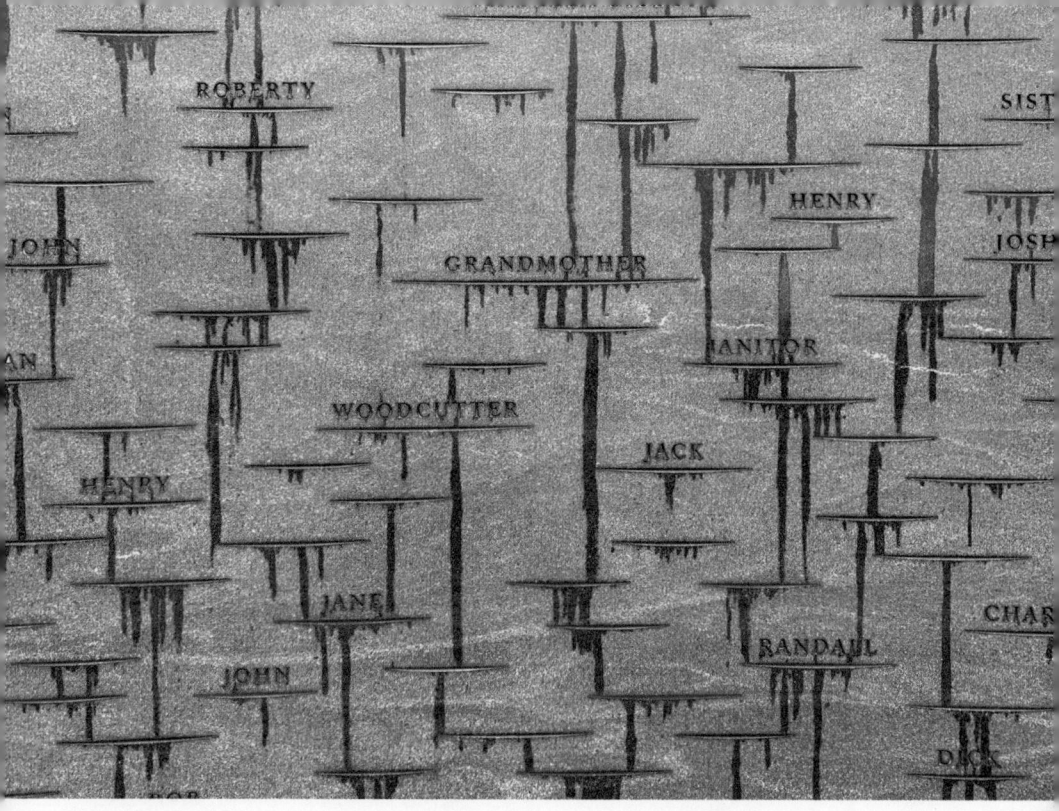

above: Water collects in the incisions of the Memorial to Enslaved Laborers
opposite: Memorial to Enslaved Laborers (aerial view, lower right), University of Virginia at Charlottesville

are unknown in terms of their names. We have only about 577 partial or full names, and partial records of the community. We presented the four thousand enslaved persons as a kind of genealogical cloud that stretches across the stone. There's a mark for every person. If we know a name, it's inscribed above the mark. If we know a skill or trade, that's also carved above. And when we know kinship, or can assume kinship, that's also inscribed. Because the marks are deeply incised, the water that collects in them during the rain is held longer. So the surface around the incisions dries relatively quickly, and then the water in the incisions begins to slowly run down the face of the stone, creating a kind of streaking, crying, bleeding quality.

There's a bench on the inside with a timeline carved into it. The timeline begins with a quote by Isabella Gibbons, an enslaved woman who was freed but stayed in the community and became a teacher: "Can we forget the crack of the whip, cowhide, whipping post, the auction block, the

Eto Otitigbe, Isabella Gibbons's eyes

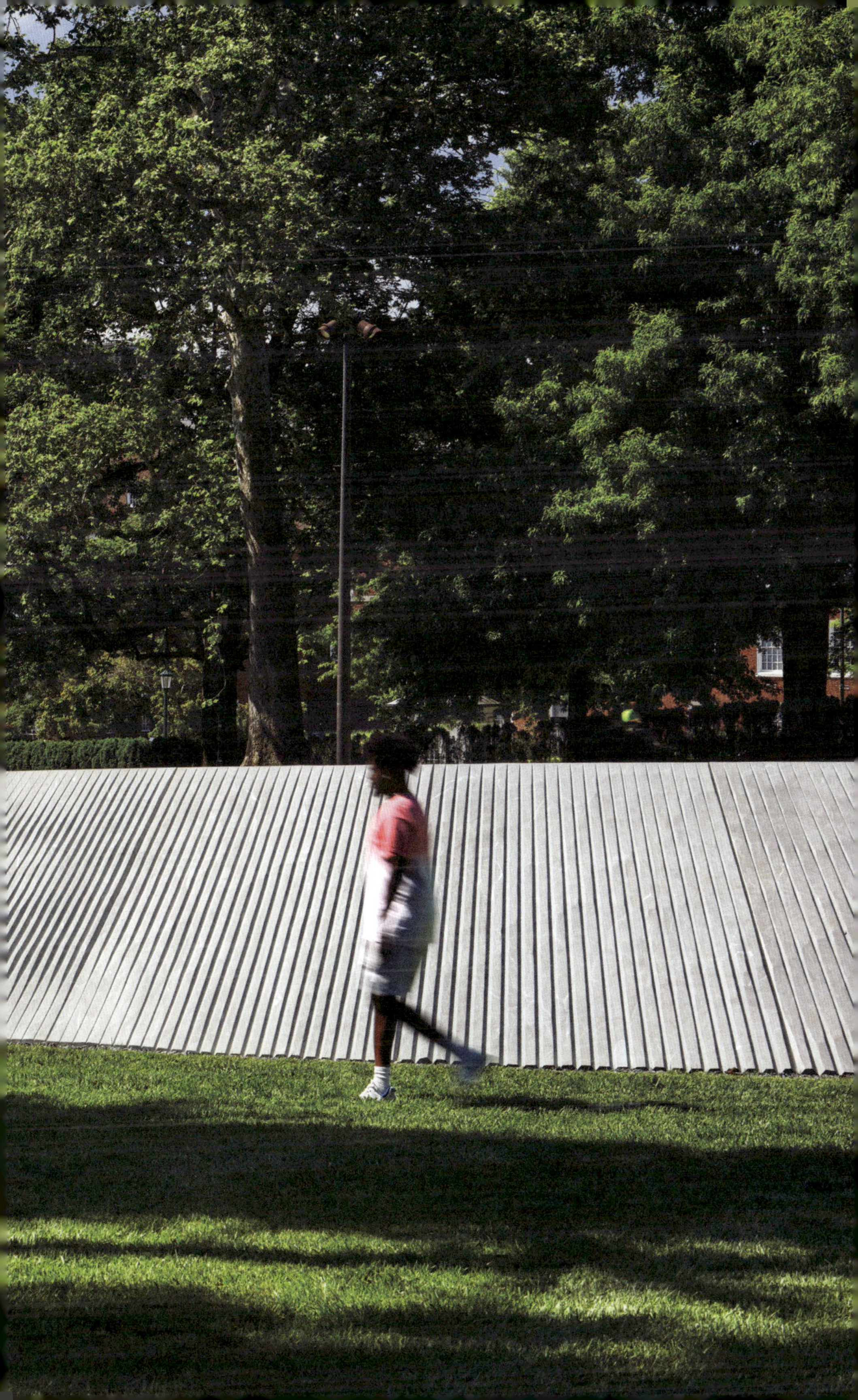

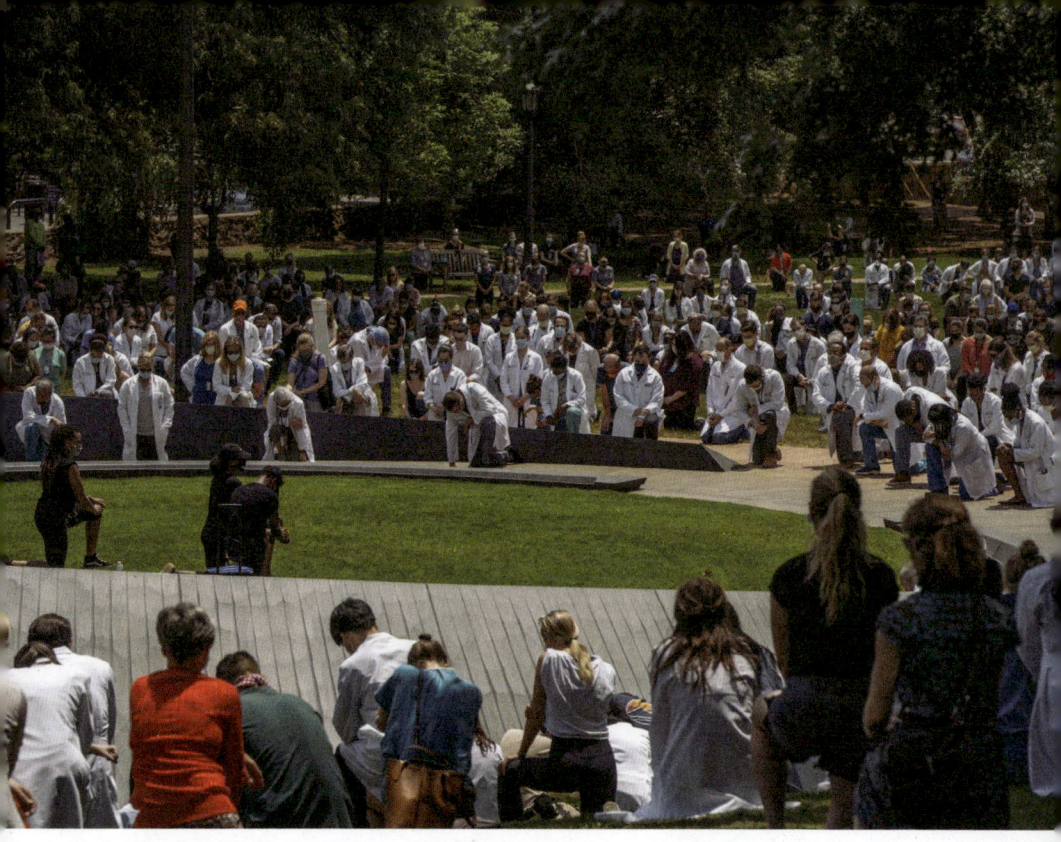

White Coats for Black Lives at the Memorial to Enslaved Laborers

handcuffs, the spaniels, the iron collar, the negro-trader tearing the young child from its mother's breast as a whelp from the lioness? Have we forgotten that by those horrible cruelties, hundreds of our race were killed? No, we have not, nor ever will." Isabella became more than a protagonist for the memorial—she is the watcher and the witness. We collaborated with Eto to begin carving her eyes at a colossal scale. There are very few enslaved persons of whom we have a photograph from this period at the university, but he made her portrait legible in memory of her and her community.

The memorial opened in 2020. It was still a construction site, but when George Floyd was killed, the Memorial to Enslaved Laborers became a site where individuals and groups came together spontaneously to acknowledge and grieve the brutality of his death. Then those groups got larger and larger, and ever since, the memorial has become a site that brings people together to recognize the injustices that persist in the wake of slavery today.

> **The memorial opened in 2020. It was still a construction site, but when George Floyd was killed, the Memorial to Enslaved Laborers became a site where individuals and groups came together spontaneously to acknowledge and grieve the brutality of his death.**

BW — How can we, as architects, do a better job of serving a broader range of people?

MY — Today there's no such thing as architecture without social, material, political, and environmental consequences. My partner, Eric, and I just published *Verify in Field*. Its title is derived from a notational convention on architectural drawings indicating that the information is subject to unknown conditions on the site. The book highlights field verification as a productive design tool to test ideas and act on the world because out-in-the-world is where architecture impacts people.

At the intersection of all the global challenges we face, we understand context as more than just the physical site. It's the historic context, the ecological context, the labor context, the material supply chain context, and so on. Fortunately, we don't have to solve these difficult and complex challenges all alone. Working from the set of values we've built over time, we put together teams whose combined knowledge, expertise, and skills suit each project we take on. Serving a broader range of people means engaging in a process of dialogue. The UVA Memorial to Enslaved Laborers is a useful project to illustrate that you always have responsibilities above and beyond your own creative imagination when you're entrusted with work that many people are invested in. And really, that describes all of architecture.

If there's anything to take away from that project, or any project, it's that you need lots of conversations over lots of time in order to build understanding and trust among people—sometimes people who are very different from one another, or, sometimes, very different from you. That kind of human connection, that trust and respect, is absolutely critical to any good design.

> If you want something,
> you have to give the same thing.
> If you want love, you have to
> give love. If you want peace, you have
> to give peace. If you want healing,
> you have to give healing.

> Phil Freelon
> FAIA

Minority Stress

Minority stress refers to a person's mental and physical response to being stigmatized due to race, ethnicity, gender, sexual identity, age, disability, and so on. Stressors vary widely, but often include workplace bias, inadequate financial resources, physical or verbal abuse, and poor social support systems. Research shows that chronic stress is closely linked to poor health outcomes.

> To get a sense of the state of opportunity for women in architecture, consider that the firm getting the most high-profile architectural commissions in the world right now has just two female principals and this web address: big.dk. Yes, BIG (for Bjarke Ingels Group) is based in Denmark (hence the "dk"), but the firm's use of this cheeky address just about sums up the situation facing many women in the architectural profession today.

Allison Arieff
contributing opinion writer, *New York Times*

> In many ways, architecture is a profession that has been the epitome of the dominant white patriarchy, from most of the celebrated starchitects to the all-too-frequent obsession with buildings that are better known for the beauty of the object than the quality of life that they enable. I'm Black and female; my existence is the exact opposite of that system. So perhaps it is no accident that as I've built my own path in this field, I've been committed to a design practice that is rooted in elevating the stories of those who have most often been neglected or silenced.

Liz Ogbu

designer and activist

Structural and Systemic Discrimination

Discrimination can be embedded in systems, structures, institutions, laws, or policies that operate in ways that lead to inequity and injustice. These forces may be racist, and can be more or less obvious in their suppression of equal rights. Examples include the legal justice system, health care, redlining of minority neighborhoods, race-blind admissions, and voter suppression laws, which may benefit the more privileged or powerful members of society but do great harm to others that continues generation after generation.

[SNAPSHOT]

A PROFOUND ACT OF SELF-PRESERVATION

Lesley Lokko

In October 2020, Lesley Lokko, a widely acclaimed educator and design leader who founded the Graduate School of Architecture at the University of Johannesburg in 2015, tendered her resignation as dean of the Bernard and Anne Spitzer School of Architecture at City College of New York, a post she had assumed in January that same year. In a statement to Architectural Record, she elucidated the obstacles that prompted her resignation.

My decision to leave Spitzer after less than a year is fairly straightforward: I was not able to build enough support to be able to deliver on either my promise of change, or my vision of it. The reasons why are more complex.

Part of it has to do with COVID-19 and the rapid lockdown, which occurred after only three months in post. It's hard enough to build social capital in a new place without having to do it over Zoom. Part of it too has to do with the wider inflexibility of US academic structures. In an incredibly bureaucratic and highly regulated context, change is as much administrative as it is conceptual.

The lack of meaningful support—not lip service, of which there's always a surfeit—meant my workload was absolutely crippling. No job is worth one's life and at times I genuinely feared for my own.

Race is never far from the surface of any situation in the US. Having come directly from South Africa, I wasn't prepared for the way it manifests in the U.S. and quite simply, I lacked the tools to both process and deflect it. The lack of respect and empathy for Black people, especially Black women, caught me off guard, although it's by no means unique to Spitzer. I suppose I'd say in the end that my resignation was a profound act of self-preservation.

> But even as we acknowledge that most people who have made it have worked hard, we must also recognize that there are many, many other people who are working just as hard—or harder—who will never make it because of an uneven playing field. And that uneven playing field has been structured and is being maintained by racism, sexism, heterosexism, capitalism, and other systems of structured inequity.

Camara Phyllis Jones
physician and anti-racism activist
"Seeing the Water: Seven Values Targets for Anti-Racism Action," 2020

[BENCHMARK]

JOINT STATEMENT ON THE SUPREME COURT'S DECISION REGARDING RACE-CONSCIOUS ADMISSIONS

American Institute of Architects (AIA)
American Institute of Architecture Students (AIAS)
Association of Collegiate Schools of Architecture (ACSA)
National Organization of Minority Architects (NOMA)

On June 29, 2023, the US Supreme Court ruled by a vote of six to three that the admissions programs used by Harvard College and the University of North Carolina violate the Equal Protection Clause of the Fourteenth Amendment, which bars racial discrimination by government entities. The court's ruling effectively makes unlawful any ongoing direct consideration of a college applicant's race in achieving student diversity in higher education. Though the court's decision speaks only to colleges and universities, the ruling has led to a wave of public and private businesses and institutions dismantling their diversity, equity, and inclusion initiatives.

For Immediate Release

Washington, DC, June 30, 2023—The American Institute of Architects (AIA) and other allied organizations recognize that even with affirmative action, the number of minorities enrolled in our nation's colleges and universities is disproportionate to our demographics. By removing these protections, we are concerned that the impact of underrepresentation may worsen outcomes for everyone.

Equity, diversity, inclusion, and belonging represent our combined core values. We will continue to advocate for inclusive collegiate admissions because its educational benefits are integral to moving the architecture profession forward. **Diverse student perspectives and lived experiences will not only enrich the next generation of architects and design professionals, but also shape our world through the built environment they will design.** We are committed to the protection of the health, safety, and welfare of the public, which includes ensuring that our future workforce reflects the population it serves.

SCOTUS rules against affirmative action in college admissions

Colleges and universities can no longer consider race in their admissions processes after the US Supreme Court ruled against affirmative action, overturning decades of precedent that has benefitted Black and Latino students.

Majority: Roberts, Thomas, Alito, Gorsuch, Kavanaugh, Barrett

Dissenting: Sotomayor, Kagan, Jackson

Source: US Supreme Court, Students for Fair Admissions, Inc. v. President and Fellows of Harvard College
Graphic: Annette Choi, CNN

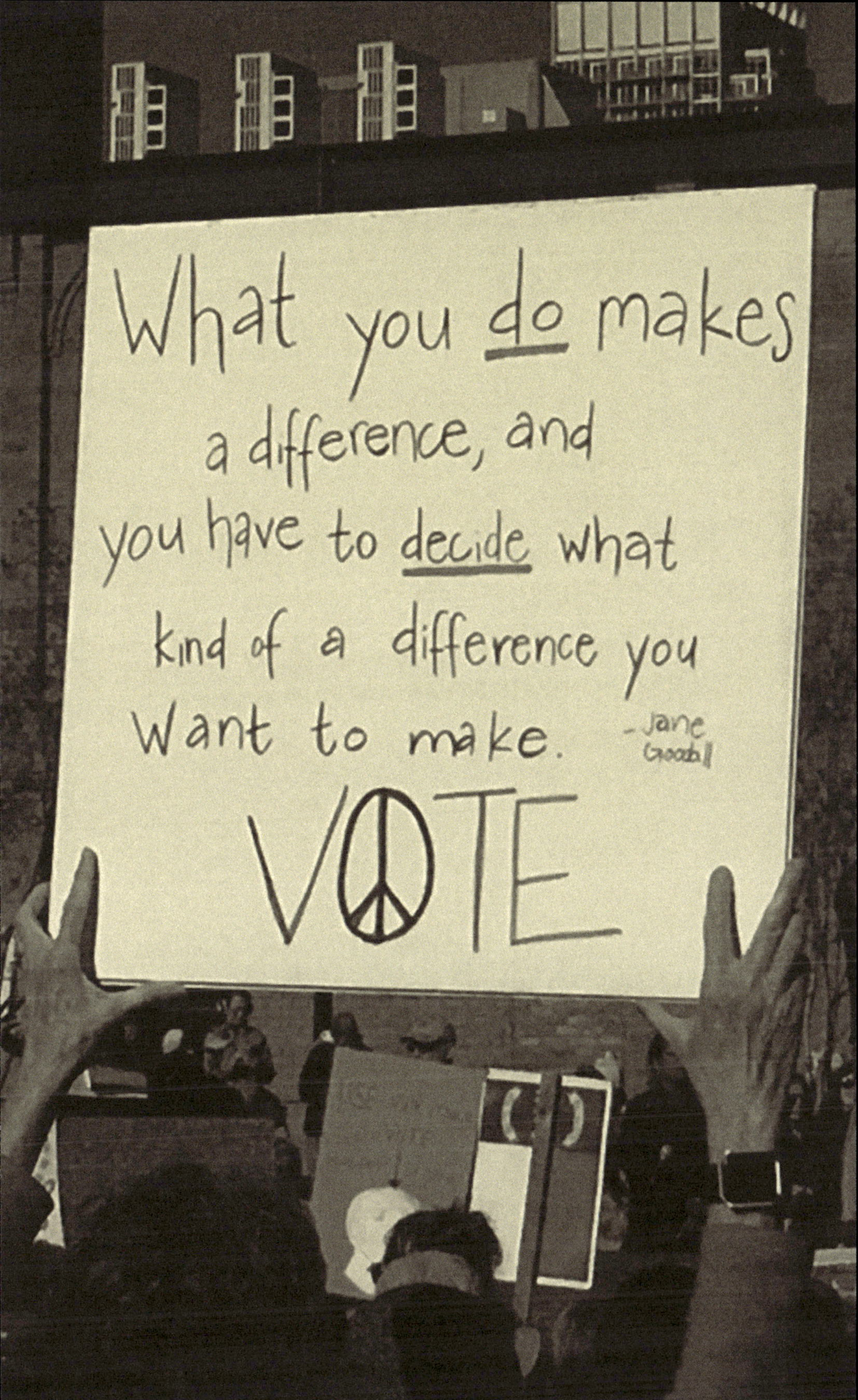
What you do makes a difference, and you have to decide what kind of a difference you want to make.
-Jane Goodall
VOTE

> [Make] ardent arguments through which to expand, refine, and acquire real outcomes for real people, tireless propaganda for the good, the just, the fair, and the beautiful.

>> Michael Sorkin
>> architecture critic
>> "Why Architectural Criticism Matters," 2014

I STAND with my BLACK, LGBT, MUSLIM, IMMIGRANT/REFUGEE, SURVIVOR, MARGINALIZED, FELLOW AMERICAN SISTERS + BROTHERS

AFTERWORD

Kelly Carlson-Reddig

This book is a space for questioning and speculation, as well as insights, ideas, methods, and projects. We began the undertaking with a few essential questions:

Who is the intended audience?
This book is aimed at the architecture profession broadly—it is for students, faculty, and architects. Readers experiencing the privileges of the majority might gain insight into the systems that maintain predominantly white and male architectural power centers. Minority readers may find hope in more inclusive views about the profession, shifting project focuses, prioritization of more varied issues, and seeking ways to better serve all populations.

What will this book add to the conversation about architecture?
Architecture—through actions, omissions, and barriers—has excluded people, practices, and cultures. A central aim is to amplify *other* voices with differing perspectives on architecture, enriched by their identity. We have been honored to work with architects, scholars, and educators who are transforming status-quo narratives about architecture and bringing their own challenging questions. Their fresh and provocative insights offer new ways to think, design, and build. Their words and work often focus on serving underrepresented populations through architecture.

Is this book primarily about buildings or people?
Decidedly, it is about both. In human terms, this book is concerned with the discriminatory and inequitable systems, structures, and practices that have existed in academia and the profession, which are surely causes of architecture's lack of diversity. Consequently it is for and about all those who study, teach, and practice within the discipline. It is also fundamentally concerned with the people that architecture should serve, and particularly those not yet adequately served or represented. In all of these regards, this book is about people.

As architecture involves the cultural production of buildings, cities, and spaces, it is clear that what we build and don't build can include or exclude, empower or disempower. We know that

> **It is clear that what we build and don't build can include or exclude, empower or disempower.**

architecture will be more diversely representative when it is inclusive—with more and different voices, cultures, viewpoints, and priorities. A better future with more diverse architecture is at the heart of this book.

Ideas about diversity, equity, inclusion and exclusion, discrimination, and identity permeate the book in three types of curated texts: *essays* by authors whose scholarship is enriching the discourse around identity, diversity, equity, and inclusion in architecture; *benchmarks* recounting events, speeches, pleas, and protests in the struggle for equality; and *snapshots* of personal events that will resonate with many. Each text, in its way, encourages a better understanding of the biases that run through the discipline of architecture, its representation, and its practices. Collectively, they demand that we reflect on our architectural priorities—where architecture is practiced, for whom it is created, and how alternative knowledge bases and design processes can yield greater multiplicity and beauty through difference. The collection portrays both the stakes involved if we fail to diversify and the potential gains if the discipline broadens its constituencies and views.

> "The language of the built environment tells a complex story of place that can either speak to our collective values and ideals or reveal persisting inequity and injustice."
> —Colloqate Design, mission statement

Architecture's omissions and barriers are surely a cause of its lack of diversity. Until recently, the long-standing "text" of architecture's history was solely focused on a selective canon of works conforming to narrow, Eurocentric standards of what was historically considered "good" and "worthy." Repeated incessantly, the exclusionary mantra became a kind of status-quo architectural truth:

- Architecture is monumental.
- Architecture's history can be grasped in a few big stylistic chunks—ancient, medieval, Renaissance,

> **"** Until recently, the long-standing 'text' of architecture's history was solely focused on a selective canon of works conforming to narrow, Eurocentric standards of what was historically considered 'good' and 'worthy.' **"**

Baroque, and modern—which follow canonical rules and sacrosanct principles, and possess formal qualities by which they are affirmed. To learn these standards well, young white men of aristocratic class went on grand tours to view, study, and draw the best work.
- Architecture across history was built by and for those with political, religious, and economic power.

In the early 2000s, the National Architecture Accreditation Board finally demanded the evolution of typically stodgy (and racist) curricula to include other countries and cultures that had clearly been excluded. This was a seminal moment for an important idea, and it felt like a real stretch at that time. Now it is clear that the centuries-long practice of omissions has been fundamentally damaging to diversity in architecture. Conventional histories were biased and subjective, crafted by those in power, in images of their own likeness to reinforce their authority and domination. Non-Western histories and cultures, as well as Indigenous and vernacular work, were long ignored. The differential power, privilege, and access underlying architecture was understood, but accepted unproblematically. The systems of slave labor, indentured servitude, and colonized people who labored for centuries to build architecture were barely mentioned. So much architecture and so many people were disregarded, ignored, and left out of the story.

Here *Margin and Text* is a poignant metaphor for architecture. We must critically ask: Who and what have been included in the text? Who writes the text? What cultures, architecture, and people are relegated to the margins or left out completely? Inclusive narratives are urgently needed, as are inclusive practices and programs in architecture's institutional, professional, and academic settings. As a discipline, we are increasingly recognizing the many ways in which we are less diverse than we should be. And recognition is leading to more studies, more questioning, more advocacy, and more programs to address the causes that underlie our lack of diversity. The findings are sometimes obvious, but often intersectional, insidious, and invisible.

> "Achieving a culture [of inclusion and equity] requires the celebration of differences among people and, more importantly, the elimination of obstacles that the underserved and underrepresented face to access the same opportunities that others have."
>
> —Alice Liao, "Increasing Diversity in Architecture: Barriers to Entry," *Architect*, 2019

In 2019, journalist Alice Liao published a three-part series in *Architect* magazine entitled "Increasing Diversity in Architecture." Her research suggests a long time frame of causes and effects, from youth through architectural education, internship, and licensure.[1] The roots of underrepresentation begin very early, starting with the choice of a career path. Underrepresentation of minorities in the profession leads to a shortage of mentors and role models in communities of color. As Bryan Lee Jr. of Colloqate Design states: "You have to know you want to be an architect."[2] Exposure to architects and access to pre-college design and mentoring programs increase the prospects for entry into architecture programs at the university level. Now preparatory programs such as the ACE Mentor Program, Project Pipeline, Drafting Dreams, and Hip Hop Architecture Camp are filling the gaps, specifically aiming to expose youth from underrepresented populations to the profession.

Access to architecture has not been equally open to all, and when it was available, its explicit practices and implicit norms required survival amid a boot-camp mentality. In already stressful environments, underrepresented students and architects are subject to subtle or overt pressures to speak on behalf of their race or gender, and being called out can further fuel a sense of separateness and isolation. Liao's research suggests that those in the minority are subject to explicit and unconscious biases steeped in stereotypes. In the professional world, such biases may limit hiring, compensation, promotions, inclusion, and opportunities for advancement, and contribute to "minority stress."

Author Michelle Joan Wilkinson speaks to the relentless burden for people of color to be continually "resilient" under such pressures—to be expected to recover from microaggressions, emotional trauma, and othering, reflected in so many forms by the texts here. Lesley Lokko resigned as

1. Alice Liao, "Increasing Diversity in Architecture: Designer-Led Solutions," *Architect*, May 13, 2019, https://www.architectmagazine.com/practice/increasing-diversity-in-architecture-designer-led-solutions_o.

2. Liao, "Increasing Diversity in Architecture."

> **Access to architecture has not been equally open to all, and when it was available, its explicit practices and implicit norms required survival amid a boot-camp mentality. In already stressful environments, underrepresented students and architects are subject to subtle or overt pressures to speak on behalf of their race or gender, and being called out can further fuel a sense of separateness and isolation.**

dean of the school of architecture at City College of New York amid a pervasive "lack of respect and empathy for Black people, especially Black women." Justin Garrett Moore was the only Black voice included in an expert AIA panel on affordable housing, and he was literally erased from the video documentation. These types of aggressions might be missed by those in the majority, but their accumulation marginalizes BIPOC, international, female, and LGBTQ+ students, creating environments that are hostile, insensitive, and discriminatory.

On the positive side, awareness of the systemic, structural, and informal barriers is increasing. Professional firms are recognizing the value of diversity, and formulating practices, policies, and programs to improve work environments. Key professional organizations, including the AIA, NAAB, and ACSA, are grappling with underlying issues and engaging in studies to better understand how to make change. Student and professional organizations such as NOMA/NOMAS, ACSA Deans' Equity and Inclusion Initiative, Designing in Color, 400 Forward, and Equity by Design are raising visibility and awareness of the issues facing underrepresented groups.

Numbers matter, and they are telling. In my thirty-two years as an educator, I have witnessed progress toward greater diversity in our student body—more Hispanic and Black students, more international students. Women now comprise 50 percent of architecture students nationally. This is very positive, and statistics validate that architecture student bodies are becoming more diverse. But gaps in representation still remain. Furthermore, statistics show that diversity diminishes over career time, with fewer women and minorities among licensed architects and faculty. Despite equitable gender representation in schools of architecture today, "the missing 32 percent" refers to the percentage of women who leave the profession between school and licensure. In 2022, the AIA reported that its membership is 71 percent male and 24.9 percent female (with the remainder not reporting). A 2020 NAAB report found that 65 percent of faculty are white, with underrepresented Black and Hispanic/Latinx educators.

In professional practice, the National Council of Architecture Registration Boards (NCARB) tracks demographics (gender, race, and age) by measuring completion of a sequence of professional credentials: 1) NCARB application, 2) AXP internship program, 3) Architecture Registration Exam (ARE), and 4) NCARB certificate holders who are registered architects (the last is noted in the table below). The American Institute of Architects (AIA) likewise reports the demographics of its membership. Both sets of statistics show that racial diversity, like gender diversity, diminishes over career time. Candidates starting an NCARB record are more diverse than those who complete their AXP internship; still less diverse are those completing the ARE; least diverse, NCARB certificate holders are 83 percent white and, of those, 63.8 percent are male.

	US POPULATION (2020 CENSUS)	STUDENTS IN ACCREDITED PROGRAMS	FACULTY (ALL LEVELS)	AIA MEMBERSHIP (2022)	NCARB CERTIFICATE (2021)
		9% unknown	12% unknown	18.1% unknown	
CAUCASIAN	58.9%	39%	65%	64%	82.7%
AFRICAN AMERICAN	13.6%	5%	0.8%	2.4%	1.9%
HISPANIC OR LATINX	19.1%	18%	9%	5.6%	5.5%
ASIAN	6.3%	9%	8%	6.8%	6.4%
NATIVE AMERICAN	1.3%	0.3%	0.3	0.3%	Not measured
INTERNATIONAL		19%	2%		
MALE	49.6%	50%	66%	71%	75.1%
FEMALE	50.4%	50%	34%	24.9%	24.9%
				4.1% not reporting	

Numbers and statistics validate that schools and offices remain more male, more white, and less diverse than the US population overall. Aspirational values and policies around diversity, equity, and inclusion have yet to translate into equal representation. And until the racial and ethnic makeup of students, faculty, and practitioners reflects regional and national diversity, we still have further to go.

This book contributes a more inclusive and equitable architectural future by amplifying diverse voices in our own profession. The included authors provide ideas and ways forward, not by specifically recasting history, but by proactively crafting alternative practices based on different knowledge bases, values, and priorities. Their ways of working can inspire us to think and work differently as well, maybe even in ways that transform the discipline.

KELLY CARLSON-REDDIG

"

Putting out statements is important because designers and architects must participate in this conversation [about racism]. But, the architecture industry can ensure sustained, meaningful change only by going beyond statements of camaraderie and solidarity, to action items. It is not enough to show up to a funeral and offer your condolences; you need to bring the lasagna, too.

Pascale Sablan

architect

ORGANIZATIONS

The following organizations represent architecture and its allied disciplines. They include national umbrella organizations responsible for the broad interests of the profession and its practice; licensure entities; educational entities; and architectural program accreditation bodies. Others serve to amplify particular interests and initiatives of women and BIPOC professionals (Black, Indigenous, and people of color). All descriptions are excerpted and/or adapted from the organizations' websites.

AFRICAN AMERICAN DESIGN NEXUS

African American Design Nexus is a platform that promotes Black designers who have made and are making an indelible contribution to our society and to how we see the world around us. Content includes podcasts, story maps, perspectives, news features, and profiles.

Mission: African American Design Nexus serves as a resource to diversify the design fields and ensure that voices of color are included as models for those studying, as well as for clients looking to hire designers. Content produced aims to elevate the awareness of Black designers and illuminate the impact of their work on our shared world. The Nexus seeks to highlight excellence, showcase inclusion, and strengthen a more diverse pipeline of people into the design fields.
https://aadn.gsd.harvard.edu/category/nexus-podcast

AMERICAN INSTITUTE OF ARCHITECTS (AIA)

The AIA was founded in 1857 and today has more than two hundred chapters around the world that support architects by lobbying on local, state, and federal matters; providing continuing education; conducting research; and setting standards and rules for practice.

Mission: The AIA has developed *Guides for Equitable Practice* as well as a series of "Where We Stand" statements that clarify its position on key issues facing the profession, including climate change, equity, diversity, immigration, infrastructure, licensure, school design and student safety, sexual harassment, and sustainability. The AIA, as part of the global community, champions a culture of equity, diversity, and inclusion within the profession of architecture to create a better environment for all. Achieving this vision has a direct impact on the relevance of our profession and the world's prosperity, health, and future.

The American Institute of Architecture Students (AIAS) operates student-led chapters dedicated to advancing leadership, design, and service among architecture students. Collectively, they represent the voices of students across the United States and around the world through international chapters and partnerships with comparable student associations in Europe, India, Australia, Africa, and South and Central America.
https://www.aia.org/about

—

ARCHITECTS/DESIGNERS/PLANNERS FOR SOCIAL RESPONSIBILITY (ADPSR)

ADPSR works for peace, environmental protection, ecological building, social justice, and the development of healthy communities.

Mission: ADPSR programs aim to raise professional and public awareness of critical social and environmental issues, further responsive design and planning, and honor persons and organizations whose work exemplifies social responsibility. Most recently, over the course of six years, ADPSR successfully lobbied the AIA to institute a new rule in its code of ethics prohibiting architects from designing execution chambers and rooms for solitary confinement.
https://www.adpsr.org/about

—

ASSOCIATION OF COLLEGIATE SCHOOLS OF ARCHITECTURE (ACSA)

Founded in 1912 by ten charter members, ACSA is an international association of architecture schools preparing future architects, designers, and change agents. Its full members include all of the accredited professional degree programs in the United States and Canada as well as international schools and two- and four-year programs. Together, ACSA schools represent some seven thousand faculty educating more than forty thousand students.

Mission: ACSA's core values include equity, social justice, climate action, teaching and learning, research, scholarship, and creative practice. ACSA seeks to empower faculty and schools to educate increasingly diverse students, expand disciplinary impacts, and create knowledge for the advancement of architecture. In conjunction with the AIA, ACSA developed an Equity in Architectural Education resource that provides actions and prompts intended to inspire discussions about creating welcoming environments to attract and retain those currently underrepresented in academia and in the profession.
https://www.acsa-arch.org/about/

—

ASSOCIATION FOR WOMEN IN ARCHITECTURE AND DESIGN (AWA+D)

AWA+D is a professional society dedicated to supporting career and educational endeavors for women working in the built environment.

Mission: To advance and support women in the allied fields of architecture and design; encourage and foster high levels of achievement by providing educational

programming, mentoring, and illuminating career opportunities for students and professionals in these fields; and cultivate awareness of the value and advancements created by the profession. AWA+D also provides scholarships and a midcareer fellowship via its sister organization, the Association for Women in Architecture Foundation (AWAF).
https://www.awaplusd.org/

—

BEVERLY WILLIS ARCHITECTURE FOUNDATION (BWAF)

BWAF advocates for gender equity in leadership and recognition in the architecture, design, landscape, engineering, technology, real estate, and construction industries. It achieves its mission by researching and documenting women's contributions and achievements in the built realm, educating the public, and transforming industry practices.

Mission: BWAF is leading a cultural revolution in the building industry that will acknowledge, cultivate, and value women's past, present, and future contributions and achievements. It develops leadership at all levels, and through its work seeks to build global change.
https://bwaf.org/mission

—

BEYOND THE BUILT ENVIRONMENT (BBE)

Founded by architect and advocate Pascale Sablan, BBE is a nonprofit organization committed to increasing diversity and equity in the field of architecture.

Mission: BBE seeks to empower women and people of color by providing opportunities for education, mentorship, and professional development. By increasing diversity in the profession, BBE is helping to ensure that the people who design our buildings and public spaces reflect the diversity of the communities they serve. This, in turn, can lead to more culturally sensitive and responsive design that addresses the needs of all people.
https://www.beyondthebuilt.com/about

—

BLACK RECONSTRUCTION COLLECTIVE (BRC)

BRC provides funding, design, and intellectual support to the ongoing and incomplete project of emancipation for the African diaspora.

Mission: BRC is committed to multiscalar and multidisciplinary work dedicated to dismantling systemic white supremacy and hegemonic whiteness within art, design, and academia. Founded by a group of Black architects, artists, designers, and scholars, BRC aims to amplify knowledge production and spatial practices by individuals and organizations that further the reconstruction project.
https://www.blackreconstructioncollective.org/about

—

BLACKSPACE

The BlackSpace collective brings together planners, architects, artists, and designers as Black urbanists—people who are passionate about the work of public systems and urban infrastructures. It breaks the silos of urbanist practices to build Black power and Black joy.

ORGANIZATIONS

Mission: BlackSpace demands a present and future where Black people, Black spaces, and Black culture matter and thrive. It created the BlackSpace Manifesto to practice new ways of protecting and creating Black spaces in the built environment.
https://blackspace.org

—

DARK MATTER U

Dark Matter U is a democratic, BIPOC-led network guided by the following principles: new forms of knowledge and knowledge production, new forms of institutions, new forms of collectivity and practice, new forms of community and culture, and new forms of design.

Mission: We cannot survive and thrive without immediate change toward an anti-racist model of design education and practice. Existing systems have not been able to transform away from centering and advancing whiteness, through their reliance on an implied dominant and racialized subject and audience. The impacts of that centering are widespread and can be felt in the inequities that global extraction, racial capitalism, and colonialism have created. The Earth and the majority of its people have suffered tremendous harm as a result. Collective liberation cannot only occur within the confines of individual institutions. Dark Matter U was founded to work inside and outside of existing systems to challenge, inform, and reshape our present world toward a better future.
https://darkmatteru.org/about

—

DESIGN ADVOCATES (D/A)

D/A is a network of experienced architecture and design firms, advising firms, and individuals who volunteer their time and expertise and collaborate on projects, research, and advocacy to serve the public good.

Mission: D/A creates inclusive and participatory community engagement processes and visioning for institutions, municipalities, and nonprofits; develops design strategy for organizations that serve communities and the public good; and advocates for more equitable and inclusive practices in the design industries.
https://designadvocates.org/community

—

DESIGN AS PROTEST

Design as Protest is a collective of designers mobilizing strategies to dismantle the privilege and power structures that use architecture and design as tools of oppression.

Mission: Co-organized by BIPOC designers, Design as Protest exists to hold our profession accountable in reversing the violence and injustice that architecture, design, and urban planning practices have inflicted upon Black people and communities. Design as Protest champions the radical vision of racial, social, and cultural reparation through the process and outcomes of design. It has developed an Anti-Racist Design Justice Index—a tool for dismantling systemic racism within our practices, organizations, academic institutions, and local governments.
https://www.dapcollective.com

—

FIRST 500

FIRST 500 exists to elevate and celebrate Black women architects and raise awareness about their distinction through community.

Mission: FIRST 500 elevates the visibility of Black women architects and provides tools and resources to support Black women and girls to increase the number of licensed Black women architects to better reflect the environments we serve. When we create opportunities for licensed Black women architects in the United States to practice in the industry, we create opportunities and equity in our communities.
https://first500.org

—

MADAME ARCHITECT

Madame Architect is an online periodical that presents interviews, reviews, and essays featuring more than four hundred female architects, urbanists, designers, and educators in academia, practice, and related disciplines.

Mission: Madame Architect is designed to break the architectural mold and show young women entering the industry the myriad choices they have in crafting dynamic, meaningful, and interesting careers.
https://www.madamearchitect.org/about

—

NATIONAL ARCHITECTURAL ACCREDITING BOARD (NAAB)

NAAB develops and implements an accreditation system for professional degree programs in architecture that enhances the value, relevance, and effectiveness of the profession.

Mission: The following principles serve as a guide and inspiration to NAAB: commitment to excellence, diversity and inclusion, effective communication, and spirit of collaboration. In 2020 NAAB released a statement on racial injustice identifying "critical and long-standing inequities" and articulating important conditions for accredited programs in relation to the shared values of equity, diversity, and inclusion, and program criteria related to social equity and inclusion.
https://www.naab.org/about/mission

—

NATIONAL COUNCIL OF ARCHITECTURAL REGISTRATION BOARDS (NCARB)

NCARB is a nonprofit organization made up of the architectural licensing boards of fifty-five US states and territories. It facilitates the licensure and credentialing of architects to protect the health, safety, and welfare of the public.

Mission: NCARB is committed to advancing diversity, equity, and inclusion in the architecture profession through its work as a regulatory organization. Public health, safety, and welfare are ensured more effectively when architecture professionals reflect the communities they serve in terms of race, ethnicity, and gender, but also age, disability status, background, and other factors.
https://www.ncarb.org/about/ncarbs-role

—

NATIONAL ORGANIZATION OF MINORITY ARCHITECTS (NOMA)

NOMA is a national organization created by minority architects for the purpose of minimizing the effects of racism in the profession of architecture. In addition to national, state, and regional NOMA chapters, the National Organization of Minority Architects Students (NOMAS) has chapters at more than ninety colleges and universities.

Mission: NOMA's mission, rooted in a rich legacy of activism, is to empower its local chapters and membership to foster justice and equity in communities of color through outreach, community advocacy, professional development, and design excellence. It calls on its members and the broader professional community to condemn racism and take an active role in eliminating the racial biases that account for myriad social, economic, and health disparities, and that result in the loss of human lives—Black lives.
https://www.noma.net/about-noma

GLOSSARY

ACCESS
Access refers to the relative availability or opportunity to have, use, or benefit from resources, services, facilities, or people in any number of contexts, from basic to profound. It affects and encompasses human needs, from essentials like safe housing, food, and health care, to education and political representation, to higher education and pursuit of a career. Access has a compounding effect, in that lack of access in any area can limit access in others. Good health and nutrition improve one's ability to learn. Success in K–12 education opens access to higher education, better jobs, and upward mobility. Access to role models, mentors, and networks reveals possibilities, provides guidance and inspiration, and opens new doors. But even protected rights are not experienced or available in equal measure. Access is facilitated or limited by where we live, the color of our skin, our gender identity, our level of education, who we know, our socioeconomic status, our obligations. Access can be limited or suppressed by systemic barriers and discriminatory structures, or thwarted by institutions and individuals. Those who have generally faced open doors will not easily understand how limits to access affect short- and long-term prospects and opportunities.

ACTIVISM VS. ADVOCACY
Though sometimes used interchangeably, activism and advocacy are different. Activism typically involves taking direct and sometimes confrontational action to bring about change. It might include marches, protests, or speeches. Advocacy likewise encompasses a range of activities aimed at addressing a specific issue, but advocates typically work within established systems and institutions over extended periods to shape policy, change laws, and cultivate resources in order to advance their cause.

ASSIMILATION
Assimilation—whether compelled through force or undertaken voluntarily—is when a minority social group conforms to the dominant social group's customs, attitudes, beliefs, language, etc. Assimilation most often affects immigrants and Indigenous peoples and can result not only in the loss of knowledge and skills, but also the eradication of entire cultures. An example of assimilation is the forced reeducation of Native Americans. Starting in the mid-1900s, approximately four hundred boarding schools were built in the United States to reeducate more than one hundred thousand Native American children, some of whom were kidnapped at

> We have a difficult problem in this profession with diversity. We have good intentions, of course. We're highly talented, highly focused on our work, but we're not so focused on our humanity.

Jack Travis

architect and educator

gunpoint. The children were forbidden to speak their Native languages, their hair was cut, and they were forced to renounce Native beliefs and their Native American identities, even their names.

BIPOC

BIPOC is an acronym for Black, Indigenous, and people of color—including but not limited to Native Americans, Asian Americans, Alaska Natives, Latinx, Hispanics, Native Hawaiians, and other Pacific Islanders—and is used as an umbrella term for people who are in a racial or ethnic minority. Prior to the Black Lives Matter movement, the shorter acronym POC was often used, but in recognition of the specific nature of Native invisibility and anti-Black racism, the POC acronym was expanded to BIPOC.

CODE SWITCHING

Code switching refers to the actions of a member of a stigmatized group or minority culture to change their behavior—speech, appearance, dress, expression—in ways that conform to the dominant culture in order to optimize the comfort of others and gain social acceptance, fair treatment, and better employment opportunities. Code switching can have significant implications for personal well-being and even physical survival.

COLONIZATION/DECOLONIZATION

Colonization refers to processes by which a foreign group settles or occupies the sovereign lands of another, seeking to subjugate the people, exploit the land and resources, and impose foreign customs, culture, or religion. By physical means—violence, occupation, displacement—and/or sociocultural or political domination, colonizers assume control over native peoples. Colonization involves sociocultural injustice through the suppression of Indigenous religions, language and customs, and political oppression, denying self-rule and basic human rights and liberties. Much of the world has been colonized at one time or another. The legacies of colonization continue to shape today's social and political structures well beyond the past physical occupation of place. Decolonization refers to complex processes of correction—both dismantling and rebuilding. Over time, colonially imposed legal, political, economic, and social systems that enable oppression become structurally entrenched, and so dismantling them can be critical. Recovery of lost languages, knowledge, and customs is indispensable to reestablishing culture and strengthening authentic heritage. Restoration of political autonomy and self-determination, taking measures toward economic justice and redress, and returning control over and ownership of land and resources are all paramount.

CULTURAL APPROPRIATION

Cultural appropriation is the inappropriate adoption of ideas, symbols, artifacts, images, art, rituals, icons, behavior, music, fashions, etc., belonging to a different culture. Appropriation can arise out of ignorance, malice, or a genuine desire to celebrate another culture. Regardless, it often involves cherry-picking aspects of the minority culture without understanding or respecting their significance. Examples could include wearing stereotypical Native American dress as costume; a white person wearing their hair in a traditional Black style such as cornrows or dreadlocks; wearing jewelry such as a cross or a bindi without acknowledging its symbolism, thereby reducing it to a fashion statement; or adopting a stereotypical likeness of a minority as a sports team mascot, as with the Washington Redskins (now the Washington Commanders) or the Atlanta Braves.

DIASPORA

A diaspora is a dispersion or scattering of a people, language, religion, or culture that was formerly concentrated in one geographic place of origin. A diaspora may happen relatively quickly or very slowly; it may be voluntary or forced. Diasporas have affected many parts of the world for better and for worse. The African diaspora refers to the movement of some 12.5 million Africans from their homes to other parts of the world, in large part due to slavery. The Great Migration of the 1910s to the 1970s was another diaspora, in which six million Black people moved from the US South, where they or their ancestors had been brought as slaves, to seek a better life in northern, midwestern, and western states. The forced migration of Native Americans from their ancestral homelands in the southeastern United States was also diasporic in nature. The infamous Trail of Tears, just one instance of forced migration linked to the Indian Removal Act, resulted in the deaths of approximately fifteen thousand Indigenous men, women, and children.

DISENFRANCHISE

To disenfranchise an individual or group is to deprive them of rights or privileges to which they are due as citizens. To be disenfranchised is to lose one's power or ability to make choices, effect change, or have one's voice heard. Disfranchisement may be accomplished explicitly by law or policy, or implicitly through exclusion, marginalization, or intimidation.

DOMINANT CULTURE

Dominant culture refers to a perceived cultural hierarchy in which one group in a diverse society, by virtue of race, ethnicity, religion, language, politics, or some other identifiable characteristic, has more power than other groups. Being part of the dominant culture carries both obvious and subtle benefits in relation to social, educational, professional, political, and socioeconomic prospects. Benefits accrue to those in the dominant culture, who have greater representation in decision-making institutions that may protect and promote their interests over time, structurally codifying and controlling the narrative. Those outside the dominant culture experience barriers, and as a result are afforded less power and more limited access to social, educational, professional, political, and economic networks.

EQUALITY VS. EQUITY

Equality means that each person has the same resources, rights, and opportunities as every other person. For example, a pie that serves eight can be divided into eight equal-sized pieces. Equity, on the other hand, recognizes that each person has different circumstances and allocates resources and opportunities as needed so each person can reach an equal outcome; it levels the playing field by identifying and addressing disparities to ensure that everyone has what they need to achieve success. An equitable cutting of the pie could mean that the slices are different sizes, allocated according to need and means.

ERASURE

Erasure is the removal of all traces of something or someone by ignoring them, rewriting history as if they had never existed or as if their role was or is unimportant, and/or removing references to them from history books (or social media). Erasure is a means of silencing ideas or presences that make a dominant or more powerful group feel uncomfortable or accused, often because they cast their past or present actions in an unfavorable light.

IDENTITY

Identity refers to the way a person perceives or defines themselves in relation to social and cultural categories such as race, ethnicity, gender, sexual orientation, nationality, religion, socioeconomic status, disability, or intersectional combinations thereof. Some aspects are factual, while others refer to beliefs or personality traits that characterize a person's sense of self. Identity is nurtured and framed by environment, and consciously or unconsciously can change over time. No two people's identities are exactly the same. Sometimes stereotypical identities, usually negative, are assigned to groups of people by other groups. These include things such as having lower intelligence, being lazy, having a tendency to be violent, and even having less ability to feel emotional or physical pain. Reducing the identity of any person or group to a small set of stereotypical traits allows extremists to demonize them more easily. Being poor or ill or elderly is not a condition of identity but a condition of circumstance, even though other people may attach value judgments to these circumstances.

IMPLICIT BIAS AND UNCONSCIOUS BIAS

Unconscious bias and implicit bias are often used interchangeably to refer to subconscious associations and perceptions of others based on race, gender, religion, age, or other differences. Unconscious bias can be shaped by societal influences, media, stereotypes, prejudices, or personal experiences, and can elicit unjustified, seemingly automatic responses to people or situations. Bias may unintentionally affect our judgment and behavior toward others in ways that include acts of discrimination.

INTERSECTIONALITY

Intersectionality refers to the idea that each person's identity has multiple facets that naturally overlap or intersect. For instance, the challenges faced by someone who is Black and female are different than those faced by someone who is white and female or someone who is Black and male. Intersections of race, gender, and sexuality identities contribute greatly to the type of systemic discrimination experienced by an individual or group. Social issues such as racism, poverty, homelessness, and so on have multivalent causes, and the nuanced complexities of their intersectional nature require distinct recognition.

MARGINALIZATION

To be marginalized is to be ignored or treated as insignificant, unimportant, or powerless. People who are marginalized are usually not part of the dominant culture; this often includes women, racial and ethnic minorities, people with disabilities, LGBTQ+ individuals, people living in poverty, and so on. Marginalized individuals and groups are actively and often systemically restricted by unfair social, cultural, political, economic, and structural barriers that make it difficult for them to advance.

MICROAGGRESSIONS
Microaggressions are intended or unintended verbal, nonverbal, and environmental slights or insults—often subtle or indirect—that communicate negative, dismissive, or exclusionary messages. These can include backhanded compliments; tone of voice, words, or gestures that convey annoyance or impatience with another's point of view; making assumptions based on stereotypes; interrupting or talking over someone during meetings or discussions; or facial expressions and body language that convey disrespect or condescension, such as crossing arms or avoiding eye contact.

MINORITY STRESS
Minority stress refers to a person's mental and physical response to being stigmatized due to race, ethnicity, gender, sexual identity, age, disability, and so on. Stressors vary widely, but often include workplace bias, inadequate financial resources, physical or verbal abuse, and poor social support systems. Research shows that chronic stress is closely linked to poor health outcomes.

OTHERING
Othering is a process of stereotyping and social exclusion based on a perception of what is normal, desirable, or comfortable, as opposed to what is unfamiliar, undesirable, or uncomfortable. Every social group, regardless of whether they are members of a majority or minority, engages in othering—defining an "us" (those on the inside who belong) and a "them" (those on the outside who don't belong). Othering is based on power relationships and is deployed to cast suspicion on, discriminate against, devalue, insult, or exclude groups due to race, ethnicity, socioeconomic status, age, gender identity, etc.

RACISM AND ANTI-RACISM
Racism is the conscious or unconscious belief that different races possess distinct characteristics, abilities, or qualities that make them innately inferior or superior. These beliefs can manifest outwardly as overt harassment, humiliation, violence, neglect, oppression, inequitable opportunities, or unfavorable outcomes. Racism is often associated with a dominant white culture, but prejudice and discrimination based on race and ethnicity exist across all cultures. Racism can be fueled by action or inaction. Doing nothing or not speaking up when something unjust is happening is, in effect, racist.

Anti-racism is the practice of acknowledging one's own prejudices, taking steps to identify and describe existing racism, and actively working to dismantle racist systems. The goal of anti-racism is to proactively change systems, institutions, laws, policies, behaviors, and beliefs that perpetuate racist ideas and actions.

REDLINING
Redlining refers to a historical practice, beginning in the 1930s in cities across the United States, in which banks and lenders created maps that identified with red outlines neighborhoods with large minority populations. These maps were used to defend discriminatory lending practices, such as denying loans and devaluing property, that effectively segregated

communities and suppressed wealth accumulation, thereby structurally limiting potential for upward mobility in communities of color. While this practice is no longer overtly practiced in mortgage lending, the term can refer to other practices that effectively discriminate or deny access.

REPRESENTATION
Representation refers to the action of speaking or acting on behalf of an individual or group, such as the way an elected politician works on behalf of their voting constituency. Equal representation suggests that all people deserve this right, and further, that proportional representation by individuals who share characteristics of identity (race, gender, ethnicity, etc.) would create fairer representation and advocacy for all people, especially those historically underrepresented. In an equitable and inclusive society, institutions and centers of power would reflect the diversity of those whom they serve. To speak of historically underrepresented groups points to the fact that the perspectives, experiences, and needs of large groups have gone unheard by those in power. The disadvantage of underrepresentation compounds over time through the concretizing of systems and structures that disempower and disable.

RESILIENCE
Resilience refers to the ability of something to recover from impact or harm; for instance, inanimate materials must be strong, tough, and/or flexible to withstand a potentially destructive force without damage. When applied to human beings, the concept is less straightforwardly positive. While it may seem like a compliment to describe a person or community as resilient, it also implies an unfair and unrealistic expectation that they should be able to recover readily from psychosocial stresses associated with bias, microaggressions, discrimination, overt racism, and violence.

SOCIAL JUSTICE
Social justice refers to the equitable experience of all people in a society with regard to quality of life, such as access to resources, protection from harm, opportunities to advance, and guaranteed civil rights. For communities that have historically been denied services and resources or that have experienced the brunt of economic or environmental harm, social justice can refer to remediation that aims to create fair and equal provision, or even the return of fundamental rights. It begins with recognition and awareness of inequitable conditions through direct work with underrepresented communities. Awareness may become action through advocacy and social and spatial reinvestment in infrastructure, institutions, or environments. In the context of architecture and design, this might include advocating for the human right to housing that is affordable, culturally sensitive, universally accessible, and environmentally sustainable.

STRUCTURAL AND SYSTEMIC DISCRIMINATION
Racism and other forms of discrimination can be personal but they can also be embedded in large-scale systems, structures, institutions, laws, or policies that operate in ways that lead to inequity and injustice. These forces may be more or less obvious in their suppression of equal rights. Examples include the justice system and health care system, the redlining

of minority neighborhoods, race-blind admissions, and voter suppression laws, which may benefit the more privileged or powerful members of society but do great harm to others that continues generation after generation.

TOKEN
A token is a minority individual who is hired, included, consulted, etc., for the sake of appearance—to suggest an absence of discrimination based on race, gender, ethnicity, socioeconomic background, gender identity, or other minority status. The individual may be highly qualified or not qualified at all; the primary intent is what determines the tokenism.

WHITE GAZE
White gaze refers to the tendency to consciously or unconsciously represent things from the perspective of whiteness, and to assume that one's audience shares that perspective. Such representations bias white experiences, aesthetics, culture, values, and attitudes. White dominance in the media space reinforces stereotypes and racialized power imbalances, and implies authority of white norms or preferences.

WHITE PRIVILEGE
Privilege is a right or benefit that is given to some people and not to others based on factors such as race, gender, sexual orientation, socioeconomic status, or religion. People who regularly experience privilege may not be conscious of it, and may fail to understand the experience of those who lack privilege. White privilege refers to the unquestioned and unearned set of advantages, entitlements, benefits, and choices Caucasians enjoy solely because of their race.

WHITE SUPREMACY
White supremacy is the idea that white people are superior to Black people, Indigenous people, and/or people of color as well as Jewish people, Muslims, and immigrants. The discrimination often extends to people who identify as non-binary or LGBTQ+, regardless of race. As a movement, white supremacy relies on a toxic sense of superiority, righteousness, and belonging. White nationalism is a form of white supremacy that champions the creation of a whites-only homeland. Other forms include violent right-wing movements—the Ku Klux Klan, neo-Nazis, racist skinheads—as well as religious fundamentalist groups such as Christian Identity. The majority of domestic terrorism and hate crimes are linked to white supremacy, but it also exists in much more insidious forms in all corners of society, from politics to finance, military and police forces, and legal and educational systems. Since the nineteenth century, white supremacy has heavily impacted school curricula in the United States, with academic disciplines across the spectrum being taught with a heavy emphasis on white culture, contributions, and experiences, and a lack of representation of nonwhite perspectives and accomplishments. Social media has made it much easier for white supremacists to organize. As of 2018 there were more than six hundred known white supremacy organizations in the United States. During the Trump presidency there was a surge of interest and visibility in white supremacy and white nationalism, with the leaders of many white supremacist organizations openly supporting him, and him welcoming their support.

> If architecture is going to nudge, cajole, and inspire a community to challenge the status quo into making responsible changes, it will take the subversive leadership of academics and practitioners….

Sam Mockbee
architect and educator

EDITOR BIOGRAPHIES

BETSY WEST holds a master of architecture degree from Yale University and is an associate professor in the School of Architecture at the University of North Carolina, Charlotte. She has practiced professionally with a number of firms, including the Freelon Group at its inception. She also served as chair of the College of Architecture at UNC Charlotte. Her scholarship and teaching focus on the relationship of architecture to its context, issues of diversity in the profession, and humanitarian design processes and projects. Her work in these realms explores the physical, cultural, historic, political, pragmatic, and poetic aspects of design as they combine to create varied conditions of wastelands, borderlands, and homelands. West has taught graduate and undergraduate studios across the curriculum and has developed a number of seminars, including "Humanitarian Design: Small-Scale Mediation in a Big-Scale World," "Wastelands, Borderlands, Homelands," and "Everything Reverberates: Ernest Hemingway, Edward Hopper, Louis Kahn." She has also taught numerous courses focused on writing in the discipline.

KELLY CARLSON-REDDIG holds a master of environmental design degree from Yale University and a bachelor of architecture from Texas Tech University. She is an associate professor in the School of Architecture at the University of North Carolina, Charlotte, and served as its associate director from 2008 to 2016. She is a licensed architect and chaired the national ACSA technology conference entitled "'Souped-Up' and 'UnPlugged': Perspectives on Architectural Technology." Carlson-Reddig's teaching and scholarship examine the conceptual dimensions of architecture's materiality and tectonics. Her current project examines the material, haptic, and aesthetic realms of mark making in the context of architecture—the intersection of materiality, technique, action, and outcome. Carlson-Reddig teaches graduate and undergraduate studios across the curriculum, and seminars such as "MARK~," "Critical Artful Materiality Tectonics," and "In the Details." She has been instrumental in curriculum reform related to the climate emergency, teaching studios related to biodiversity and adaptive reuse.

JOSÉ L.S. GÁMEZ holds a bachelor of environmental design from Texas A&M University, a master of architecture from the University of California, Berkeley, and a PhD in architecture and urban design from the University of California, Los Angeles. His teaching and research explore artistic and spatial models of praxis rooted in cross-cultural expressions. He has published widely in both books and academic journals, including in *Aztlán: A Journal of Chicano Studies*; *Places: A Forum of Environmental Design*; *Journal of Urbanism*; *Journal of Applied Geography*; *Plan Journal*; and *Collaborations: A Journal of Community-Based Research and Practice*. He was the recipient of a Provost's Award for Community Engagement from the University of North Carolina, Charlotte, and he has served on the Dean's Equity and Inclusion Initiative, as a Provost Faculty Fellow, and as a research fellow with both UNC Charlotte's Institute for Social Capital and its Urban Institute.

IMAGE CREDITS

Page 6: Chris Cornelius

Page 10: Paul Decker

Page 17: Leonard Lenz

Page 18: Betsy West: Dee Blackburn; Kelly Carlson-Reddig: Tom Carlson-Reddig; José L.S. Gámez: Zach Allred; Sekou Cooke: Bobby Quillard; Michelle Joan Wilkinson: Maggie Janick; Manoj Kesavan: courtesy Z. Smith Reynolds Foundation; Aneesha Dharwadker: Sachin Dharwadker; Whitney M. Young Jr.: courtesy AIA Archives; Melanie Reddrick: courtesy Little Diversified Architectural Consulting; Jack Travis: Sojourner Joy Travis; Pascale Sablan: Aundre Larrow; Chris Cornelius: C. J. Foeckler

Page 19: Dhalia Ndoum: Vadym Guliuk Photography; Ronald Rael: Minesh Bacrania Photography; Michelle Magalong: Kay Meyer; Ghazal Jafari: Ali Fard; Teddy Cruz & Fonna Forman: courtesy Estudio Teddy Cruz + Fonna Forman; Zena Howard: Arsalan Abbasi; Lauren Neefe: Liz Bullock; Isabel Strauss: Tara Raghuveer; Meejin Yoon: Conor Doherty; Lesley Lokko: Festus Jackson-Davis; The Supreme Court Justices, 2023: Fred Schilling

Page 22: Fibonacci Blue

Page 23: Chad Davis

Page 25 top: Tyler Merbler

Page 25 bottom: US Dept. of Homeland Security

Page 29: Mike Licht

Page 35: Tim Pierce

Pages 41–42: Alan Karchmer

Page 44: Ruppert Landscape

Page 47 left: © 2020 Catlett Mora Family Trust/Licensed by VAGA at Artists Rights Society (ARS), NY

Page 47 right: © Kennedy Yanko; photo courtesy the artist, Salon 94, and Devals

Page 50: Alisdare Hickson

Pages 62–64: Chicago Design Office and Hinterlands Urbanism and Landscape, 2018

Page 65 top, center left, and bottom right: Zachary Keltner, 2022

Page 65 lower left: Aneesha Dharwadker, 2019

Pages 66–67: Chicago Design Office and Made in Englewood, project design

Page 68: Brian Griffin/Griffin Imaging Studio

Page 70: Greg Snyder

Page 76: Jonathan McIntosh

Page 80: Lorie Shaull

Page 82: Photographer unknown

Page 88: Frederic Schwartz Architects

Page 90: Paul Warchol Photography

Pages 91–95: Jack Travis

Page 98:
top left: Paul Becker
top right: Don Sniegowski
middle left: Peter Burka
middle right top: Miki Jourdan
middle right bottom: Wolfgang Bayer
bottom left: Singlespeedfahrer
bottom right: Paul Becker

Page 99:
top left: Daniel Lobo
top right: Taymaz Valley
middle left: Duncan Cumming
middle right: Bdward3
bottom left: Lorie Shaull
bottom right: GoToVan
Page 102: Paul Becker
Page 105: Alisdare Hickson
Page 110: Elvert Barnes
Page 119: Andrew Ratto
Page 120: Earl Campbell III, MD
Pages 125–26: Chris Cornelius
Page 128: Tom Harris
Pages 132–33: Chris Cornelius
Page 137: Nick Zukauskas
Pages 140–41: Chris Cornelius
Page 144: Loco Steve
Page 154: Ron Rael
Pages 157–61: Ron Rael
Page 172: Fibonacci Blue
Page 174: Ivan Radic
Pages 183–85: Ghazal Jafari
Page 192: Latent Design and *Archinect*
Page 195: *Archinect*
Page 200: Clemson University Archives
Page 202: Anthony Crider
Pages 206–14: Estudio Teddy Cruz + Fonna Forman
Page 218: Anthony Crider
Page 221: Backbone Campaign
Page 226: Kelly Jordan
Pages 229–33: Courtesy Perkins&Will
Page 234 top: Courtesy Perkins&Will
Page 234 bottom: Keith Isaacs
Page 242: Roger Jones
Page 253: Prints & Photographs Division, Library of Congress
Page 256: Marc C. Monaghan
Page 258: Alan Karchmer
Page 259: Courtesy Höweler+Yoon
Pages 260–61: Alan Karchmer
Page 262: Sanjay Suchak / UVA
Page 272: Graphic: Annette Choi, CNN; image source: US Supreme Court
Page 273: Kelly Carlson-Reddig
Page 275: Collection of the Smithsonian National Museum of African American History and Culture (Object number 2017.85.11)
Page 283: Leonard Lenz

Published by Princeton Architectural Press
A division of Chronicle Books LLC
70 West 36th Street
New York, NY 10018
papress.com

© 2024 Betsy West, Kelly Carlson-Reddig, José L.S. Gámez

All rights reserved.
Printed and bound in China.
27 26 25 24   4 3 2 1   First edition

No part of this book may be used or reproduced in any manner without written permission from the publisher, except in the context of reviews.

Every reasonable attempt has been made to identify owners of copyright. Errors or omissions will be corrected in subsequent editions.

Editor: Jennifer Thompson
Design: Natalie Snodgrass, Paul Wagner

Library of Congress
Cataloging-in-Publication Data
Names: West, Betsy (Writer on architecture), editor.
Title: Margin and text : amplifying diverse voices in architecture /
  [editors] Betsy West, Kelly Carlson-Reddig, José L.S. Gámez.
Description: [New York] : [Princeton Architectural Press], [2024] |
  Includes bibliographical references and index. | Summary: "BIPOC voices
  in architecture discuss issues of diversity, equity, access, and social
  justice embedded in and related to the built environment"
  —Provided by publisher.
Identifiers: LCCN 2024006006 | ISBN 9781797227665 (hardcover) | ISBN
  9781797227672 (ebook)
Subjects: LCSH: Architecture and society—United States. | Cultural
  pluralism—United States.
Classification: LCC NA2543.S6 M3585 2024 | DDC
  720.1/030973—dc23/eng/20240404
LC record available at https://lccn.loc.gov/2024006006